THE FRENCH ARMY AND
ITS AFRICAN SOLDIERS

FRANCE OVERSEAS: STUDIES IN EMPIRE AND DECOLONIZATION

Series editors: A. J. B. Johnston, James D. Le Sueur, and Tyler Stovall

THE FRENCH ARMY AND ITS AFRICAN SOLDIERS

The Years of Decolonization

RUTH GINIO

UNIVERSITY OF NEBRASKA PRESS | *Lincoln and London*

© 2017 by the Board of Regents of
the University of Nebraska

Library of Congress Cataloging-
in-Publication Data
Names: Ginio, Ruth, 1966–, author.
Title: The French army and its African soldiers:
the years of decolonization / Ruth Ginio.
Description: Lincoln NE: University of Nebraska
Press, [2016] | Series: France overseas: studies
in empire and decolonization | Includes
bibliographical references and index.
Identifiers: LCCN 2016032569
ISBN 9780803253391 (cloth: alk. paper)
ISBN 9780803299498 (epub)
ISBN 9780803299504 (mobi)
ISBN 9780803299511 (pdf)
Subjects: LCSH: France, Armée—Colonial
forces—Africa—History—20th century. | Africa,
French-speaking West—History, Military. |
Blacks—France—History—20th century.
Classification: LCC UA709 .G55 2016 | DDC
355.3089/9604409045—dc23 LC record
available at https://lccn.loc.gov/2016032569

Set in Lyon by Rachel Gould.
Designed by N. Putens.

For Eyal, Nitai, and Ophir

CONTENTS

ILLUSTRATIONS

ACKNOWLEDGMENTS

The journey of this book began almost a decade ago in a visit to the Musée des Forces Armées in Dakar. This museum exposed me to the complex and fascinating ways in which the story of the African soldiers who served in the French army during the colonial period is officially told today in Senegal. After studying for a while the manner in which these soldiers were both commemorated and somewhat ignored in France and in Senegal, I began to notice a major lacuna in the field, including my own study, namely, the period of decolonization. I then began working on a manuscript that would fill this lacuna by examining the relations between the French army and its African soldiers after World War II and the role the army played in the political processes in the federation from which most of its African soldiers originated, French West Africa.

On the long road to completing my book I gathered a number of debts. The research that led to this book was financed by the Israel Science Foundation (grant 882/09). The index was financed by a grant from the Tamar Golan Africa Center at Ben Gurion University of the Negev. I received kind assistance from the staff of the Centre des Archives d'Outre-Mer in Aix-en-Provence and the archives of the Musée des Troupes de Marine in Fréjus, France, and from the employees of the Archives Nationales in Dakar, Senegal.

Sokhna Sane from the Department of History at Cheick Anta Diop University in Dakar put me in contact with her student Cheick Anta Mbaye, who conducted some of the interviews included in this book. Ibrahima Thioub kindly allowed me to use one of the interviews conducted during the African oral workshop, funded by the British Academy. Ousmane Sene invited me to give a lecture on my research in the West African Research Center in Dakar, and Daha Cherif Ba directed the ensuing discussion, which allowed me to better understand the Senegalese point of view on my research topic. I am especially grateful to one person who participated in this discussion, Sadiq Sall, who kindly agreed to meet me a few days after my talk and shared with me the experiences of his late father in the French army. The conversation I had with him opened my eyes to many of the issues I discuss in my book and helped me see them from a very different perspective. Still in Senegal, I would like to thank Cheick Bamba Dioum, whose blog discussed the military involvement in pilgrimages to Mecca and with whom I had a fascinating e-mail exchange on this issue.

There are many colleagues in the United States, Canada, France, the UK, and Israel to whom I am indebted, first and foremost for providing me with a vibrant, warm, and supportive community that is essential for conducting research. Their names are too numerous to mention, so I will concentrate on those who contributed most to my research. Denis Charbit, Rick Fogarty, Eric Jennings, Greg Mann, Lynn Schler, Martin Thomas, Romain Tiquet, and Sarah Zimmerman all provided invaluable help by answering questions I had difficulty finding answers for, by sending me material that was inaccessible to me, or by reading parts of my manuscript or its entirety and providing helpful comments and suggestions for revisions. While I meet most of these wonderful colleagues only at conferences and while on research trips to France and to Senegal, Lynn Schler and I work closely on an almost daily basis. We share not only our research interests but also the challenging and happily successful mission of reviving African studies in Israel. Working with her is a privilege one rarely finds in academic life.

I extend my warmest thanks to my research assistants Guy Roufe and Debora Elhadad-Aroshas, who helped me in many of the technical aspects of my work. Debora's efficient method of classifying the daunting number of archival documents allowed me to extract the maximum data from my primary sources. I would also like to thank my English editor, Carolyn Gross-Baruch, who helped me overcome the difficulties in writing in a foreign language. At the University of Nebraska Press I am grateful to the anonymous readers of my proposal and later of my entire manuscript. Their valuable and knowledgeable comments contributed to improving my text. My thanks also to Bridget Barry, the acquisitions editor for history, geography, and environmental studies, for her encouragement and readiness to assist me in the process of my book's publication; to editorial assistant Emily Wendell; and to Ann Baker, Rachel Gould, and Martyn Beeny. My special thanks to Mary M. Hill, the press-assigned copyeditor, who painstakingly and prudently polished the final text of the manuscript.

On a more personal note, I would like to thank Eyal, Nitai, and Ophir. Eyal, who was working on his book on the social history of the Balkan Wars at the same time that I was working on my own, lovingly shared with me, along with all other aspects of life, this long and sometimes frustrating road of research. Reading his fascinating manuscript and receiving his helpful comments on my own were a source of endless inspiration. My son, Nitai, and my daughter, Ophir, helped me keep my work in perspective and accompanied me on various research trips. Growing up with this research on African colonial soldiers, they were always supportive and understanding and were even patient when I dragged them to see a cemetery for African colonial soldiers during a vacation in France. To these three most important people in my life this book is dedicated with love.

ABBREVIATIONS

AEF	Afrique Équatoriale Française
AERDA	Association des Étudiants du Rassemblement Démocratique Africain
AGED	Association Générale des Étudiants de Dakar
ANS	Archives Nationales du Sénégal
ANSOM	Archives Nationales, Section d'Outre-Mer
AOF	Afrique Occidentale Française
BAA	Bureau des Affaires Africaines
BDS	Bloc Démocratique Sénégalais
CFA	(Franc de la) Communauté Française d'Afrique
CHETOM	Centre d'Histoire et d'Études des Troupes d'Outre-Mer

CGT	Confédération Générale du Travail
DRV	Democratic Republic of Vietnam
EET	Écoles des Enfants de Troupes
EFORTOM	École de Formation des Officiers du Régime Transitoire des Territoires d'Outre-Mer
EMPA	École Militaire de Préparation Africaine
FEANF	Fédération des Étudiants d'Afrique Noire en France
FLN	Front de Libération Nationale
IOM	Indépendants d'Outre-Mer
MDRM	Mouvement Démocratique de la Rénovation Malgache
OAS	Organisation Armée Secrète
PCF	Partie Communiste Française
RDA	Rassemblement Démocratique Africain
SFIO	Section Française de l'Internationale Ouvrière
SHAT	Service Historique de l'Armée de Terre
UGEAO	Union Générale des Étudiants d'Afrique Occidentale
UGTAN	Union Générale des Travailleurs d'Afrique Noire

INTRODUCTION

On April 15, 1974, Lt. Col. Seyni Kountche, an ex-sergeant in the French colonial army, committed a successful coup d'état against Niger's president, Hamani Diori.[1] Diori had been on good terms with the French government ever since he had imposed draconian measures against the African opposition parties, which had called for immediate independence during the 1950s. Despite this, the French units stationed in Niger did not intervene and allowed Seyni Kountche to take power. Diori's request for assistance was refused because of his demand to renegotiate the price of uranium, which his country supplied to France. This insistence caused the French to take their chances with a new leader, one who had once been part of France's colonial units and who they believed might be more accommodating.

This was not the first nor the last time in the postcolonial period that the French government instructed the military units stationed in its ex-colonies in Africa to choose sides according to its interests. The critics of this policy, known as Franceafrique, accused France of meddling in African conflicts in a manner that did not consider the welfare of the populations in these countries. In fact, after the end of French colonial rule in sub-Saharan Africa in the early 1960s, the French army intervened forty-eight times in various conflicts and crises on the continent within the context of this policy. The French support of the extreme Hutu government, which led the Genocide against the Tutsis and moderate Hutus in Rwanda in 1994, only intensified this criticism.[2]

Gen. Charles de Gaulle and his advisor for African affairs, Jacques Foccart, initiated the policy of Franceafrique after de Gaulle's return to power in 1958.[3] Foccart was to become the most controversial figure related to France's manipulations in its ex-African colonies. The term itself was actually borrowed from the first president of the Ivory Coast, Félix

Houphouët-Boigny, who was in favor of maintaining close relations with France, although not in the sense of securing French interests exclusively.[4]

As demonstrated by the successful coup d'état of an ex-African colonial soldier in Niger under the auspices of the French army, the military aspect of this French policy was not only evident but crucial. Immediately after independence France had signed military agreements with most of its ex-territories in sub-Saharan Africa. These agreements allowed it to hold a monopoly over the sales of arms to the newly independent countries and over important minerals such as uranium.[5] These stipulations reflect the lingering military aspect of France's relations with its ex-colonies. It is therefore surprising that so little attention was given to the role the French army had played in the federation of French West Africa (Afrique Occidentale Française, AOF) in the years prior to independence. While numerous studies have dealt with the army in other parts of the French empire such as Indochina and Algeria, practically none have considered the role it played in the political processes within AOF. The reason for this void is rather obvious. An army's principal role is to fight wars; therefore, the importance of the French army in Indochina and Algeria, where two of France's most vicious imperial wars took place, is evident, and the role of the army in these two parts of the French empire attracted much scholarly attention. In AOF, on the other hand, the army had no war to fight, and so it seems that it had a less important role there as a colonial agent. This could not be farther from the truth. Fighting wars was certainly not the only role of the French military units in the empire. In its attempts to defeat its enemies, the French army in Indochina, and even more so in Algeria, did not limit its activities to traditional warfare. Under the guise of what was termed "psychological warfare" the army assumed other roles in domains that were supposed to be under civilian responsibility, including education, social assistance, and health. It was also deeply involved in colonial decision making and in shaping the colonial agenda.

As I intend to show in this book, this important part of the military mission was also relevant to AOF. Maintaining control over the federation was crucial in the eyes of the colonial army's command. The fact that many of the army's colonial troops originated from this territory enhanced its importance and turned these soldiers into a link between the army and the African population of the federation. It is true that no war broke out in

AOF, but the army's fear of losing control over this part of the empire was still significant and was reflected in various ways. In the eyes of the military command of the federation, this was a space that was to be defended and saved from what it perceived as the negative influences of the anticolonial struggles taking place in other parts of the French empire and in other European colonial empires. In addition, both main rivals in the Cold War, the Soviet Union and the United States, were beginning to grow hostile toward France's colonial project. Therefore, the military policy, agenda, and aims in AOF at the time of decolonization are indispensable to our understanding of this important period in the history of the region.

This book contributes to our understanding of the three main themes mentioned in its title: the French army, its African soldiers, and decolonization, focusing on the army's agenda, policies, and activities during the last fifteen years of French colonial rule in the federation of AOF. Thus it examines the army as a significant political agent during this period and demonstrates the often-blurred boundaries between the military and civilian authorities in the federation. I will show that even though the army did not have to wage war in the federation and the level of violence it had to handle was limited, it still played a major part in the attempts to control the political processes that took place in the federation. Military officers often criticized the civilian authorities for not protecting the federation enough from what they perceived as negative influences of other politically more sophisticated and more dangerous parts of the French empire, most notably, Indochina and Algeria. A thorough examination of the army's role in the political processes in AOF in the post–World War II years will enhance our understanding of the continued military presence and involvement in France's ex-colonies in the region after independence. My focus will be on the nonmilitary activities of the army in AOF, such as education, propaganda, and attempts to control the civilian administration. I will also examine the military policies toward West African soldiers during the Indochina and Algeria wars.

Another major theme of this book is the participation of African soldiers in the wars of decolonization. African soldiers who served in the French colonial army were a vital component of the military attempts to keep AOF French. The African soldiers' service in the French army gained much scholarly attention during the last decade as public awareness of these soldiers in France and West Africa increased, thus encouraging academic research and popular debate on the subject.

A notable example is Rachid Bouchareb's 2006 film *Indigènes* (*Days of Glory*), which revived public debate regarding the African veterans' demands to equate their pensions to those of French veterans after those pensions were frozen just before independence. However, the main goal of this new awareness, at least in France, is to remind the French public of the sacrifices these soldiers made for France and therefore of the right of their "descendants" (i.e., African immigrants in France, most of whom in fact had no relation to the veterans) to be regarded as part of the French nation. It is not surprising, then, that the focus of both public remembrance and academic research is on the soldiers' roles during the two world wars (the second more than the first) rather than on their participation in France's controversial wars of decolonization.[6]

While it is definitely important to shed light on the African contribution to the war effort in the two world wars, focusing mainly on these episodes in the history of African soldiers' service in the French army might anachronistically conceal a large part of the picture. This focus turns the story of the soldiers into a French or European one; it relates their service to the history of metropolitan France rather than to the history of the regions from which these soldiers originated. It also makes us forget that the original aim of recruiting Africans to the army was to conquer the empire and maintain order in it by utilizing the supposedly violent nature of the Africans as a screen behind which colonial violence and brutality could hide.

When studying the role of African soldiers in the two world wars there is a tendency to present them as unsung heroes, exploited but brave colonial subjects who came to the motherland's rescue but whose reward was not recognition but rather discrimination and later oblivion. This depiction, which is largely accurate, must be completed by further research. Otherwise it is quite easy to marginalize the fact that African soldiers also took part in the occupation of the French empire and in maintaining order in its territories. These soldiers also participated in the post–World War II repression of anticolonial movements in Madagascar, Indochina, and Algeria, in which France tried to save its empire. African soldiers participated in the brutal repression of the revolt in Madagascar; they fought in Indochina against the Viet Minh and in

Algeria against the Front de Libération Nationale (FLN), where they were assigned the most abhorrent jobs; they were also sent to subdue protests in AOF. In fact, in the most infamous repression of African ex-POWs in Camp Thiaroye near Dakar at the end of World War II (a subject that I will deal with in chapter 2), African soldiers brought from other regions were those who opened fire on their protesting comrades under the command of French officers. I have no intention of denying that African soldiers, even those who had participated in such brutalities, were in a way also victims of the colonial system. They were assigned these roles by their French commanders in order to pass the responsibility of violent repression onto them. Nevertheless, I maintain that ignoring the less heroic and glorified activities of African soldiers prevents us from understanding their story in the context of the French colonial project, in which they played an essential part. Furthermore, examining the French colonial army and its African soldiers at the time of decolonization allows us a more nuanced perspective of both the army as a political agent in AOF and the story of the African soldiers serving in its ranks.

The third theme that this book explores is the ongoing academic debate around the term "decolonization" and its various definitions. In the past this term was largely considered to describe the struggle of colonial peoples to achieve political and so-called national independence. However, during the last fifteen years the emphasis in this field has largely shifted from the national story of an anticolonial struggle ending "happily" with independence to the perception of decolonization as the culmination of a history of interaction and conflict between colonizers and colonized.[7] The uniqueness of this point of view is that it also gives weight to the variation among the colonizers and among the colonized. Frederick Cooper, one of the main scholars contributing to this historiographical shift, noted in 2002 that the outcome of decolonization should not be regarded as the only possible and inevitable one: "Africans cannot be reduced to stick figures in a drama with two actors, colonizer and colonized, or a story with one plot line—the struggle for the nation."[8]

The study of the army's political involvement in AOF after World War II contributes to this debate on the nature of decolonization from several perspectives. First, as we shall see, the military vision of the future of AOF was based on the military reforms of the 1950s, which equated the service conditions of African and French metropolitan soldiers. The success of these reforms in appeasing African soldiers and veterans who were contesting against the army after World War II allowed military officers to believe that a policy of reforms that advanced equality between the French and Africans could indeed become an alternative to independence.

Second, the significance of the army as a political agent in AOF that did not always see eye to eye with other agents such as the civilian authority, the French governments, and various African politicians demonstrates that the political struggles that took place in the federation during this period were not necessarily between oppressed Africans and oppressing French. Various views with regard to the political future of the region existed both among the French and the Africans, and coalitions were sometimes made across these two groups.

Third, 1960 is usually seen as a significant year in the history of AOF, as during this year all of the territories of the federation became independent (except Guinea, which had gained its independence in 1958). The study of the army in AOF shows that in fact other events and processes in the history of the region were no less significant. From a military point of view, the truly problematic turning points in the political processes in the federation were the Loi-Cadre of 1956 and the establishment of the Franco-African Community in 1958. When independence came in 1960 the military authorities were already planning their next steps, which included military agreements meant to preserve the army's influence in the area. In this sense, 1964 was much more important from a military perspective, as this was the year in which all African soldiers who served in the French army were demobilized, some joining the armies of the newly independent countries. This was not, of course, the end of the military presence in AOF, and as we shall see in chapter 7, the army continued to control the politics of the former French colonies. The different chronology that this study offers supports the thesis that decolonization did not necessarily mean the struggle for independence and that in fact the actual year of independence did not always mark the commencement of essential transformations in the history of the region.

The discussion of the French army and its African soldiers in the period of decolonization in AOF sheds light on these three important themes: the army's political involvement in AOF after World War II, the participation of African soldiers in the wars of decolonization, and the study of decolonization in AOF. It also connects these three themes and thus contributes to our understanding of the postcolonial military relations between France and its former colonies in West Africa.

Sources and Methodology

There are several studies on the army's general involvement in the establishment of the French empire in Africa, as well as specific ones on the French military involvement in certain French colonies before and after independence, that were helpful for my research.[9] This is, however, the only study to date that examines the involvement of the French army in the decolonization process in AOF.

While the recent focus has been on African participation in the two world wars, there are a few important studies that deal with African soldiers in the post–World War II period. One is the pioneer research of Myron Echenberg, *Colonial Conscripts* (1991), in which the last three chapters are dedicated to the period 1945–60. The other is Gregory Mann's more recent *Native Sons* (2006), which also touches upon the period of decolonization. Sarah Zimmerman's doctoral dissertation examines African colonial soldiers from the establishment of their first battalions until the end of the colonial period, including their experiences in Indochina and Algeria.[10] In the final part of his book, Echenberg offers us a glimpse into the military reforms of the 1950s, the major changes in the way in which the military command viewed African soldiers, and the attempts to professionalize the African units. Mann sheds light on the complex relations between the army and its veterans before and after World War II, and Zimmerman examines the actual experiences of African soldiers in the Indochina and Algeria wars and their adjustment to the independence of their own territories. While these important and rich studies served as a vital source for this book, my own focus is on the army's attempts to use its African soldiers as a means of influencing the general population of AOF and as proof of the validity of the army's vision with regard to the political future of this federation. As I will show, the army saw the general loyalty of the African soldiers after the military reforms as evidence that it was possible to maintain AOF as part of the French empire.

As noted, while much scholarly attention has been given to the decolonization struggles in Indochina and Algeria, the relatively quiet and nonviolent parallel political process in AOF was somewhat neglected until recently.[11] In 2010 Charles Robert Ageron and Marc Michel edited a volume on the subject titled *L'heure des indépendances*, and several more studies in French dealt with specific issues regarding decolonization in AOF, but few studies on this theme were published in English. A notable exception is Tony Chafer's *The End of Empire in French West Africa: France's Successful Decolonization?* published in 2002, which demonstrates that in spite of the nonviolent character of the process it was nevertheless full of tensions and contradictions that merit our analyses. In her book *Cold War and Decolonization in Guinea*, Elizabeth Schmidt thoroughly examined the decolonization process in French Guinea, the only French colony that rejected de Gaulle's idea of a Franco-African Community and gained full independence by 1958. A more recent study on decolonization in AOF, although the word does not appear in its title (perhaps not by chance), is Cooper's latest book *Citizenship between Empire and Nation: Remaking France and French Africa, 1945-1960*. In this book Cooper describes the political debates regarding the postwar form of the old colonial system. He also focuses on the various meanings and interpretations of other key concepts such as citizenship, empire, nation, and sovereignty. None of these studies discusses the army as a significant factor in the process of decolonization in AOF.

In this book I plan to examine the army as an influential political agent in AOF during the post–World War II years. My analysis will be based on the above-mentioned studies, and my conclusions considering the army's role in the federation will enforce the idea of decolonization as a complex struggle between various groups that did not consider independence as the only possible remedy to the evils of colonialism.

The importance of the military aspect of the decolonization process in AOF was acknowledged by Chafer and Alexander Keese in their edited volume *Africa at Fifty*. In the introduction Chafer and Keese present three major narratives that have developed over the years regarding the decolonization of French sub-Saharan Africa. Their book challenges two of these narratives, which in spite of being conflicting are based on the same assumption. One narrative is that of the successful and well-planned decolonization, the other that of French manipulation and conspiracy. Both narratives assume that the French had some sort of control over the political process of decolonization in AOF. The third narrative is that of the military bond. According to this narrative, military relations were established between France and its territories in AOF as a result of the service of African soldiers in the two world wars and in the Indochina and Algerian wars, during which a narrative emphasizing brotherhood in arms and shared glory and sacrifices was encouraged. This may explain to a large extent both the colonial and the postcolonial relations between France and these territories.

In my own study I accept the rejection of the first two narratives and certainly accord much attention to the idea of the military bond. Nevertheless, I do not consider this concept as a narrative that explains the decolonization of AOF but rather as an additional perspective from which we can examine this process as one that is much more complex than a struggle between French oppressors and their African victims. The military perspective of the decolonization of AOF complicates the story of decolonization and therefore adds an important aspect to the debate around the meaning of this concept.

In this book I connect the three themes—the army as a political actor, the African soldiers who served in it, and the process of decolonization. My main primary sources are military and administrative documents that deal with the military involvement in various domains within AOF, such as education, propaganda, and social assistance, with policies that relate to both African soldiers and veterans and with dilemmas regarding the service of Africans in Indochina and Algeria. These documents are found in archives in France and in Senegal. Newspapers from the period, especially those that were designated for soldiers and veterans, also serve as a basis for my research. Although my main focus in this book is on French military policy, I also use some oral sources and veterans' memoirs to examine the perspectives of Africans who served in the French army after World War II. These sources often expose the irrelevance of some of the concepts that are commonly used in relation to decolonization, such as nationalism, resistance, and collaboration. The struggles against colonial discrimination and mistreatment did not always involve a sense of brotherhood with other colonial peoples. The identity of many of the African soldiers who served in the French army was complex and flexible, and their main concern was often social and economic rather than "national."

It is my hope that *The French Army and Its African Soldiers* will contribute to the ongoing debate around the notion of decolonization, as well as deepen our understanding of the major role the French army and its African soldiers played in this process.

The Book's Structure and Its Logic

Chapter 1 offers the reader a political and historical background of the period covered in the book and provides basic information regarding each of the three main themes discussed. I begin with a short survey of French colonial rule in West Africa and its main characteristics. I then discuss the French army's role in the colonization of the region and its structure. Next I present the African soldiers' service in the French army until the end of World War II. Finally, I offer a brief overview of the main stages of the decolonization process in AOF.

Following this historical introduction, my starting point is the aftermath of World War II in AOF and the attempts of both the military and civilian authorities to control the thousands of disgruntled African soldiers returning home from France. Chapter 2 thus covers the years 1944 to 1949, during which relations between the army, its soldiers, and its veterans hit rock bottom. The abovementioned Thiaroye rebellion and its brutal repression marked the lowest point in these relations, but the situation remained extremely tense in the following years. Only in 1950, with extensive military reforms and especially the equation of the pensions, did this period of mistrust and resentment end. Chapter 3 deals with the implementation of the military reforms in AOF and their significance. It examines the revised policy of recruitment, the attempts to professionalize the colonial units and to attract Western-educated Africans to the army, and the reforms in the military schools of the federation, known as the Écoles des Enfants de Troupes (EET). In this chapter I consider the question of how much had really changed in the military's perceptions of African troops. The fourth and fifth chapters take us away from AOF to Indochina and Algeria, where a large number of African soldiers were sent to fight against the Viet Minh and the FLN, respectively. This diversion from the main line of the story is important, as the army's policies toward its African soldiers in the two conflicts are necessary to understand its views on the decolonization of AOF, which will be discussed in the two final chapters. The army's position toward AOF cannot be understood without appreciating the difficulties and dilemmas it faced in the other parts of the French empire and its attempts to "protect" African soldiers from the messages they received from the liberation movements in the two regions. Chapter 4 discusses the military policy toward Africans serving in the Indochina war and the attempts to keep their morale high and their loyalty intact despite the physical and mental difficulties these soldiers faced. Chapter 5 presents similar questions regarding the Algerian war. In addition, it discusses the notion of psychological warfare, which targeted not only the Algerian population but also African soldiers. This form of warfare was formalized in the French army toward the end of the Indochina war and played an important role in the Algerian conflict. Due to the Islamic religious affinity between many of the African soldiers and the Algerians, this chapter also deals extensively with the place of Islam in the military propaganda aimed at the soldiers, focusing on the pilgrimages to Mecca and Medina organized by the military.

Chapter 6 takes us back to AOF and examines the military vision of the political future of AOF and its concerns regarding the influence of political events in the international arena on Africans, specifically on African soldiers, whose loyalty was vital. I begin this chapter with the response of two colonial officers to the suggestion of the army's representative in Washington DC, at the time, Gen. Jean-Étienne Valluy, who formerly served in the colonial army, to abolish the colonial units and transfer their soldiers to newly established African armies. The two vehement responses help us understand the colonial military position on the decolonization process in AOF. Next, I examine the attempts to control the population in AOF through surveillance and the spread of propaganda, indicating that even in the mid-1950s the army assumed the continuous colonial presence of France in the federation. Finally, I deal with the military attempts to encroach on civil administrative responsibilities in AOF. Chapter 7 examines the final years of French colonial rule in AOF, focusing on the period between 1958 and the early 1960s. It explores how the army chose to deal with the official loss of AOF, its attempts to establish the new armies of the independent states and to control them, and the compensation it sought for the loss of direct control over the military power of the federation. This chapter will also examine the ways in which African soldiers and veterans dealt with the changing reality of newly found independence. Finally, I will briefly discuss the phenomenon of military coups in former French colonies led by African veterans of the colonial army as a means of exploring the influence of the military bonds created in the colonial period on postcolonial politics. In the conclusion I will deal with the significance of the three-way relationship between the army, its soldiers, and the federation of AOF and its contribution to our understanding of decolonization in this part of the French empire.

1

Historical Background

*The Army, the Empire, and the
Decolonization of French West Africa*

The French arrived on the shores of present-day Senegal in the seventeenth century and settled along the coast. Like other Western powers at the time, the French used trade and trading posts rather than military power as a way to establish their presence in the area. Their inability to penetrate the hinterland due to transportation difficulties and diseases for which there was yet no cure, principally malaria, forced them to rely on African intermediaries in order to perform their trading activities. Up until the mid-nineteenth century the French presence was felt mainly along the coast of Senegal in four towns, later to be known as the four communes: Dakar, Gorée, Rufisque, and Saint Louis (locally called Ndar). A municipal decree from 1872 accorded a commune status to Saint Louis and Gorée; Dakar and Rufisque joined them a few years later. During this early period of French presence, two local groups emerged as significantly influential within the four communes. One was the *métis*, descendants of French men and African women who had gained political, social, and economic power. The other group was comprised of Africans known as the *originaires*, who happened to reside in these four towns when France was overwhelmed once again by the revolutionary tide in 1848. The *originaires* gained French citizenship without being required to renounce their personal status. This meant that even an African who did not speak a word of French, was Muslim, and was married to a few wives would automatically become a French citizen just because he happened to be in the right place at the right time. Many colonial officials would later lament this measure, uncharacteristic of republican France, and some would try to revoke it, as this was quite a privileged status within the harsh colonial reality. Nevertheless, the *originaires* did not lose their privileged status during the Second Empire or even under Vichy rule in the early 1940s. These *originaires* were allowed to vote and be elected to local assemblies and could send a representative to the French parliament. In fact, in 1914 Gorée-born Blaise Diagne (1872–1934) was the first African elected to this post after a series of *métis*.

The *originaires* were also allowed to organize and establish newspapers. But most important, they were exempt from the two most repressive colonial practices that the French implemented when they began to extend their rule to the entire area of AOF and later to the territory that became the neighboring federation of French Equatorial Africa (Afrique Équatoriale Française, AEF): the *indigénat* and forced labor.[1] The *indigénat* was a legal tool that ensured administrative control over colonial subjects. It allowed administrators and other French representatives residing in the federation to arrest a colonial subject for a period of up to fifteen days or fine him for a listed offense (in general, women were exempted from the *indigénat*). As one of these offenses was disrespect for colonial authority, this punishment could be applied to virtually any act a colonial subject had performed that may have upset a colonial official. The *originaires* were not subject to this law and therefore enjoyed much more freedom than the colonial subjects.[2]

The other colonial practice *originaires* were exempt from was that of forced labor. The French recruited Africans by force to work in agricultural tasks that were considered undesirable, such as cotton cultivation and certain public projects. They paid these workers very little and forced them to work under difficult conditions, often subjecting them to brutal treatment. This practice was abolished by the French parliament only in 1946 on the initiative of Félix Houphouët-Boigny, the parliamentary representative of the Ivory Coast.[3]

Being exempt from these two colonial tools of repression was indeed a

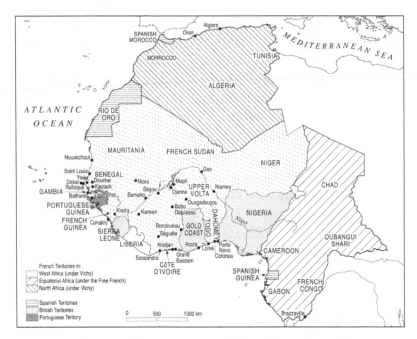

FIG. 1. French West Africa, 1940–42. Map designed by Tamar Soffer.

privilege, but it came with its own set of responsibilities. As French citizens, the *originaires* were required to serve in the French army. Their service conditions were far better than those of the African subjects who either were recruited by force or volunteered to serve. While the *originaires* served in metropolitan units alongside French soldiers, the other African soldiers were drafted into a special force called the Tirailleurs Sénégalais (Senegalese Infantrymen), established in 1857, when France desperately needed African help to extend its control in West Africa.[4]

The Structure of the French Colonial Army

During the nineteenth century the French and other Europeans acquired the means to leave the shores of Africa and reach the inland sources of their trade, thus releasing them from dependence on African intermediaries. The development of steamboats enabled Europeans to travel through narrow rivers to the hinterland, and the discovery of quinine as a means of preventing and treating malaria permitted them to do so with diminished anxiety. Although the French tried to employ diplomacy and sign dubious contracts with African local leaders in order to establish French authority, they soon encountered resistance in several areas: Haj Umar and Samori Touré in the area of present-day Guinea and Mali and King Behanzin in the region of Dahomey (Benin) were the fiercest resistors of the French expansion. The French had no choice but to use force, but they found it increasingly difficult to rely on European soldiers. They therefore began to recruit Africans, who they believed were far more resilient to the climate and geographical conditions in West Africa. They were also much cheaper to use, and their death did not raise criticism in France against unnecessary colonial adventures.[5] African recruits thus became the backbone of the colonial army.

As shown by Anthony Clayton, there was a contradiction between France's imperial aspirations and its need for military force to fulfill them, on the one hand, and the public objections in France to sending French soldiers outside the metropolitan territory, on the other. According to French legislation, a conscript from the metropole could not be sent to sub-Saharan Africa, Syria, or Indochina (until 1945) except under special circumstances. In order to reconcile this contradiction, two new forces were established, independent of the metropolitan army, that remained responsible only for the defense of metropolitan France. One was the Armée d'Afrique, which was actually the army of Northwest Africa. This force was established by the July monarchy (1830–48) after France landed in Algeria in 1830. It was responsible for the occupation and defense of North Africa and included Algerian, Tunisian, and Moroccan conscripts, known as Spahis (a term borrowed from the Ottoman traditional army), as well as other units such as the Foreign Legion. The second force responsible for the French empire was the Troupes Coloniales or La Coloniale. Prior to 1900 and after 1957 this force was known as Troupes de Marines. Its origins go back to the seventeenth century, and its units were sent to garrison French colonies in Africa, the Caribbean, and elsewhere. These units were formalized under the Restoration monarchy (1814–30) and increased considerably in the middle of the nineteenth century, when they began to recruit local soldiers in the French colonies. This was the force that in 1857 had incorporated the units of the Tirailleurs Sénégalais, which included soldiers from all over AOF and to a lesser extent Equatorial Africa. It also included separate units of metropolitan soldiers, largely volunteers, referred to as

La Coloniale Blanche (The White Colonial Army). The Troupes Coloniales were responsible for defending the rest of the French empire, excluding North Africa, which was under the responsibility of the Armée d'Afrique.[6] As the focus of this book is on the AOF region, this will be the force to which I am referring when I use the term "French colonial army," "colonial units," "French army," or simply "army."

The Deployment of African Soldiers in Europe

In theory, then, it was the French metropolitan army that was responsible for defending metropolitan France, while the other two forces were assigned to conquer and maintain order in the growing French empire. But when in the beginning of the twentieth century the clouds of war began to darken European skies, Col. Charles Mangin (1866–1925), later a well-known general, expressed an idea to use colonial units of African soldiers to defend the motherland. In a book titled *La force noire*, published in 1910, Mangin maintained that the falling birthrates in France made it necessary to recruit African soldiers to defend its borders.[7] He regarded the deployment of black soldiers in the defense of the motherland as the pinnacle of France's civilizing mission.[8] Referring to the pseudoscientific racial theories of his time, Mangin claimed that several so-called natural attributes of Africans made them excellent soldiers. Among these he included their ability to live in harsh climates and their capacity to carry heavy loads over great distances, explained by the belief that a supposedly underdeveloped nervous system allowed them to withstand pain. He argued that these ostensible qualities made African soldiers valuable for deployment as "shock troops" (*troupes de choc*) and that their appearance on the battlefields of Europe would have a considerable effect on the enemy's morale.[9]

Mangin was not alone in claiming that African soldiers could contribute to France's war efforts in Europe. Gen. Joseph Gallieni (1849–1916), who commanded many of the colonization campaigns in Africa and Indochina, stated in 1910 that "the warriors' qualities of the Senegalese can no longer be contested. They are proud to serve under the orders of the French leaders, so it is impossible to treat them as simple mercenaries; in the service of our flag, they constitute, on the contrary, elite troops that it would be regrettable not to deploy."[10]

After a heated debate among military and political circles in France, it was finally decided to support Mangin's proposal. African soldiers were recruited and sent to Europe right from the beginning of World War I, but mostly after 1916, when French casualties became heavy and mutiny in the ranks was on the rise. Over the five years of the war, AOF supplied 170,891 soldiers to the military forces.[11]

The main objection to this draft came from the then governor-general of AOF, Joost Van Vollenhoven, who was later killed in action in World War I. Van Vollenhoven did not see the logic in sending Africans to fight in a European war instead of leaving them to work their lands in Africa.[12] However, the recruitment campaign in AOF was led by the first African deputy in the French parliament, Blaise Diagne. Diagne estimated that recruiting Africans to World War I would encourage the extension of civil rights in the colonies. He therefore took it upon himself to convince Africans that volunteering for the army would contribute to their well-being in the future, and he succeeded in attracting a great number of volunteers, although in fact most Africans who served in the war were eventually forcibly recruited.[13]

Sending African colonial subjects to defend the motherland dramatically changed the rules of the "colonial game"—although it seemed at the time that the French did not yet realize this. The French military and administrative officials legitimized the idea of sending Africans thousands of kilometers away from their homes to fight a war that was not theirs by emphasizing what officials called the "blood debt." This was a supposed debt Africans owed the French for bringing civilization to their people and saving them from local and ruthless tyrants. It wasn't long before this idea was reversed, and the blood debt became one that France owed its colonial subjects for coming to its aid against its German enemies. A debt to colonial subjects is certainly not something any colonial power would easily admit to, but the contribution of tens of thousands of Africans to the war effort required some sort of gratitude, at least from the military perspective. This was manifested right after World War I by military efforts to commemorate African soldiers. Much later, on the eve of World War II, the African veterans' contribution was acknowledged by a decree giving them the right to be judged before French courts of law, thus allowing them to avoid the constant threat of the *indigénat*.[14]

It would take a while until this gratitude would be translated into massive reforms, but Africans who served in World War I gained a patron in the form of the military command in AOF. This did not simplify matters for the colonial administrators, who often found African veterans difficult to control. The experiences the Africans underwent in Europe and especially their relations with white women made them seem arrogant and disobedient in the eyes of members of the administration, especially in their behavior toward the African chiefs who did not go to war. Africans who served in Europe blurred colonial boundaries, as their experiences during the war reshaped their perceptions of colonialism and challenged their categorization as "colonial subjects." This suspicion toward veterans sometimes caused friction between administrators and military officials. One prominent example is the reluctance of colonial governors to participate in commemoration projects in AOF held for the African soldiers who had perished in the war due to their concern that such attention would only increase the veterans' disrespect toward the colonial authorities.[15]

The war also elevated the significance of the army's role in the colonial arena. As was the practice when the army occupied new territories, military officers took over the administration of the territory that was to become AOF and shaped colonial policy. When the federation of AOF was established in 1895, colonial rule was gradually transferred to civilian administrators in most of the colonies of the federation. The army thus lost much of its control over the shaping of colonial policy.[16] World War I and the mass participation of local soldiers from AOF in this war changed the situation and again increased military influence over the administration of the federation. One event that exemplifies the army's comeback is a tour to AOF in January 1925, led by no other than the hero of Verdun, later to become the collaborator of Vichy marshal Philippe Pétain. The aim of this tour was to formulate a report on the quality of the "black army" that Pétain was to submit to the minister of overseas France, Édouard Daladier.[17] The decision to send the most important military figure that emerged from the war to conduct this tour and write the report is hardly trivial. It demonstrates the new significance and respect the army had gained in the colonial arena. From now on the colonial civilian administration had to take the army's positions into account, and not only in strictly military matters. The military and the civilian administrations in AOF often saw eye to eye, but occasionally there were clashes. As we shall see later in this book, these frictions became more frequent during the tense years of decolonization.

Unlike the situation prior to World War I, when a heated debate ensued around Mangin's proposal to send African soldiers to defend metropolitan France, as World War II approached both colonial and military circles agreed that a massive draft of African soldiers was necessary. African soldiers' experiences in this war and its influence over their perception of French colonial rule upon their return will be examined in the next chapter. Suffice it to say that unlike World War I, which occurred at a very early stage of the French presence in West Africa, the second world conflict broke out when African politicians, students, and workers had already been challenging the legitimacy of colonial rule and the inherent discrimination it entailed. Its effects on the Africans who fought in this war were therefore much more significant than those of the previous war on their predecessors.

Major Watersheds in the Decolonization of AOF

In 1944, toward the end of World War II, Free French leader Charles de Gaulle convened a conference on colonial reforms in the capital of AEF, Brazzaville.[18] Although the eventual reforms were rather limited and no African representatives were invited to participate in the debates, in retrospect this conference can be seen as the beginning of a process that resulted in independence. This was not de Gaulle's intention, though. It was not even the preference of many Africans at the time, who only wished to become equal citizens in the newly established French Union. Nevertheless, fifteen years later, all of the colonies of AOF became independent states.

In the various chapters of this book, I will refer to the major events and political developments in the post–World War II years in AOF and briefly analyze their significance and impact. So as not to disrupt the discussion with detailed explanations each time I refer to such an event or development, I provide here a brief outline and background information of several important watershed events in the years of decolonization.

The first colonial reform after the Brazzaville conference, mentioned above, was the new constitution of 1946 and the establishment of the French Union. Although the constitution that was finally approved in October of that year was much less liberal than the first draft proposed six months earlier, the colonial reform abolished some of the most hated aspects of French colonialism, notably the *indigénat* and forced labor. Africans were no longer considered colonial subjects but rather "imperial citizens," though this limited citizenship accorded them no rights in metropolitan France. The voting rights to representative institutions in AOF were gradually extended after 1946. Trade unions that were authorized under the Popular Front between 1936 and 1938 and had been dissolved just before the war were again permitted to become active. The reauthorization of trade unions encouraged Africans to organize and demand improved pay and work conditions. They were often supported by French metropolitan unions. Trade unions organized several significant strikes in the post–World War II years, including a general strike in Dakar and Saint Louis during January 1946 and a railway strike that encompassed the entire federation and lasted from October 1947 to March 1948.[19] Both strikes were based on a demand of equal pay for equal work rather than a call to end colonial rule. In fact, during the late 1940s African workers managed to gain benefits by evoking the principle of equal pay for equal work, thus abolishing racial discrimination. Some of these reforms were endorsed thanks to the pressure of African deputies in the French National Assembly. For example, as we have seen, the Ivory Coast representative, Houphouët-Boigny, was the leader of the movement to abolish forced labor. The ability of these deputies to bring about changes in French colonial policy encouraged Africans to focus their political demands on the Paris channel rather than act within AOF. Residents of the French Union were still considered citizens thanks to a bill passed by the Senegalese deputy Lamine Guèye. The significance of this citizenship, however, was not clear, as it did not include the same voting or residence rights of French citizens.[20]

The first federal African party—the Rassemblement Démocratique Africain (RDA), headed by Houphouët-Boigny—was also established in 1946. Although this party mainly advocated more equality and political rights within the French Union and did not call for either autonomy or independence, the French administration saw the RDA as a threat and tried to weaken it by supporting other political parties that were considered more moderate. This hostility and lack of cooperation pushed the RDA to align with the Partie Communiste Française (French Communist Party, PCF), even though Houphouët-Boigny, who was a wealthy planter, was hardly a Communist. This alliance only intensified French suspicion and repression of the RDA until 1951, when the minister of overseas France, the young François Mitterrand, realized this alliance was practical rather than ideological and changed the French attitude toward the RDA. Suspicion of the RDA did not completely disappear, and within military circles the party was still considered radical and dangerous. The RDA's main rival was the Indépendants d'Outre-mer (IOM), a parliamentary group formed with French encouragement to counter the RDA, although it had no party organization in AOF. As we shall see, the military authorities saw it as moderate and much less threatening than the RDA.[21]

The next major political reform, which is also often considered as a turning point in the history of AOF, was the Loi-Cadre (Framework Law) of 1956. This law proposed to reorganize the institutions of the French Union without revising the constitution. The key issue in formulating this law was the debate between maintaining the federal structure of the political system and the "territorialist" approach, which called for transferring power to territorial governments. This approach finally gained the upper hand, as most African deputies supported it. The only exception was Léopold Sédar Senghor, later to become the president of Senegal. Not all powers were transferred to the territorial government. Several major areas became the direct responsibility of the French government: defense, the police (except rural and municipal police), the customs service, financial and monetary organizations, communications, the media, and higher education. Thus, the French government succeeded in maintaining dominance over strategic areas while at the same time shifting the responsibility for unpopular decisions from the colonial administration to the African territorial governments. This solved the problem of having to deal with workers' strikes and demands, as from now on demands had to be presented before the meagerly budgeted African governments.[22]

The two years between the Loi-Cadre and the next major colonial reform were characterized by the inherent instability of the French Fourth Republic. The crisis in Algeria escalated, and governments rose and fell in France every few months. This crisis reached its peak in May 1958, when military representatives and French settlers established the Comité de Salut Publique (Committee of Public Safety) in Algeria and demanded the return of de Gaulle to power. The May 1958 crisis and the army's part in it will be discussed in chapter 7. For our purpose here, suffice it to say that this crisis resulted in de Gaulle's return to power and in the end of the French Union. In September 1958 de Gaulle invited the African territories of AOF to join a new political framework, the Franco-African Community, in which they would gain full autonomy, leaving the areas of defense, diplomacy, and monetary policy in French hands. De Gaulle stated that territories that would join the community would be able to negotiate independence at a later stage. He warned, however, that the consequences of declining his invitation would be grave. De Gaulle stood behind this statement, as Guinea was to learn after rejecting de Gaulle's offer. The French reaction was hostile and vindictive. All the other territories of AOF voted for joining the community, though within two years all of them became independent. By joining the community in 1958, these territories, unlike Guinea, were able to maintain close contacts with France, which no longer objected to their independence.[23] In chapter 7 we will examine in depth these two years in order to explain the shift in French colonial policy, to which the army fiercely objected.

The reforms in the French colonial system in AOF outlined above were not the result of a calculated French plan. As Tony Chafer and Alexander Keese rightly indicate, these reforms do not represent a successful and organized decolonization that led to independence without bloodshed. Nor do they reflect a conspiracy to manipulate the political aspirations of Africans in order to continue French control over its territories after independence. In fact, each of these reforms, from the Brazzaville conference to the 1958 referendum, was an improvised response to a rapidly changing political reality that the French were not able to anticipate.

The French colonial military command was unhappy with this chain of political reforms, which made its missions in AOF difficult and prevented it from realizing its own colonial vision in the federation. As we shall see, the army viewed its improved relations with African soldiers and veterans as proof of the successful adjustment of the French colonial rule to the post–World War II reality and the creation of a common future for France and its African territories that would not rely on coercion and repression. It could be argued, of course, that this vision was unrealistic and paternalistic. Such a paternalistic attitude to Africans had been dominant among French commanders of African soldiers ever since the establishment of the African units within the colonial army. There is no doubt, then, that this military vision ignored the aspirations of many Africans, who did not share it and who rejected the military's tutelage. Furthermore, the success of the military reforms, which will be discussed in chapter 3, was based on the army being a nondemocratic and highly hierarchic institution. It then became possible to implement reforms without the risk of further demands on the part of the African soldiers, who did not have the right to strike or protest as civilian workers. Nevertheless, taking into account this vision and the desperate military attempts to promote it enhances our ability to see the entire picture of the decolonization years in AOF. In the following chapters, I will examine the army's role in the decolonization process in AOF and the ways in which it used African soldiers and veterans to preserve its control over the population of the federation at a time when it was fighting against anticolonial movements in other parts of the empire.

2

The Aftermath of World War II

Frustration, Protest, and Rebellion

World War II is often considered a milestone in African colonial history, as it ushered in a set of processes that eventually ended colonial rule, though this was not their original purpose. As recent studies have shown, the war had transformed the lives of many of the continent's inhabitants and had significant repercussions on the political, social, and economic developments in most of its regions.[1] While the war did not have the same influence everywhere within the colonial empires, in the French case it definitely changed the course of the colonial project.

The war naturally affected the relations between the French army and its African soldiers. As we shall see, it significantly increased the level of distrust and hostility between these two parties. In fact, the aftermath of World War II, especially in its final stages, constituted the lowest point in these relations. In order to properly understand the army's postwar colonial policy concerning its treatment of African soldiers and veterans, it is imperative to understand the experiences of the Africans who fought in this war, their arduous demobilization, and their disenchantment after it ended.

This chapter aims to analyze the general resentment of demobilized

Africans at the end of World War II, the various manifestations of this anger and frustration, and the military and administrative attempts to deal with them. The shared feeling among the military commanders of African soldiers in France, and even more so in AOF, was that they were losing control over these soldiers, who were becoming increasingly alienated from France and its army. Initial attempts to repress such protests by force, sometimes with tragic results, proved counterproductive, and the military authorities pressed for reforms that would mend the breach between the army and its soldiers. The war and its aftermath are thus a crucial stage in the relations between the army and its soldiers, and a thorough examination of this period can help us understand later military policies and attitudes toward African soldiers and veterans.

As I noted in the introduction, most of the research about African colonial soldiers to date focuses on their military service during the two world wars. In addition, much of the current discourse referring to the commemoration of African soldiers and the link between the sacrifices of the past and the present-day rights of African immigrants in France is based on the experiences of Africans in World War II. I will avoid repeating stories told elsewhere and focus on the ways in which African experiences in the war and the problems that arose during soldiers' demobilization affected subsequent developments, up until the end of the decade, in the relations between the French army and its African soldiers and veterans.

I will first describe briefly some of the experiences that African soldiers endured during the war and how these experiences influenced colonial relations and then move to examine the complex issue of demobilization and the conflicts it caused. I will begin with the most famous tragedy related to Africans' demobilization—the brutal repression of the soldiers' revolt in Camp Thiaroye near Dakar in December 1944—and continue by investigating subsequent French colonial dilemmas concerning the problematic process of demobilization.

To demonstrate France's precarious political position in the colonial realm I will also examine French and British negotiations regarding the French African subjects who had crossed the border into the British colonies during the Vichy period and were drafted into the British army. While the war ended officially in 1945, the aftermath of demobilization was felt until the end of the decade, as the colonial administration and military command had to continue tackling problems related to the demobilized African soldiers. As noted, the ongoing crisis encouraged the military authorities to initiate a series of reforms that transformed the relations between the army and its African soldiers and veterans. I will discuss these reforms in the following chapter.

African Soldiers in World War II

World War II brought the European conflict into the African continent and carried Africans into the battlefields in Europe and Asia. Of all the Allied powers, France was the only one that took full advantage of the manpower its colonies offered. It was also the only European power to deploy African soldiers on Continental soil. While the French had already deployed Africans in World War I, the complex position of France as a defeated colonial power in the second global conflict made Africans' participation in this war especially problematic. Africans fought in the battles of 1940, witnessed France's defeat and the German occupation of its soil, spent considerable time in German POW camps, and, finally, took part in the liberation of France within the ranks of the Free French forces. Their experiences on and off the battlefields reshaped their views of French colonialism.

According to rough estimates, 100,000 soldiers were mobilized in AOF from the outbreak of the war in September 1939 up to the fall of France in 1940, in addition to the standing army of 50,000. After the signing of the Armistice most of the soldiers who survived the battles of 1940 were demobilized. Others remained in the military forces the Vichy regime was allowed to keep in order to defend the federation. After November 1942, the Free French recruited 100,000 additional soldiers. Altogether, 200,000 soldiers were recruited to fight the war. Between 15,000 and 16,000 African soldiers fell into German captivity, and between 20,000 and 25,000 died.[2]

During the battles of 1940, African soldiers had been the victims of German atrocities directed specifically against them. The image the Germans held of African soldiers as savage barbarians who do not follow international rules of warfare and German memories of Africans as part of the occupation forces in the Rhineland after World War I reinforced the basic racism of German soldiers and commanders. In some cases, such as after the battle near Chasselay, a village near Lyons, the Germans massacred African soldiers who were taken captive.[3] African POWs were occasionally subject to medical experiments in German POW camps. This adverse treatment was short-lived, however, and German treatment of African POWs improved considerably, mainly due to the ulterior motive of causing anti-French contention among the colonial prisoners.[4] Unlike most other prisoners in the POW camps, Africans' communication with home was highly sporadic and often nonexistent because postal connection with the colonies was slow and unreliable and because many of the soldiers could not provide accurate addresses. According to Raffael Scheck, African POWs often accused the French authorities of being responsible for all of the Africans' difficulties and of indifference to their fate. They also believed that French metropolitan soldiers were receiving more benefits than they were due to intentional discrimination. Scheck suggests that these feelings were unfounded, as in fact many of the decisions regarding the fate of African POWs were in the hands of the Germans, and the Vichy regime was not responsible for most of them.[5] Logic would dictate that even if the Vichy regime could have some control over the fate of African POWs, it is hard to imagine how it could have allowed itself not to give metropolitan French POWs precedent over colonial ones, as this regime was attempting to preserve its eroding legitimacy during that period through the release of French POWs. In any case, we can see here that at this stage African soldiers had already developed resentment toward the French authorities and accused them of deliberate discrimination toward them.

The war not only affected the fate of African soldiers but also had a major influence over the colonies from which they had originated. Shortly after the signing of the Armistice in June 1940, the governor-general of the federation of French Equatorial Africa, Pierre Boisson, affirmed his loyalty to the new leader of France, Marshal Pétain, and was consequently transferred to the more strategically important federation of AOF. Until Boisson's departure in July 1943, eight months after the Allied landing in North Africa, this federation was under Vichy rule.[6] Concurrently, Félix Eboué, the governor of Chad, announced in August 1940 his loyalty to de Gaulle, who appointed Eboué the new governor-general of AEF. Each of the French federations in Africa was now under a different and opposing colonial administration, each claiming to be the "real" France. This unusual and unprecedented situation was particularly damaging from a colonial point of view, especially since a large part of metropolitan France was now under German occupation, exposing the colonial power as weak and vulnerable. It is therefore not surprising that both Vichy and the Free French invested enormous propaganda efforts to restore at least some French colonial prestige.[7] This situation was most confusing for African soldiers who served in the initial stage of the war and later found themselves on the opposing side of their former comrades, who had returned to Free French–ruled AEF. In the Syrian campaign, which the British and the Free French forces launched in June 1941 with the aim of taking Syria and Lebanon away from Vichy rule, for example, Africans who previously fought on the same side now fought each other. This change of purpose in the course of the war certainly did not enhance the African soldiers' trust in their colonial ruler.[8]

While under these conditions of military defeat it was difficult to convince Africans in the colonies that France was as powerful as ever, it was almost impossible to counter the accounts of demobilized African soldiers who had experienced France's defeat firsthand. These were divided into three main groups. The first group included the soldiers who came back to AOF after the fall of France and were the concern of the Vichy authorities. No less worrisome were the experiences of African soldiers who were taken captive following the battles of 1940. These soldiers were mostly discharged toward the end of the war and were therefore the concern of the Free French, who had already taken over the federation at that stage. The third group, which was also demobilized as the war ended, included the soldiers who fought with the Free French during the war and were part of the forces that liberated France in 1944. Although these soldiers had participated in the French victory and the fall of Germany, their experiences as the liberators of France were no less troubling for the colonial administration. From the colonial perspective, having African subjects as part of the heroic forces of liberation to which the civilian metropolitan population owed its gratitude was mostly disadvantageous. This was the main motive behind de Gaulle's order to "whiten" the liberating forces entering Paris in August 1944. De Gaulle determined that African soldiers should not be allowed to enter Paris so as not to cause demoralization among the civilian liberated population. This decision enraged African soldiers and contributed much to their deep resentment of their French commanders.[9] In fact, as Eric Jennings shows, the policy of whitening the forces designated to liberate Europe was already implemented a year before in Algeria, when the military command replaced all the African soldiers in an entire unit of the Free French forces with French metropolitan and North African soldiers.[10]

However, the colonial administration was worried by more than the military experiences of colonial soldiers. It was also deeply concerned by the warm relations some African soldiers had forged with French civilians. Soldiers were often invited to French homes, and the attitude toward them was radically different from the racist and paternalistic treatment the representatives of the colonial administration and other Europeans residing in the colonies had shown them at home. African soldiers developed friendly and even intimate relations with French women, some marrying these women and having children with them. In a few cases, women who had forged relationships with African soldiers during the war asked the colonial administrators for permission to join them in the colonies. Such requests were always refused, even though legally the French colonial administration could not have prevented French women from moving into the colonies. Colonial administrators often found it more convenient to send African veterans who wished to renew these relationships to France. This preference was aimed at avoiding the repercussions interracial couples might cause in the colonies and resulted from the fear of damage to colonial prestige. While the colonial authorities did not attempt to prevent reunions of African ex-soldiers with their French wives or girlfriends, they nonetheless preferred that these problematic couples reside far away from the eyes of other colonial subjects.[11]

The warm relations that often developed between French civilians— both male and female—and African soldiers threatened to blur the already precarious boundaries between colonized and colonizers and were therefore seen by the colonial administration as a real threat to colonial stability after the war. As we shall see, this state of affairs influenced African soldiers' perceptions of the treatment they received from the French military and colonial authorities. They were not patient, to say the least, when they encountered numerous difficulties stemming from neglect and discrimination in the course of their demobilization. When they expressed their discontent during their long process of demobilization, the colonial and military authorities often linked these emotions to the experiences the soldiers' had undergone during the war. Official documents contain many references to the connection between the defiant behavior of African demobilized soldiers and their relations with French civilians, especially with women, who according to these documents were one of the catalysts of this questioning of colonial authority and the rigid colonial categories. As we shall see, this analysis was embedded with numerous misunderstandings and was clouded by ongoing paternalism toward the soldiers.

Turbulent Demobilization in AOF

African soldiers were already involved in serious incidents and protests before their repatriation at the end of the war. The chaos that reigned in France right after the liberation affected the ability of the military and civilian authorities to take proper care of the soldiers and accord them their rights. The delays in sending the soldiers back to their colonies made them restless and impatient. The conditions in the camps in France in which the African soldiers waited before repatriation were terrible; the food was very limited, and some soldiers bitterly claimed that even the conditions in the German prisoner of war camps had been better. In 1944 and at the beginning of 1945, several incidents and mutinies occurred in various camps in France where African soldiers were stationed, including Morlaix, Versailles, and Fréjus. African soldiers disobeyed orders, organized protest marches, and occasionally had violent altercations with French soldiers and civilians. French civilians, for their part, sometimes claimed that African soldiers demanded to receive their groceries for free.[12]

It is no wonder, then, that by the time the soldiers arrived in AOF the colonial authorities were extremely concerned regarding what they perceived to be the soldiers' rebellious state of mind. In October 1943 AOF secretary-general Léon Geismar, representing Free France, informed the governors of the colonies that demobilized soldiers who had fought with the Free French forces were causing disturbances in Senegal. Geismar reminded the governors of the problems caused by demobilized soldiers after the previous world war due to their difficulties readjusting to their former lives. He asked the military authorities to inform the administration upon the arrival of demobilized soldiers at AOF and requested that the governors do all in their power to prevent undesirable incidents.[13] In spite of the vigilance of the colonial administration and their concern that demobilized African soldiers might cause certain instability in colonial rule, it seems that no one in the French colonial administration or in the colonial army could have predicted the scope of the African soldiers' discontent and the tragic results their mistreatment in France and in AOF would create.

In November 1944, after long stretches of imprisonment in German camps located in France during the war, 1,280 African soldiers returned to Dakar and were interned in a camp in Thiaroye, approximately 15 kilometers from the city. The poor conditions in the camp, along with the refusal of their French commanders to grant them the payment they justifiably demanded, led the soldiers to protest. In order to alleviate the situation, the camp commanders tried to move five hundred soldiers to Bamako, but the soldiers refused to leave the camp. The soldiers then blocked the path of Gen. Marcel Dagnan, the commander of the Senegal-Mauritania division, and demanded their due payments. The general finally promised to handle this matter and was allowed to leave. After this incident, Dagnan declared that the soldiers were in a state of revolt and suggested taking severe steps to remedy this dangerous situation. He could not tolerate the idea of armed soldiers contesting French colonial authority so close to the federal capital. On the morning of December 1, 1944, additional units entered the camp, many of which consisted of African soldiers brought from other parts of the federation. The idea was to surprise the "rebels" and demonstrate the power of the military command in order to repress them. The soldiers refused to be impressed, and for a couple of hours they insulted and jostled the European commanders. Finally, the forces brought into the camp opened fire. According to French official figures, thirty-five of the rebelling soldiers involved in the revolt were killed, but most historians estimate that the number was actually around seventy. Many more were wounded.[14]

Documents from the period just before the revolt of Thiaroye and its brutal repression demonstrate the inability of the French military and administrative authorities to understand the mental state of the African soldiers and the immense effect their war experiences had on their perception of themselves, their French commanders, and their right to both better treatment and full equality. Just a month prior to the revolt in Camp Thiaroye, the minister of the colonies had informed the high commissioner of AOF that only a quarter of the soldiers' salaries would be paid to them in France and that they would receive the rest in their villages. In addition, he explained that the plan was to give each of the demobilized soldiers a certain amount of fabric, a useful commodity that was limited during the war, but due to the scarcity of fabric in France this plan would not be implemented. The minister anticipated some kind of trouble due to the long absence of the soldiers from their homes and the new habits and ways of thinking they had acquired, which turned them, according to the minister, into a "very special element." He pointed to the confusing situation in which they had lived since the liberation of France, which contributed to their becoming extremely demanding, especially with regard to their material conveniences, such as requesting better clothes and food. The best solution to the problem, he felt, was to send the soldiers as quickly as possible to their villages.[15]

The great number of soldiers who were still in France also concerned the minister. These soldiers belonged to two main categories: the first included ex-POWs who had been in German captivity since the battles of 1940, 8,000 of whom were designated to be demobilized in AOF. The second category was comprised of soldiers who had not been in captivity. Originally, 2,000 of them were supposed to be sent to AOF, but their numbers were constantly growing. All in all, over 10,000 quite belligerent African soldiers were due to arrive in the federation. The French intention was to send these soldiers back home as soon as possible, but the shortage of ships prevented this. In the meantime, the army invested some efforts in improving the living conditions of the soldiers camping in France, waiting to be sent back to West Africa. The French command offered these soldiers social assistance; opened clubs, training centers, and medical services for them; and gave them parcels containing all sorts of treats, such as biscuits and cigarettes.[16] However, such measures were hardly enough to satisfy the African soldiers. The French refusal to pay them their full salaries and demobilization grants and the lack of satisfactory food and clothing reinforced their anger. The soldiers were further enraged when French commanders, realizing that some soldiers had large sums of money in their possession, accused them of theft. Indeed, only two days before the tragedy in Thiaroye, an information report pointed to the low morale of the soldiers who had already arrived at Dakar, some of whom even threw the biscuits and cigarettes they received into the ocean. The main concern voiced in the report was the potential subversive propaganda that the soldiers had been exposed to during their short stay in Morocco.[17] Other reports mentioned the repercussions of the German propaganda that the soldiers had encountered during their captivity. The simple idea that all the soldiers wanted was respectful treatment and the payments that they legally deserved did not occur to the minister or to the other representatives of the military and civil authorities.

Preventing Another Thiaroye

Even after they brutally killed more than three dozen former POWs who had sacrificed several years of their lives for France, the French authorities still hoped to appease the demobilized soldiers with somewhat insignificant means. Immediately after Thiaroye, the commandant of the Podor district (*cercle*) in northern Senegal, for example, granted permission to eight ex-POWs to buy sugar and fabric, a special privilege, as these products were limited after the war due to their scarcity. When four of the ex-POWs also asked for a position in the administration, he vaguely requested them to wait until their military situation cleared. The commandant of the Bas-Senegal district was rather disappointed that the authorization he gave to six *originaires*—demobilized soldiers from Saint Louis—to buy 15 meters of fabric did not seem to have the desired effect on them, as they expressed their frustration over their existing conditions after their return. In his report, the commandant remarked that one could have expected people who returned home after five years of suffering to be rather more cheerful and enthusiastic.[18]

The French response to the Thiaroye rebellion demonstrates the administrative and military shock at the turn of events, despite some expectation of trouble. It also shows genuine attempts to prevent the recurrence of such troubles. A few days after the revolt, the high commissioner reported on the events to the minister of the colonies. He determined that the operation was necessary not only in order to avoid the consequences of the armed African soldiers' unruly behavior so close to the center of Dakar but, on a larger scale, because French sovereignty was at stake.[19] While the French military and administrative authorities expressed no remorse or regret regarding the action they took against the soldiers, they did attempt to examine what went wrong and to determine how to avoid such incidents in the future. Immediately after the shooting, the governor of Dakar suggested to the high commissioner that he should postpone the demobilization of the soldiers, as they might spread their discontent among the civilian population. He was especially concerned about the population of Dakar, which he considered as "rather emotional." He therefore recommended fortifying the soldiers' discipline before their final demobilization. A hand-written comment added next to this suggestion expressed its writer's skepticism in these words: "I do not think this is possible in the current situation of the military personnel."[20]

On December 12, 1944, less than two weeks after the rebellion in Thiaroye, the high commissioner submitted several ideas intended to prevent such incidents from reoccurring. This report seems to demonstrate that the military authorities were already beginning to accept the fact that the main catalyst for the rebellion was the commanders' refusal to deliver to the soldiers their due payments. The minister suggested paying full salaries to the demobilized soldiers already in France. Among his other proposals was the suggestion that the soldiers would be better controlled if French officers who were experienced in working with Africans supervised them. Only at the end of the report did the high commissioner mention the so-called negative effects of the German propaganda that African POWs may have been exposed to during their captivity, previously considered as the main cause of the soldiers' discontent.[21]

In the aftermath of the revolt and its repression, the administration was concerned about the potential repercussions it might have among the African population. The high commissioner briefed all administrators, up to the level of the district commanders (*commandants des cercles*), as to how they should explain these events. Some reports mentioned the local population's deep sadness at the news about the revolt. In other reports, the high commissioner warned administrators that they would have to contend with spreading rumors, according to which the French had killed hundreds of African soldiers while suppressing the insurgency.[22]

It seems that the tragic events in Thiaroye made the French much more cautious both in France and in AOF. Discontent among African demobilized soldiers continued as late as 1948, and the longer it lasted, the more far-fetched the theory that the German propaganda was the main culprit seemed, even to the colonial authorities. Some reports sent from AOF to Paris attempted to transmit an aura of reassurance regarding the situation. Such was a letter from the high commissioner of AOF, Pièrre Cournarie, to the minister of the colonies, dated August 23, 1945, in which he explained that the colonial administration had taken necessary measures and that the demobilization was running smoothly. The main subject of this letter was an attempt to explain why the visit of Madame Jane Vialle, who had offered to work with African former POWs in AOF as she had in France, was completely superfluous.[23]

Born in 1906 to a French father and a Congolese mother, Vialle was the representative of Ubangui-Shari (contemporary Central African Republic) in the French parliament. She graduated from Jules Ferry High School in Paris and during the war joined the Resistance movement in Marseille. After the Germans arrested her in 1943, she spent a year in a concentration camp and was later awarded the Medal of the Resistance for her activities. Vialle entered politics following a tour she made with a member of the French parliament, Senegal's deputy, Léopold Sédar Senghor, in Senegal in 1945.[24] Cournarie's outright rejection of the suggestion that Vialle meet with African ex-POWs during that tour, accompanied by an obviously false description of his total control over the situation in the colonies, reveals the threat a figure such as Vialle posed for the administration. After all, the administration was attempting to present the soldiers' protests as a temporary outrage influenced by their uprooting from their so-called natural environment rather than a real and permanent change in their perception of the colonial and racial relations in AOF. As a mixed-race woman, a hero of the Resistance, and a politician fighting for Africans' rights and equality, Vialle had crossed both racial and gender boundaries. Such a figure was not someone the high commissioner wanted African ex-soldiers to meet.

In spite of the high commissioner's efforts to reassure the minister that he was in total control of the demobilized soldiers' discontent, information describing the situation in Thiaroye more than a year later casts serious doubt on this idyllic description. The 2,700 African soldiers who arrived in the camp in November 1946 were in a very bad state of mind. They were aggressive toward the European personnel, did not respect their officers, and refused to salute them. European women, so the report emphasized, had lost all esteem in their eyes, supposedly because the soldiers had developed intimate relations with these women during the war.[25]

Around the same time, a report from Dahomey dated March 1946 expressed bewilderment at the negative attitudes of demobilized soldiers. Four hundred African soldiers returning to Africa by ship recounted to everyone they met onboard that the Americans were the ones who had fed them and supplied their uniforms in France, while their French commanders totally neglected them. They felt the French were unappreciative people who treated the soldiers badly because the French believed that the blacks of West Africa, especially those from Dahomey, were the most backward of all races. At this point, the writer of the report remarked that this attitude was surprising because these soldiers had not been in German captivity.[26] Here it is evident that the idea that German propaganda was the main motive for the demobilized soldiers' discontent had not completely faded away even by 1946. The fact that soldiers who were not exposed to such propaganda were still complaining about the French seemed to the French writer of the report to be highly surprising. These four hundred returning soldiers also caused concerns about the possibility of an armed rebellion in AOF. Although it seems that the French military and civil authorities in AOF did not consider the occurrence of such a rebellion very probable, they also did not rule out the possibility altogether. This same report included information describing the weapons the soldiers on the ship had acquired in order to stage a protest if they did not receive their demobilization grants. Only when their comrades from Dakar warned them that the French response would be harsh did they decide to throw their grenades, revolvers, and bullets into the sea. Nevertheless, the French authorities found sixteen supposedly stolen revolvers onboard after the ship had anchored in Dahomey. A similar case of arms theft occurred in another unit, and although the report mentioned that the authorities found no connection between the two cases, they were both somewhat alarming.[27] Shortly afterward, in April 1946, the chief of the military security service, Lieutenant-Colonel Bonnefous, reported on a rumor spreading among soldiers from Dahomey suggesting the establishment of an anti-French movement in AOF. According to the rumor, members of this movement intended to start a rebellion against the French in Dahomey with the purpose of taking over the army. The potential rebels supposedly received their orders from Paris through students serving as emissaries. Although Bonnefous suggested that this rumor not be taken too seriously because it was being spread by people who were influenced by the currents of nationalism and the events in Indochina and the Levant, he still recommended that propaganda within the military be controlled and weapons be guarded more vigilantly.[28]

Monitoring African Soldiers after Thiaroye

This fear of revolt, especially at a time when anticolonial struggles were taking place in Algeria, Madagascar, and Indochina, prompted the military authorities to watch demobilized soldiers closely. In the period after Thiaroye the French administration made genuine attempts to closely monitor the mental state of the demobilized soldiers and to take measures to prevent another outburst of discontent. In Guinea, for example, French administrators invited World War I veterans to welcome the returning soldiers and mentor them, handed out food and cigarettes to the demobilized soldiers, prohibited the sale of alcohol, and provided immediate transportation in order to transfer the soldiers as quickly as possible to their villages. In addition, secret police officers toured the area to monitor any sign of protest.[29] The colonial administration continued to monitor the soldiers who had been in the camp during the rebellion even after their return to their homes. This was done for two reasons. One was to ensure that these soldiers would not cause additional problems. The other was to understand from these demobilized soldiers what they felt was the source of the uprising. The attempt to hear these soldiers' perceptions seems to show that the official French interpretation of the events, as reflecting German anti-French propaganda and/or the immorality induced by questionable French women and excessive consumption of alcohol, was not offered wholeheartedly. A month after the revolt in Thiaroye a report was submitted to the high commissioner discussing several ex-POWs who had either participated in the revolt or witnessed it. According to the report, all ex-POWs were behaving well and had not performed any subversive activities or expressed dangerous political views. One of them, described as a relaxed and serious fellow, was reported to be living with his mother (a fact that perhaps somehow rendered him less dangerous). This demobilized soldier was indeed followed closely, as the writer of the report noted that he and his mother visited a man who wrote letters to POWs during the war in order to thank him. The ex-soldier was also reported to have bad memories of the Germans and not to have spent exaggerated sums of money. The last remark was related to the large amounts of money that some of the rebellious soldiers in Thiaroye had in their possession and that, according to the French, were proof of a German conspiracy to turn the soldiers against the French. This, of course, contradicted the claim made by some of the French commanders, that the soldiers had stolen the money.

Military representatives also directly questioned another ex-POW, Momar Guèye, about the sources of the soldiers' discontent. Guèye claimed that he was on leave at the time of the revolt. This did not prevent him from speculating that the soldiers who initiated the revolt were the same soldiers who caused problems while stationed in Versailles. He was not so sure, though, about their motives. He doubted the theory claiming that German propaganda had influenced them and said that he had never witnessed any German attempts to persuade African soldiers to revolt against the French after their liberation. However, he did volunteer that the Germans sent some African POWs to study German. As for the weapons and money the rebellious soldiers had in their possession, Guèye did not think that the Germans distributed them. He said that many weapons were left on the battlefields and that the money was probably stolen from dead bodies or from abandoned institutions.[30]

Other intelligence reports further undermined the theory of a German or a Communist conspiracy. Several ex-POWs from among the *originaires* who were returning by train to their homes in Saint Louis were overheard during their journey and were reported to be anti-Russian and deeply pro-French. It turned out that the Russians delayed them in the Soviet Union after their release from German captivity. They claimed that the Russians treated them even worse than the Germans had. They told the other passengers that the French in France opposed the current colonial policy, and many of them worked to improve life in the colonies.[31] Another report stated that *originaires* who returned from France commented on the difference between the way the French treated them and the way the Germans did. They recognized the importance of a continued French tutelage, which they openly admitted encouraged and advanced the development of the colonies. They did not favor the Americans, because they knew that they would never sit at the same table with a black man, while French fraternity allowed blacks and whites to study and work together. None of the demobilized soldiers was in favor of Nazism, and they all had bad memories of the Germans.[32] These short reports relate to almost all the French fears of the period. They express fear of the influence of German propaganda over African soldiers who were POWs during the war, fear of Communists encouraging Africans to revolt, the concern about American intentions with regard to the French colonial project, the horror of miscegenation, and finally the concern of losing prestige in the eyes of colonial subjects.

Despite the reassurance these reports gave French colonial administrators, they also indicated continued dangers. Even the ostensible love for the French in France included hostility to the French of the colonies. Many of the French civilians African soldiers had met during the war were opposed to colonial rule and treated them with respect. Such treatment only reinforced the African soldiers' expectations when they returned home. In one case, demobilized soldiers from Dahomey expressed their excitement about the warm welcome French families had given them. They therefore expected large demobilization grants and employment in AOF upon their return.[33] Other soldiers from Dahomey, demobilized two months later, spoke about their regret at leaving France due to economic motives. They worked there as builders and mechanics, earning between 6,000 and 9,000 francs, which was considered quite a good salary, and were not happy to settle for a much smaller salary in the colonies.[34] Some reports emphasized the demobilized soldiers' continued discontent over their material conditions and the inequality between them and their French metropolitan comrades, which contrasted with some of their wartime experiences. One report, for example, noted that demobilized African soldiers were returning to their villages somewhat bedraggled, wearing only shorts and torn shirts.[35] The issue of uniforms was important, as the French commanders asked African soldiers to return the uniforms they received at the end of the war from the American army. These uniforms were a source of pride for the soldiers, who hoped to impress their friends and relatives when they returned to their villages.

The clothing issue was especially disturbing, as African soldiers returning from France compared their miserable uniforms not only to those of French metropolitan soldiers but also to those of Nigerian soldiers demobilized from the British army. These soldiers crossed the border into French territory, donning new uniforms from head to toe, displaying at least three or four medals on their chest, and carrying a sum of 70 pounds in their pockets. The provider of this description was no other than the minister of the colonies, who wrote about this to High Commissioner Cournarie. He noted that all these soldiers had done was work on the roads in Burma, and their appearance in the French colonies caused justified resentment among the demobilized soldiers who served as combat troops for France.[36] The high commissioner, for his part, was concerned about the possible temptation demobilized soldiers might have to move into the British colonies after acquiring a profession in the army due to the much wider range of employment opportunities the British offered to demobilized soldiers in their colonies. In a letter to the commander of the French forces in AOF, he mentioned the tremendous efforts the British administration invested for the benefit of demobilized soldiers, ensuring their employment and according them high standards of living.[37] For the French administration, Britain's colonial policy and practice served as another source of threat to the relations with their African veterans. The French colonial administration at its highest levels was thus aware of the unsatisfactory and often ungrateful treatment it accorded demobilized soldiers, but apparently it either could not or would not make the necessary efforts to compete with its British neighbors. This competition with the British became especially problematic, as a large number of soldiers, serving in British territories either under the Free French forces or in the ranks of the British army, were also returning to their villages in AOF during that period.

Demobilization of Africans Who Served in
AEF and in the British Colonies

Though the French had many concerns regarding soldiers returning from France, not all the soldiers who served in the war returned to AOF from the metropole. Some Africans from AOF found themselves either voluntarily or accidentally in the ranks of the Free French in AEF, the Free French Resistance movements operating from either AEF or British-ruled colonies, or even the British army. Among these were mostly West Africans who were either sent or arrived by themselves to AEF before the Free French took over the federation in 1940 and were then recruited into the army by de Gaulle's followers.[38] Others were Africans who for some reason, probably financial, crossed the border into the British colonies and then joined the Resistance (or at least claimed to do so) or were recruited into the British army even though they were French subjects. These soldiers posed problems not only for the military authorities but also for the colonial administration. As soldiers who fought on the winning side of the French inner conflict between Vichy and the Free French during World War II, they were supposed to receive special benefits. A special committee established that, once demobilized, these soldiers would be in the next preferred employment category after wounded soldiers.[39] Colonial administrators did not always implement this affirmative action, as can be gleaned from the many complaints about discrimination against Free French soldiers. In response, the minister of the colonies expressed his disapproval of the situation in a letter he sent to the high commissioner, stating the fact that Free French soldiers did not get preference in employment and sometimes found themselves at a disadvantage compared to other soldiers.[40]

Beyond the differential benefits offered to different categories of demobilized soldiers lay a deeper problem: the difficulty these soldiers, especially those who fought with the Free French Resistance groups operating in British colonies, had proving that they indeed belonged to the Free French forces. Soldiers who submitted requests for benefits to the colonial administration in their colonies received the assistance of Mr. Orcel, the French consul in Bathurst, the capital of the Gambia, and of Mr. Plozin, the representative of the association of the Free French combatants in Niger. On July 20, 1946, Orcel wrote to the high commissioner on behalf of Chief Sgt. Djibril Guèye, a former master mason in the Dakar municipality who had crossed the border to Gambia in 1940 and had joined the Free French forces there. He now asked to receive compensation for his service in the Resistance. The consul wrote that as his commander he could testify to his exemplary conduct and that Guèye served as a model of real and selfless patriotism.[41] Three months later the consul sent a letter to the president of the newly established committee responsible for the benefits for Free French African soldiers in which he expressed support of eleven additional requests of Africans who did not possess documentation to prove their claims either because they had lost them or because they never had them.

The consul attested that they had given statements in his presence and had been corroborated by witnesses.[42] The lack of documentation sometimes required the assistance of colonial administrators who had to confirm the timetable the soldiers presented attesting to their whereabouts during the turbulent years of World War II. Apparently, not all administrators were enthusiastic about filling in endless forms in support of African soldiers' requests. Mr. Plozin expressed his dissatisfaction with these administrators to the above-mentioned committee in 1947 after thirty-nine Free French combatants complained about the lack of cooperation they encountered while attempting to attain proof for their requests. In one case, a soldier who had traveled 200 kilometers (124 miles) in order to have an administrator fill in a questionnaire was sent home with the questionnaire still blank.[43]

Even more complicated than the status of Africans who served under the Free French was the issue of Africans who had crossed the border to British colonies during the war for a variety of reasons—often to avoid forced labor or military service or to engage in illicit commerce—and found themselves drafted into the British army. This was more complex, as another colonial power was involved and the French administration depended on its goodwill when it discussed the demobilization of these soldiers with British administrators. The long correspondence between the French and British authorities and the detailed British reports discussing this issue reveal its complexity for both sides and presumably even more for the soldiers. The French were anxious to return to AOF all Africans who had deserted from the army or had simply disappeared when called to the flag (referred to as *bons absents*). They were concerned about losing these men to the British, who often offered them better pay and employment opportunities after their discharge. The British, for their part, were not interested in giving up soldiers who had served in their army, especially those who had been sent to other parts of the British empire and whom British authorities now had to transfer back to West Africa. The British authorities also claimed that it was hard to identify French subjects, as their physical appearance, names, and languages were similar to those of British African subjects.[44] Eventually, in September 1944 the British agreed not to renew the mobilization of French subjects to the British army.[45] This did not solve the problem of those French subjects who were already serving under the British flag. British and French negotiations on this issue resulted in the establishment of an effective date: July 24, 1943. All French subjects drafted to the British army before that date were to continue serving in the British army, while those who were drafted after this date were to be immediately returned to the French authorities.[46] The British took upon themselves all the expenses of the demobilization of African soldiers from the British army and their return to French territory. In fact, the only role French administrators were assigned was to keep in contact with their British counterparts and report to the high commissioner on every demobilized soldier.

The negotiations between the British and the French regarding the demobilization of the African soldiers who were drafted into the British army demonstrate the fragile position of the French authorities and, to a greater extent, that of the Africans who were the subject of these negotiations. It seems that the main wish of the Africans who returned to French territory after serving in the British army was to evade service not only in the British army but also in its French counterpart.[47]

To conclude, the demobilization of African soldiers who had served either in France or in other parts of the colonial world was an arduous process, with some disastrous results. The brutal killing of the soldiers in Camp Thiaroye, after they had sacrificed several years of their lives for France and lost their friends in battle, is the clearest evidence of that. Even soldiers who were not involved in the violent revolts often felt deep frustration both during and after demobilization. Many did not receive the payments due to them, and their nutrition and clothing while en route to the colonies were sorely lacking, especially in comparison to those of metropolitan soldiers and even their counterparts serving under the British flag. Their commanders often accused them either of being encouraged to revolt by the Germans or of stealing money and weapons. Although racist or paternalistic attitudes played a large role in this inadequate treatment of the soldiers, it also stemmed from France's dire situation after the war. The difficult economic situation in France at the end of World War II and the political turmoil that overtook the nation prevented both the military authorities and the colonial administration in AOF from properly attending to the needs of African soldiers. As we have seen, the French authorities were somewhat aware of the mistreatment of the demobilized African soldiers and the advantages enjoyed by Africans serving in the British army. Nevertheless, they were only partially successful in remedying this unfortunate situation. The resentment of African soldiers and veterans toward the French military and administrative authorities continued until the end of the 1940s, when the latter began to take more significant measures to remedy the situation. These measures included a series of reforms that, according to the military authorities, aimed to drastically change the character of the colonial army. In the next chapter we will examine these reforms and the "new" colonial army they created. We will also look at the essence of this "new army" and investigate how new it actually was.

3

The Military Reforms

A New Army in French West Africa?

Even though World War II had ended, the challenges for the French army were not yet over. On the very day on which Europe celebrated the end of the war (May 8, 1945), riots began in the town of Sétif in Algeria, followed by the massacre of thousands of Algerians. A few months later, in August, with the end of the war in the Far East, the Japanese retreat from Indochina created a vacuum, which the Viet Minh filled quite easily. Soon the French army found itself involved in a full-scale war with this organization. In addition, in 1947 a revolt erupted on the island of Madagascar. The army had to rely on West African soldiers to deal with all these challenges of French authority.

As we have seen in the previous chapter, during this same period relations between African soldiers and the French military command hit rock bottom. In spite of French administrative and military efforts to prevent the recurrence of revolts after the tragic events in Thiaroye, serious discontent still existed among demobilized and active soldiers, and occasionally smaller-scale revolts did flare up. In order to improve their relations with the African soldiers, the military authorities decided to initiate a series of reforms that aimed at radically transforming the nature of the colonial army.

In this chapter, I will examine these reforms and the manner in which they were implemented. My aim is to demonstrate that the difficult situation in which the army found itself in the aftermath of World War II forced this institution to advance massive and significant reforms, which changed the nature of the relations between the army and its soldiers and veterans. My main argument is that the reforms actually reflected the military command's perception of the transformation of its African units and in a way also its vision of the political future of AOF. The new army was supposed to become a modern and equal institution and as such to represent the new form of French colonial rule. While, as we shall see in this chapter, the lingering paternalism and disrespect for Africans on the part of some of the French commanders hindered the reforms and slowed down this transformation, the military reforms represented a major change in the French military mind and the army's new approach both toward its African soldiers and toward the manner in which France should rule over AOF. After presenting the military's preliminary efforts to improve relations with African soldiers and veterans at the end of the 1940s, this chapter will examine four main areas affected by the reforms: recruitment policy, improvement of the federation's military schools, attempts to form an African military elite comprised of officers and skilled soldiers serving in elite units, and the army's efforts to present a new image to the population of AOF. We will see how the recruitment policy changed after World War II and what measures were taken to attract candidates skilled in various crafts that could be useful in the army and encourage volunteers rather than relying only on forced recruitment. We will also look at the initial attempts to entice Africans from the Western-educated elite into the army and away from administrative careers.

As the initial efforts to attract such candidates did not bear fruit, the army invested efforts in improving its own system of education, establishing schools aimed at training African youth to become NCOs. Although the army had established schools, known as the Écoles des Enfants de Troupes (Schools for Soldiers' Sons, EET), in 1923, during the period discussed here these establishments underwent significant reforms, and additional funds were invested in them. The new name designated for the schools, École Militaire de Préparation Africaine (Military School for African Preparation, EMPA), suggested the professional objective of the schools and the extension of the target audience of these school beyond the sons of serving soldiers. These reforms and the debates surrounding them will be examined in depth in the following pages.

The third part of the chapter will deal with the later attempts to increase the numbers of African officers, beginning in the mid-1950s, when it became apparent that the process of Africanization of the officer ranks and the special units (such as the air force) in the colonial army was slow and unsatisfactory. I will discuss the measures that were taken to attain this goal, as well as the obstacles to this policy.

The fourth part of this chapter will examine the attempts of the military to project its new image to the population of AOF. I will consider the various means through which the army tried to present itself as modern and professional to Africans, including the organizations of tours, ceremonies, celebrations, and sports events. Finally, I will determine the ways in which this image reflected reality. In other words, to what extent was the "new army" truly new, and how much of the "old army" still persisted?

Initiating Military Reforms

The political situation in France and in other parts of its empire during the immediate post–World War II years made appeasing African soldiers and veterans a political necessity. In France the postwar purge was followed by the creation of the Fourth Republic and later by de Gaulle's retreat from politics. Political turbulence continued with the expulsion of Communist ministers from the government in 1947. Major rebellions erupted in Indochina and Madagascar, and violent incidents occurred in North Africa and the Levant.[1] During this precarious period the French needed African soldiers and the support of African veterans. The soldiers were needed in order to protect the empire, and the veterans played an important role in the local West African political scene. The colonial administration saw the veterans' alliance with African political groups that challenged the French colonial rule in the federation as a significant threat to political stability in a region that, at the time, was still relatively calm.

To this end, from 1947 onward various French authorities took a series of steps aimed at gaining the support of soldiers and veterans alike. The army played a significant part in these efforts. In March 1947, after a preliminary survey of the veterans' complaints, Gen. Raymond Delange reported that the veterans were still supportive of France but should not be underestimated, as they felt they were being abandoned to their fate.[2] The following three years saw an unprecedented administrative effort to change this situation, as veterans were showered with attention and their monetary demands finally dealt with. This campaign took quite some time to implement, as the military and administrative authorities first had to establish connection with the veterans and try to estimate their numbers. This irregular situation resulted from a lack of reliable and organized data regarding demobilized soldiers and their exact addresses. A French officer, Henri Liger, was entrusted with the overwhelming mission of traveling over 48,000 kilometers (30,000 miles) across AOF and examining the cases of some 175,000 veterans and their families. Liger's mission emphasized the complete bureaucratic chaos that existed regarding veterans and their rights. Liger encountered many difficulties and often had to compete with local African political representatives over the veterans' support. Nevertheless, in spite of the almost impossible conditions under which he acted, Liger managed to convince African veterans that their interests would be best served by the French authorities. His survey laid the groundwork for implementing a myriad of benefits for veterans, such as allocated loans and cash advancements, as well as the establishment of veterans' centers and a variety of public honors. Other military figures, such as Capt. Michel Dorange, used the political potential of the African veterans to their own advantage. Dorange protected the interests of the many veterans living mainly in French Sudan and Upper Volta (contemporary Burkina Faso), working closely with the African veterans' leaders. He cultivated friendly and close relations with many veterans and reacted severely against any veterans who attempted to get involved in politics.[3] Although some veterans did engage in political struggles, as we shall see in chapter 7, the main veterans' organization, based in Dakar, the capital of AOF, adopted this stance and claimed to be "apolitical."

Many of these actions can be seen as a continuation of the French military's paternalistic attitude toward African soldiers and veterans. In addition, this campaign favoring veterans obviously accorded the French significant political advantages. Still, these efforts should not be viewed too cynically. French officers such as Liger and Dorange seem to have truly believed in their duty toward the veterans. Dorange had commanded

African soldiers during the war and thought that the French army and nation should be grateful to them. The military command's attempts to grant the veterans benefits and eventually equate their pensions with those of French soldiers, while facing objections from some French politicians, cannot be completely understood if they are viewed solely as a political maneuver. There were certainly some military officers who genuinely believed in the importance of brotherhood-in-arms.

Following the actions of officers such as Liger and Dorange, the military authorities initiated a series of reforms, which will be discussed in the following pages. But more than anything else it was the decision of the French government to subscribe to the principle of paying equal pensions to veterans in the metropole and in the colonies that marked the end of the hostility and mistrust that prevailed among soldiers and veterans in the aftermath of World War II.

This remarkable achievement was an indirect result of the soldiers' protests described in the previous chapter. The atmosphere of anger and resentment among the demobilized soldiers, combined with France's precarious situation in other parts of its empire, caused the military command to change the course of its thinking and press for what could only be described as revolutionary reforms. These reforms reflected the acceptance of a principle that was totally rejected in the French colonial mind: the principle of equal pay for equal work (at least concerning the payment of pensions, though not necessarily the salaries of serving soldiers) and the automatic applications of metropolitan legislation in the empire. As an example, due to the extension of all metropolitan legal texts concerning the rights of veterans to the colonies, financial assistance was offered to war orphans and children of African war invalids and ex-POWs. These children received the status "pupils of the nation" (*pupilles de la nation*), which had already been given to their French counterparts in 1917. This status accorded many benefits to the children whose fathers died in active combat during their service in the French army, such as care of their basic needs should their families not be able to supply them, education scholarships, and even paid vacations.[4] In 1952 almost 3,000 African children enjoyed this status and its accompanying benefits.[5] Until then, the French administration had implemented this principle only with regard to Africans holding French citizenship. The reforms thus accorded veterans privileges hitherto inaccessible to colonial subjects and therefore blurred the boundary between African citizens and subjects.

The following concerned note written by the minister of the colonies on December 1, 1952, demonstrates this shift of the regular colonial policy represented by the military reforms of 1950. The minister refers to the gradual implementation of various legal texts concerning metropolitan veterans to veterans in the colonies. While he accepted that this new policy was a fait accompli, he mentioned his concern regarding the dangerous precedent it had created, which might invoke similar demands from other sectors of the colonial populations. The minister mentioned the more elevated cost of life in France, which made equal pensions illogical.[6] However, he also mentioned the ostensible disadvantages that the application of metropolitan legal texts might have for the colonial subjects who were affected by these texts if they were not adjusted appropriately. This was a rather pathetic attempt to pretend that the reforms were problematic not only because of their financial consequences but also because they might harm African veterans whose living conditions were not taken into consideration. It is hard to imagine, though, what difficulties a raised pension could have caused African veterans.

The minister's concern regarding the military reforms and the potential consequences demonstrates their revolutionary nature. The only metropolitan legislation that had been automatically implemented in the colonies until then was the Vichy anti-Jewish laws of October 1940 and June 1941.[7] These, of course, did not apply to Africans. The idea of transferring a law designed for French citizens to the colonial arena with no adjustments whatsoever was inconceivable at that time. But it did happen in a rather unexpected institution: the colonial army, in which the hierarchy between French metropolitan and African soldiers had been carefully maintained. The recent debate in France regarding the French decision in 1959 to freeze the pensions of African veterans tends to overshadow the significance of these reforms.[8] While there is no doubt that freezing the veterans' pensions was unjust, equating them with those of metropolitan soldiers a decade earlier was highly uncharacteristic of the French colonial mindset of the time. It was a remarkable victory on the part of African soldiers and veterans, whose unrelenting protests even after the butchery in Thiaroye won them an achievement no other sector within colonial society managed to emulate.

The uniqueness of the military reforms within the French colonial policy was not lost on the military and colonial authorities, and they aimed to take full benefit of these measures. To this end, the French authorities tried to ensure that African political leaders would not take credit for this important achievement. On September 21, 1950, the high commissioner sent the governors of the federation a circular referring to an article published in the RDA's journal *Le Reveil* a few weeks before in which a delegate of this party, Yves Mathieu, tried to take credit for the matching pensions. The high commissioner asked the governors to publish the decree from February 4, 1950, explaining the uniformity of the pensions in order to correct this misinformation. This text made clear that equating the pensions for all veterans was not a result of any action by a particular political party, especially not the RDA. Rather, this was the result of a governmental initiative backed by all of the French authorities, including the high commissioner. In fact, the PCF (the French Communist Party) and several of the RDA members of parliament, including Hamani Diori, Ouzzan Coulibaly, and Félix Houphouët-Boigny, voted against this law. African veterans, said the high commissioner, should know who was truly working in their best interests.[9] Records of the debates in the French National Assembly verified the high commissioner's version. The PCF resisted the government's proposal, as it suspected this was an attempt to lay the groundwork for another war. Since the RDA was a political ally of the PCF at that time, its members voted in accordance with the Communist policy, despite their obvious opposing political interests.[10]

As we can see from this struggle between the RDA and the colonial administration over the right to claim credit for the uniform pensions as a political achievement, this was a crucial milestone in the more general struggle over the hearts of African veterans. A new period had begun and was marked not only by this tremendous political achievement of the African veterans but also by the army's heavy reliance on African soldiers in other parts of the empire. The revolt in Madagascar in 1947 was repressed with the help of these soldiers, and thousands of them took part in the Indochina war and in the Algerian war that followed. The military reforms were meant to change the serving conditions of African soldiers so as to ensure their loyalty. We should remember, though, that without the African soldiers' protest and their challenge of French military paternalism and discrimination, these reforms would probably never have materialized. It was this protest, which grew out of genuine rage and disappointment, that urged the military authorities to create a "new army," although this involved a heavy financial burden. In order to form this "new army," military authorities tried to make the recruitment to the African units more selective by attempting to entice more volunteers who could become skilled soldiers, as well as Africans who had graduated from the colonial education system.

Recruitment in Post–World War II AOF

After World War II the mission of the African units in the French army remained basically the same: to control AOF and protect the French empire wherever needed. The major change was that the inclusion of France in NATO in 1949 decreased the need for African soldiers on European soil. This meant that fewer African soldiers were needed and that French recruiters could allow themselves to be more selective. For example, while the minimum height requirement for recruits was officially 1.72 meters (5 feet 8 inches), in practice only candidates of 1.75 meters and above were recruited after World War II. Between 1946 and independence in 1960, 4,000 soldiers were recruited on average every year (as opposed to 12,000 annually before the war). Out of the total of 34,000 African soldiers who served in the French army after the war, 15,000 served in AOF, and 19,000 served in other parts of the empire.[11] Nevertheless, as the war in Indochina continued, the army needed more and more soldiers for its African units. This recruitment was especially challenging after the so-called Indochina amendment of November 11, 1951, according to which African soldiers could no longer be dispatched against their will to a territory defined as "a theater of active operations." This was true only for conscripts. Once a soldier volunteered for the army he had no say as to where he would serve.[12] After World War II recruited Africans also had to be more professional and educated than the average soldiers recruited in the past, as the Indochina War proved to be strategically challenging for the French. While earlier the percentage of volunteers in the African units could not surpass 25 percent, this restriction was canceled in 1946. In 1948 37.6 percent of the soldiers in the African units were volunteers, although they did not evenly represent all of the territories. While 84 percent of the recruits from Guinea were volunteers, the percentage of volunteers from Senegal, Dahomey, Mauritania, and French Sudan was lower than 20 percent.[13] We should bear in mind that the term "volunteer" is somewhat ambiguous in this situation. African intermediaries, such as canton chiefs (*chefs de cantons*), coerced young Africans into the ranks of the colonial army, gaining material and political benefits for themselves. They recorded these young men's status as "volunteers," although in reality they were nothing of the sort.[14]

As of 1926, even before World War II, recruitment to the army was divided between proper military units and units referred to as the second portion (*deuxième portion*). The second portion was a quasi-military system of forced labor that officially existed until 1950. Africans who were forcibly recruited to this service faced two years of difficult and dangerous labor. Public projects such as the notorious Office du Niger relied heavily on these recruits.[15] The colonial administration's dependence on the second portion's workers was, in fact, the reason this system survived four years after the Houphouët-Boigny law officially abolished forced labor in AOF.[16] Several colonial administrators objected fiercely to the abolishment of the second portion because they feared they would have no African labor force at their disposal. Edmond Louveau, the governor of French Sudan, from which most recruits originated, went as far as to claim that Africans confused "the liberty of work with the option to never work again at all, especially for the administration."[17]

Recruitment for the second portion continued in the aftermath of World War II under the heavy protests of African politicians. Newspapers such as the RDA's *Le Reveil* and the more moderate *L'AOF*, published by the Section Française de l'Internationale Ouvrière (the French Section of the Workers' International, SFIO), included articles against this blatant bypassing of the anti–forced labor legislation. During 1946, for example, 6,804 Africans were recruited from French Sudan to serve in the second portion. In other territories the numbers were much lower; in 1948 the breakdown included 742 recruits from Senegal, 500 from Guinea, and only 149 from Mauritania. The fact that under the Vichy regime the number of second portion workers was especially high (over 13,000 in 1942) made the case for protesting against it stronger, as it was possible to link this practice with a regime the French government wished to disassociate itself from.[18] Africans recruited to the second portion after World War II often protested about the inequality between them and regular soldiers, who were gaining more and more rights. They demanded to be treated with the same respect as soldiers returning from the war, even though, as we have seen in chapter 2, the latter did not actually share this view about their ostensibly respectful treatment.[19]

Eventually, recruitment for the second portion gradually diminished, and by February 1950 this practice was officially canceled. As the military reforms were just implemented around the same time period, Africans who served in the second portion did not have adequate opportunity to benefit from them. It is doubtful that they would have gained the same benefits even had the reforms been implemented earlier. As for the supposed cancellation of the second portion, according to several documents the practice of recruiting to these units by lottery was still taking place in December 1950. One possible explanation is that despite the decision to stop the practice, the necessities of the labor force required that it be continued. The instructions regarding recruitment in Senegal that year cautioned against detaining recruits from the first portion in the recruitment posts in order to perform forced labor.[20] The need for these instructions demonstrates that administrators actually considered soldiers as potential forced laborers even when they were not designated as such and testifies to the blurred boundaries in AOF between the use of Africans as soldiers and their recruitment as forced laborers. At a time when forced labor had officially been banned in the federation, obligatory military service enabled the continued exploitation of Africans for so-called public works and for agriculture.

The escalation of the war in Indochina after 1949 put pressure on the military authorities in AOF to increase African recruitment to the regular military units in order to reinforce the French units there. On August 2, 1951, the governor of Senegal informed the commandant of the Thiès district about a military advertising campaign about to be launched in order to encourage Africans to volunteer for service in Indochina. He noted that previous campaigns had been unsuccessful and that army units in Indochina lacked skilled soldiers. Thus, a ten-day campaign would begin on August 15, though no pressure would be put on the population. The campaign was to be run by soldiers who would contact the subdivision chiefs and the district's commandant.[21]

It seems that recruiting soldiers for service within the confines of AOF was rather less problematic, as this did not have to rely on so-called volunteers. In a report regarding the enlistment of 1950, the Ziguinchor district commandant noted that the number of Africans eligible for recruitment exceeded the army's recruiting abilities. The problem was that all the candidates wanted to serve in the first portion, but it was impossible to accept all of them due to financial limitations. The recruitment to the second portion was, for understandable reasons, quite unattractive to Africans.[22]

The number of positions allocated for the first portion for the entire federation in 1950 was 5,000 men. All eligible candidates were supposed to participate in a lottery that decided whether they would be recruited for the first or the second portion. As part of the army's efforts to attract Western-educated Africans to its ranks, the *grandes écoles* graduates were exempt from this lottery and were automatically sent to the first portion.[23] Volunteers were recruited first (probably because those were the men who could be sent directly to Indochina) and received a signing bonus of 1,400 francs.[24]

I will examine the motives of Africans to volunteer to the army, knowing that they might be sent to fight in Indochina and later in Algeria, in the next chapter. In the meantime, suffice it to say that economic considerations, stemming from the improvement of service conditions, dominated this decision. The different allocation between the various territories of the federation demonstrates that the army still preferred certain territories to others. Guinea, as always, was the leading territory with 1,100 allocated soldiers, then Upper Volta with 900, followed by Senegal and Sudan with 700 each. At the bottom of this list were Ivory Coast with 600, Niger with 500, and Dahomey with 400 soldiers. No soldiers were recruited in Mauritania.

Still, most soldiers were recruited in the "traditional" manner of sending a recruitment commission to various districts within the federation. The major innovation was that recruits were not transported to the training bases by foot but rather by motor vehicles and trains. This enabled the army to distribute recruits within the federation and thus ensure an ethnic mix in the various African units. This planned heterogeneity was required in order to prevent interethnic tensions in case of military activity in a certain region.[25] The process of the actual recruitment was conducted by French officers accompanied by African soldiers. Recruitment dates were set for each subdivision in each district, and the district commandant was notified well in advance so that he could advertise these dates. Candidates for recruitment arrived at the predetermined location, where they would first undergo physical examinations in order to establish their eligibility for the draft. In some cases, when candidates wished to apply to specific prestigious units such as the air force, they would also have to undergo psychometric exams. These recruitment campaigns demanded much planning and cooperation between the military and administrative authorities. Such cooperation was not always assured, as we can see from the following example.

On March 9, 1955, a very angry administrator of the Velingara subdivision in the district of Ziguinchor (Casamance, Senegal) sent a letter to his district commandant complaining about the total lack of cooperation on the part of two officers who were supposed to participate in the recruitment delegation in his subdivision. The administrator, Desanti, described the frustration of the dozens of candidates who had waited for these officers for six days while in great danger of being exposed to the epidemic of cerebrospinal meningitis that was rampant in the region. Desanti initially explained to the impatient candidates that the officers had a flat tire, but this excuse was only good for a few hours, and the young men began to lose patience. The chief, who had worked hard to bring these candidates to the recruitment post, could not understand the meaning of this delay. When the two officers finally arrived, they had a series of lame excuses: the telephone in the railway station was out of order, and they were unaware of the time they were expected to arrive, for example. One of the officers, who was also a physician, claimed that he did not work on Sundays. Eventually, the recruitment session had to be canceled, as local authorities were concerned that the candidates might become infected with meningitis. According to Desanti, it was later discovered that the two officers took advantage of their mission to tour the beautiful region of Casamance in southern Senegal. Desanti insisted in his letter that sanctions should be taken against the two officers, who by their negligence had sabotaged the recruitment efforts and created a highly negative impression among the potential recruits.[26]

Other problems emerged during a recruitment campaign in 1952 in the same region when many of the candidates did not arrive and the Diourbel district commandant complained of infractions among the Serer.[27] It had also been difficult to locate the canton chief due to the sudden death of his eldest son. Still, this operation was considered to be somewhat successful, as the commandant noted that among the volunteers who did arrive was one of the grandsons of Lat Dior, an ardent resister of the colonial regime in the nineteenth century.[28]

Even though the percentage of volunteers rose after the war, the percentage of absenteeism and desertion also continued to grow, rising from 18.5 percent before World War II to around 30 percent after the war. Although in 1945 the governor of French Sudan maintained that this problem was a result of the radicalization of West African politics, these deserters were in fact usually poor and rural Africans who had no other ways to be exempted from military service and would probably have been recruited to the second portion. In any case, it seems that due to the relative ease with which the French military authorities filled their quotas of recruits, this problem was not considered serious.[29]

Another problem that persisted after the war was the somewhat common practice of presenting a false identity, especially the tendency to replace designated conscripts with others. This practice was quite acceptable among families from the higher socioeconomic status who could afford to either pay potential replacements or send younger brothers instead of the real candidates so that they would fail the physical exams.[30] In order to combat this, the military instructions regarding the recruitment of 1950 required that each candidate have his two index fingers fingerprinted in order to prevent these switches and to make sure that the candidates in question had not already served in the army.[31]

As we saw at the beginning of the chapter, one of the characteristics of the new recruitment policy was the careful selection of Africans who wished to volunteer. The new colonial army intended to change the French public's perception of the typical African soldier. One example of the manner in which African soldiers had commonly been perceived previously could be found in an advertisement for a French chocolate drink, Banania. This advertisement featured a grinning *tirailleur* stating in faulty French, "Y'a bon" (for "C'est bon," meaning "It is good"). The ad presented the African soldier as rough and somewhat primitive, childish and naive, but also good-hearted and loyal. It was believed that childishness and naïveté made the *tirailleur* a valuable soldier, as he was not sophisticated enough to feel fear. After World War II the military authorities in AOF wished to change this image. In October 1945 the Department of Colonial Troops published a document in which it encouraged the authorities to recruit only Africans who spoke French fluently. The document noted that "nothing impresses the French bystander who still holds the concept of the *tirailleur y'a bon* more than meeting a *tirailleur* who is able to express himself just like him."[32] Recruiting soldiers whose level of French was high was meant to help change the public image of the entire force, turning the soldiers into living proof that a new colonial army now existed.

Enticing or forcing Africans who studied in the colonial educational system to serve in the army was not sufficient for ensuring a high educational level among the African forces. The army had to create its own elite by beginning schooling at an early age. Such a military educational system was already in existence, having been founded in 1923 under the name of Écoles des Enfants de Troupes. However, in the period under discussion it underwent massive reforms in order to render it more attractive to African families from higher socioeconomic milieus.

Reforming the African Military Schools

The EET educational system was originally intended for sons of career soldiers (*militaires de carrière*, or soldiers who served at least fifteen years in the army), as well as for the sons of chiefs who graduated from their designated school system (*écoles de fils de chefs*) and obtained a *certificat d'études primaires* (certificate of primary education, CEP). Initially there were three schools: in Saint Louis in Senegal, Bingerville in the Ivory Coast, and Kati in French Sudan. In 1949 the chief commander of the armed forces in AOF proposed to close the school in Bingerville and open in its stead a school in Ouagadougou (Upper Volta), a territory from which many past recruits had originated. This decision was reversed after the governor of Ivory Coast protested, as he was worried that the RDA would use the closing down of the school in Bingerville to attract angry veterans to its ranks.[33] Eventually, the army decided to open a fourth school in Ouagadougou. In 1953, when the EETs celebrated thirty years of existence, the military authorities in AOF decided it was time to enlarge its pool of students and improve the academic level of the schools. This was part of their general efforts to create an African elite that would be able to take upon itself roles of leadership and command within the army. The first step within this reform was to change the name of the schools so as not to create the impression that they were only intended for sons of soldiers. The new school system became the EMPA. All youth whose fathers had fulfilled their military duties were eligible for these schools, even if the fathers were not career soldiers. This meant that even sons of Western-educated Africans who only served for one year could apply to these schools. There were no school fees, and the students received free lodging, clothes, and food. Once they graduated, between the ages of eighteen and twenty (depending on when they had begun their studies), they had to enlist and serve in the army for five years. Those who refused to enlist were sent back home, and their parents were required to reimburse the school for half of their child's expenses. It is quite easy to imagine what kind of pressure was put upon these adolescents to fulfill their military duties. Indeed, there are very few registered cases of such refusals.[34] Students who excelled in their studies received a certificate that enabled them to pursue their education in an officers' academy in France. It should be noted that applicants to the EMPA had to take special entrance exams, and not all were accepted. In 1954, the first year in which these schools functioned in their new form, there were 1,000 candidates for the four schools, out of which only 248 were accepted.[35]

As the main aim of the study program at the EMPA was to train African NCOs and in rare cases also lower-level officers, the program included basic military knowledge, physical training, and moral, intellectual, and technical education. Sports and games were employed to encourage qualities of perseverance and energy that would assist the students during their military service. According to the instructions given to military guides in the schools, team sports were the most essential part of physical education because of the way they encouraged teamwork, a crucial quality for military service. As such, these sports both fulfilled the natural need of the students and contributed to their education. Target shooting, closely supervised by the staff, was also included in the sports curriculum. Competitions between the different schools were encouraged, as they contributed to the feelings of loyalty the students had for their school, and each school had its own colors, aiming to create esprit de corps. It seems that it was quite important for the military to present these pupils as excelling in sports.[36]

Sports competitions with other schools or institutions took place frequently. In February 1957, for example, a friendly football match was organized in Ouagadougou between the EMPA team and that of the Catholic mission. The EMPA won 3–1.[37]

Moral education, an important subject in the French educational system since the establishment of the Third Republic, seems to have flourished in the military schools. However, the teachers were instructed to be aware that in the current situation of evolution of the "native sector" this subject was very delicate and necessitated good knowledge of the students' psyche and milieu. This reference to "a certain state of evolution" and "the special psyche of African children," which appeared in the written instructions given to the teachers in the EMPA schools, demonstrates the problematic nature of the military educational reforms. While the military authorities felt that African soldiers should receive better education and that more of them should reach commanding positions within the army, old colonial perceptions refused to disappear, and Africans were not really perceived as potentially equal to Europeans.

The main purpose of moral education, as far as the directors of the EMPA were concerned, was to develop in their pupils a sense of loyalty, solidarity, respect, military duty, and professional pride. Music lessons were also offered as part of the ostensibly African traditional curriculum within the area of moral education. It was especially important that the students be able to sing and play an instrument. Every school was supposed to have its own orchestra, which would reflect the school's spirit and preserve its tradition. The instructions explained that military education was supposed to be simple and practical in a way that would penetrate deep into the young minds and imprint these tendencies in their subconsciousness. The directors of the EMPAs also voiced their concern about the students' mental capacity and recommended that military education be provided only on Thursdays so as not to overburden the young students.[38]

The military command and the directors of the schools disagreed somewhat about the desired level of studies in the EMPAs. One senior commander in AOF suggested adding to the curriculum courses taught in France in order to improve the academic level of the schools. The director of the EMPA of Saint Louis objected, saying that while this was relevant for the federation schools, whose students intended to continue their studies after graduation, it was completely superfluous for the military schools, because their students did not intend to do so. On the contrary, the addition of such courses would only come at the expense of other courses that would contribute much more to their military training.[39] The director obviously did not think that the academic level required of metropolitan military schools was appropriate for their African counterparts. He also did not seem to believe that the EMPAs' academic program should be equivalent to that of civilian schools in the federation. To these academic concerns the director added some financial ones, pointing to the fact that such new courses would also require the purchase of new books in history, mathematics, and sciences and thus entail heavy expenses.[40] On the other hand, when the military authorities suggested cutting down the hours in mathematics and French in the same school, Captain Mazeline, the school's commander, objected, his reasoning being that the students' educational level was already lower than that of students studying in other schools in the federation. Cutting the study hours further in these two important subjects would be extremely harmful to his students.[41] We can see here the dilemma between raising the schools' academic level, on the one hand, and maintaining their basic goal, military training, on the other. Another possible concern was that a high educational level might entice students to pursue alternative options after graduation, though this concern was somewhat alleviated by the students' obligation to enlist for five years upon graduation.

The young Africans who were accepted to the EMPAs studied under rather harsh military discipline. They wore uniforms and were punished for every breach of a rule. Military instructions regarding the functioning of the schools warned commanders not to forget that they were dealing with children and that the punishments they inflicted on them should be suitable to their age. We can assume that the fact that this appears in formal written instructions insinuates that such "unsuitable punishments" were indeed commonly practiced. The instructions allowed severe punishments for students over sixteen who had committed serious infractions. In these cases it was possible to lock up students in a cell for up to eight days or in solitary confinement for up to four days. Those who were put in solitary confinement were not allowed to study and were only let out for an hour in the morning and an hour in the evening. Students received three months' vacation every two years, which they spent at their homes. They were required to write to their parents once a month, and the school supplied the paper, envelopes, and stamps. These letters were censored so as to monitor the students' morale. In general, these pupils were closely observed. They were subjected to regular medical examinations, were not allowed to leave the school premises without permission, were never allowed to go out after dark, and were prohibited from reading certain newspapers deemed dangerous for their political inclinations.[42] The diet in the schools was mostly African, but French food was served on Sundays and holidays. As students who lived far away from school could not go home during the Christmas and Easter breaks (which most did not celebrate in any case), trips were organized for them during these vacations. At the Bingerville school in the Ivory Coast, for example, the pupils were taken on camping trips on the shore of the nearby lagoon.

Some information about the physical conditions in the schools can be gleaned from an article extolling the Bingerville school published in the military journal *Tropiques*. The author, a Lieutenant Woutaz, noted that each pupil had a corner with a bed and a small desk on which he could put all sorts of memorabilia from home, such as photos of his family and village and the postcards he had received.[43] While the purpose of this description was to demonstrate how lucky these adolescents were, given the opportunity to gain a good education in a modern and healthy environment, it actually conveyed an image of lonely children torn apart from their families and friends at a much too early age and sent to a harsh, disciplined environment that dictated a military future for them.

Although the EMPAs were open to all African youth, it seems that these schools were attractive mostly to the families of veterans and to certain segments of the African population whose access to the administration schools was limited. Applicants were accepted to an EMPA according to the results they achieved in a special examination, in which they were required to get a minimum of 60 percent correct answers in order to pass. As we shall see, though, while the army was concerned about the level of its educational establishments and took care to keep underqualified candidates out of its schools, the administration had to be sensitive to the wishes of its colonial subjects, whether these were local dignitaries or families who had lost one of their sons fighting for France.

Although passing the entrance exam was the only official way to get into these schools, in some cases members of the colonial administration tried to bypass this obstacle and asked the military authorities to accept sons of African dignitaries with whom they hoped to maintain good relations. In 1953 the governor of Upper Volta asked the high commissioner to recommend to the superior commander of the AOF forces that Moumouni Congo, son of the *morho naba* (a traditional ruler of one of the Mossi Kingdoms in Upper Volta) who was studying at the EMPA of Ouagadougou, be moved to the EMPA of Saint Louis, which was considered a better school. The governor asked the high commissioner to emphasize to the commander the political significance of accepting the boy to the school in Saint Louis. In this case the request was to move a student from one school to another, but in other cases colonial administrators requested that certain candidates be admitted to an EMPA without having to take the examinations.[44] In 1951 the same governor asked that the army admit war orphans to the EMPA in Ouagadougou. In his letter he mentioned the pressure he was under from families of candidates who were not accepted to the school. The governor asked that war orphans who were under twelve or under fifteen but with no CEP (certificate from a primary school) be admitted even though they were not qualified for the EMPA. The superior commander rejected this request, explaining that orphans already enjoyed precedence over other candidates, as long as they were qualified candidates and passed the entry exams to the school. The commander even rejected the governor's suggestion to enlarge the school in order to accommodate these applicants and reminded the governor that the matter in question was not space but rather ensuring that graduates possessed solid knowledge and techniques. Overloading the school with war orphans would not secure this aim and would create an imbalance between this school and the others regarding the number of students enrolled. The request was thus rejected so as not to harm the school's academic level.[45] A letter from the high commissioner to all of the territories' governors mentioned similar complaints and special requests from other governors as well and seems to show that this was quite a widespread phenomenon. All in all, this is another good example of the different interests of the military and administrative authorities.

Demands to bypass the formal EMPA entrance process also came from a different direction: the African veterans' organizations, which will be discussed in detail later. Papa Seck Douta, the head of the veterans' federal organization, complained to the high commissioner in July 1954 that he could not ensure the admittance of several of his comrades' sons to an EMPA and that he was told that the recruitment was over for that year. At the end of his letter Douta suggested to the high commissioner that the organization's newspaper, *La Voix des Combattants,* would participate in advertising for recruitment to the schools, in this manner reminding the administrator of the power held by the veterans' newspaper and the advantages of cooperating with the veterans in general. This friendly reminder did not impress the administration much, as the response, which came from the military cabinet, included a polite recognition of the suggestion to advertise the schools in the veterans' paper, followed by a firm reminder that all candidates for the schools must pass an exam, and only those who received the highest grades would be admitted.[46] However, while in most cases the military authorities refused to ignore the official procedures to admit children to the EMPA system in response to various administrative requests, occasionally they made an unusual exception and agreed to admit a son of an African dignitary.[47]

Generally speaking, the EMPAs managed to attain their quotas even if they did not lure many Africans from among the Western-educated elite. During the 1950s most of the graduates of these schools served in the army as NCOs. In 1955 the exam results of the pupils in the EMPA of Saint Louis surpassed those of comparable civilian schools. More important, these results began influencing the level of African NCOs. While in 1953 only 2 percent of them were considered first category, meaning having the same training as that of French NCOs, in 1956 a third of the African NCOs reached this level.[48] Yet Western-educated Africans continued to present a challenge for the military authorities. They were heavily courted because the army needed them to increase the number and level of African officers. The army also wished to gain control over them, as they often presented a threat to the continuing rule of AOF due to their "dangerous" tendency to follow international news and engage in politics. In fact, one of the guiding lines of the military policy in AOF during the 1950s was to establish good contacts with this elite and with the general population of AOF so as to prevent this population from being influenced by the political complications in other parts of the French empire. When it became clear that the new recruitment policy and the reforms in the EMPAs were not enough to attract educated Africans to the army and significantly raise the numbers and level of African officers, additional measures had to be taken.

The Attempts to Form African Military Elite: The Special
Forces and the Promotion of African Officers

The army's main difficulty in recruiting Western-educated Africans stemmed from the alternative and more attractive career options available to them. Africans who graduated from the *grandes écoles* of the federation could develop a career in the colonial administration and in the slowly developing private sector and therefore were not particularly tempted by the prospect of a military career. They often looked for ways to avoid conscription and sometimes even chose somewhat extreme means such as behaving eccentrically or expressing radical political views.[49] The army often had no choice but to settle for the education system's dropouts; whenever an African student dropped out of school he was immediately recruited. Another obstacle the army encountered was the competition with the civilian administration over the limited number of African *grandes écoles* graduates. The colonial administration desperately needed Western-educated Africans for its own purposes and tried to lure them to its own ranks. The administration frequently requested special exemptions for Africans who wished to pursue their studies abroad, mainly in France, as can be seen from the list of nine graduates Léopold Sédar Senghor transferred to the high commissioner in 1945. Senghor mentioned that these graduates wished to pursue their studies in France and therefore asked that they be released from service. The high commissioner sent the list to General Magnan, the chief commander of the armed forces in AOF, who approved all the requests but one.[50] Even when educated Africans were supposed to be drafted by law, the army's ability to use their services for the entire three years was limited by a decree issued on March 28, 1933. This decree allowed graduates of the *grandes écoles* of the federation to take a two-year unpaid leave after finishing their first year of service on condition that they work for the administration. If they left their administrative post during these two years, they would have to complete their service. Otherwise, these two years would be considered as active military duty.[51] In 1954 the high commissioner of AOF asked the minister of the colonies to extend this decree, which provided the administration with desperately needed educated African employees. Although the minister expressed his understanding of the advantages this arrangement held for the administration in AOF, he explained to the high commissioner that the decree deprived the army of talented young Africans. In light of the difficult situation of the army, whose African personnel was severely lacking in its abilities, it was necessary to act immediately to improve the level of the local military forces. Therefore, it would not be possible to increase the number of Western-educated Africans who received this unpaid leave unless the service period of other such soldiers was extended to eighteen months.[52]

This decree and the minister of the colonies' refusal to extend it demonstrate the conflicting interests of the administrative and military authorities, both of whom competed for the small number of the educated elite of AOF. While this refusal to extend the decree marked a small victory for the military authorities, it did not do much to improve the educational level of African soldiers. In 1953, for example, out of the thirty-eight African officers serving in the French army, twenty-one had completed ten years of schooling, and five had graduated from primary school. The rest had not even completed primary school.[53]

Such obstacles negatively affected the new military policy of progressively upgrading the quantity and quality of African officers. During the first decade after the war, European officers continued to outnumber African officers within the colonial army. Moreover, in 1954 there were fewer African officers than in 1946. The military authorities blamed this situation on the tight military budget, which did not allow for salaries comparable with those paid in the civilian sector. Myron Echenberg claims that this was not the only reason. Part of the problem, he maintained, was that French military officials had considerable difficulty in accepting a new African army based on assimilationist principles.[54]

In October 1954 Lieutenant-Colonel Villard, the military attaché to the high commissioner of AOF, issued a secret report in which he argued that upgrading the EMPAs had not proved sufficient to form a genuine African military elite and that African intellectuals rejected military careers because they did not believe that even if they became officers they would attain the same status as their metropolitan counterparts. In order to resolve this situation, the army launched an advertisement campaign aimed at young educated Africans, using film screenings at schools, newspapers advertisements, and pamphlets in an effort to entice young educated Africans to its ranks. It also issued glossy new magazines such as *Soldats d'Outre-Mer* and *Frères d'Arme*, which presented the advantages African officers could enjoy in the army, portraying them as living in a European style.[55] In general, this campaign was part of a larger scheme to publicize the new image of the colonial army among young educated Africans and veterans, which will be discussed in detail later.

Such campaigns were not sufficient to remedy the situation quickly. In 1955 the high commissioner of AOF, alarmed at the news that it would be another decade before it would be possible to bolster the number and quality of the African officers in the colonial army, called for immediate action to promote Africans to the ranks of NCOs or officers, even at the price of lowering standards.[56]

The Loi-Cadre published the next year gave a significant boost to the professionalization of the African forces and to the promotion of African officers. Among other measures taken to increase the Africanization of elite units within the colonial army, the new law revived the École Spéciale des Sous-officiers Indigènes at Fréjus as the École de Formation des Officiers du Régime Transitoire des Territoires d'Outre-Mer (EFORTOM).[57] This school offered Africans a venue at which they could undergo a two-year officer training course without having to compete with the talented and highly motivated metropolitan candidates who benefited from preparation at the best French high schools. EFORTOM opened its doors to its first class in October 1956. It included fifty-four candidates, thirty-four of whom graduated. Most candidates were either NCOs who had already served for two years or promising graduates from the EMPAs. They were usually sons of veterans and did not belong to the elite from which the army hoped to attract potential officers. Unfortunately, the study program at the EFORTOM was inferior to that of the metropolitan officers' academies and did not contribute much to the education level of African officers.[58]

EFORTOM continued to train African officers five years after the independence of the territories from which they originated as part of bilateral military agreements between France and most of the newly independent countries, which will be discussed in chapter 7. Between 1958 and 1965 174

Africans graduated from the school. Some of its graduates later became African military presidents following coups d'état they led. Seyni Kountché from the class of 1959 became president of Niger in 1974; Mathieu Kérékou, who graduated in 1960, became president of Benin in 1972; and Moussa Traoré, from the class of 1961, became president of Mali in 1968.[59]

Another way to advance African officers quickly was to give them a promotion for meritorious service. While there is scant information regarding this form of promotion, two future African military presidents are known to have been promoted in this manner, as they both had very limited education and were not suitable for the military academies. These were the notorious Jean-Bedel Bokassa, who committed a coup d'état in 1966 in the Central African Republic, formerly a territory in AEF, and Sangoulé Lamizana, who became president of Upper Volta in 1974.[60]

As noted, the Loi-Cadre also tried to advance the recruitment of Africans to elite corps within the colonial army, such as the air force and paratroopers units. In this case, the army insisted on allowing only suitable candidates to enter these units even if this meant limiting their number. Recruitment instructions from 1956 specified that only candidates between the ages of nineteen and twenty-two should be considered as volunteers for elite units, and they would have to pass a medical examination. Candidates had to understand French, be able to answer questions rapidly, and be able to understand orders. These intellectual abilities were to be verified by a special officer who interviewed all the candidates.[61] In some cases, soldiers were rejected on a medical basis even though they had passed the medical exams when recruited, as sometimes the earlier medical examination was not thorough enough. Such was the case of volunteers for the paratroopers, a unit that managed to attract a great number of African volunteers. In 1956 10 percent of the volunteers who had successfully passed the medical exams were declared unfit for service. In an angry letter to the health department of the ground forces in AOF, the superior command rebuked the unit's physicians for neglecting to disqualify these volunteers. The letter reminded the doctors of the standards successful candidates should meet: they should not be too thin or too fat (under 80 kilos, or 176 pounds), and they could not be suffering from any kind of disease or any physical flaw. The angry tone of the letter stemmed from the fact that the army spent 300,000 francs to train each paratrooper, and the superior command wished to prevent unsuitable candidates from being recruited.[62] The detailed description of the desired candidates also demonstrates the efforts of the military authorities to control even the physical image of the "new army."

Mamadou Niang, who signed up for the paratroopers unit in 1955, vividly described his fear of the medical exam in his memoirs. The French doctor who performed these exams was known to be very severe. He wore silver-rimmed glasses, which gave him the appearance of a scientist, and he sported a moustache yellow from cigarette smoke. Niang did everything he could before the test to ensure that his body contained no trace of substances that might be linked to any African diseases common at the time. When he finally arrived at the doctor's office, he was relieved to discover that the intimidating doctor had left for France. He had been replaced by a much more pleasant, clean-shaven, unbespectacled man.[63]

Another measure the army took after 1956 to accelerate the Africanization of the staff of certain prestigious forces, such as the air force and the navy, was the creation of a special committee known as Army-Youth (Armée-Jeunesse). The Army-Youth committee recommended that African students studying in France should not be recruited into the infantry or the artillery but rather into these more prestigious units. The director of political affairs in AOF agreed with this proposal and admitted that despite the military authorities' intentions, these units had not participated previously in the army's Africanization process.[64]

Although the army put much effort into attracting Western-educated Africans, this official military policy was also occasionally challenged by a few direct commanders of African troops. Apparently, some of these commanders did not share the higher hierarchy's enthusiasm regarding the military value of Western-educated Africans. This is demonstrated by a letter of complaint written by a representative of 180 Ivoirian soldiers posted in Bouaké and sent to the general commandant of the second brigade in Abidjan in July 1957. Out of these 180 soldiers, so the letter stated, 80 were in prison for no reason at all other than the wish of their commanders, a captain and a colonel, to ruin their military dossiers and rob them of their meager salary. Supposedly, these commanders plainly stated that they did not want these soldiers in their unit. The complaining soldiers claimed that this was because they were educated, and their commanders wanted only uneducated soldiers, referred to by the writer of the letter as "Gobits." A footnote added to the letter explained that this was a derogatory term referring to peasants from Upper Volta. The soldiers complained about the long working hours and the difficult nature of their work and compared this to the forced labor that was practiced under the Third Republic. They also complained about the low quality of the food, the lack of sugar and milk for their coffee, and the absence of lighting in their rooms. They asked the general commandant to transfer them to Dakar so that they would not have to serve as uneducated soldiers but could learn a profession, thus enjoying the same benefits as their equivalent metropolitan brothers who, like them, served under the French banner.[65] Reading this letter one could only imagine the frustration of the French commanders, as they were used to dealing with African soldiers whose normal living conditions were either similar or inferior to those that the military offered them. These commanders were unaccustomed to hearing complaints about sugarless coffee and insufficient lighting. Attracting Western-educated Africans to the army was one thing; dealing with their supposedly unrealistic expectations of military life was another.

This was not the only time the attitudes of Western-educated Africans and *originaires* caused their commanders frustration and were perceived as unsuitable for military life and duties. All the morale reports contained a special section dedicated to these soldiers, frequently mentioning their shortcomings, such as their deep awareness of their rights and total ignorance of their duties.[66]

As can be seen, the policy of recruiting Western-educated Africans to the colonial army to increase the number of African officers encountered many difficulties. This group remained mostly alienated from the military, and its commanders continued to be suspicious toward it up until independence. On the other hand, the military authorities' attempts to nurture relations with the African veterans, who were the principal beneficiaries of the military reforms, were much more successful.

Improving Relations with African Veterans

An important part of the military reforms was focused upon improving veterans' conditions. The military authorities in AOF accorded tremendous importance to nurturing good relations with veterans. This stemmed from the belief that the veterans could influence the general population of AOF, especially regarding its perceptions of the army, and therefore treating them in a positive manner could turn them into a useful tool of propaganda among this population. Apart from this practical view of the veterans' usefulness, one cannot ignore the fact that at least some of the military officials genuinely believed that the veterans should be acknowledged for the sacrifices they made for France and that these sacrifices were equal to those made by their French metropolitan comrades. I will now examine the methods the army used in its attempts to establish trust among the veterans.

Although they had a great deal in common, veterans were not a homogeneous group. First and foremost, not all demobilized soldiers were considered veterans by the French army. In fact, there were two types of ex-soldiers that belonged to this status, and each received a different title: *anciens militaires* and *anciens combattants*. The *anciens militaires* were a relatively small minority within the general category of veterans and were professional soldiers who had served at least fifteen years in the army. After fifteen years of service, soldiers who retired were entitled to half a pension. If they served for twenty-five years, they received a full pension. This pension did not depend in any way on whether the *anciens militaires* had served in a war. The *anciens combattants* were ex-soldiers who had served at the front for at least ninety consecutive days or spent at least six months in POW camps. Members of this category were entitled to a small pension. The large number of Africans who had served in the two world wars and later in Indochina and Algeria made this group quite significant. In 1959 there were 96,397 *anciens combattants* in AOF.[67]

Not only were ex-soldiers split between these two groups, each with its own set of interests, but there was also a demarcation between organized and nonorganized veterans. Urban veterans who were closer to the center of the colonial administration were usually better organized and could pay membership fees to the various territorial veterans' organizations, while many rural veterans were not so well represented and did not enjoy the benefits of the social networks urban veterans had managed to create for themselves. Nor was unity always assured among organized veterans. African veterans had begun to organize only after World War II. The first and most powerful veterans' organization, Anciens Combattants et

Victimes de Guerre de l'Afrique Occidentale Française, was established on October 7, 1945, in Dakar and was in fact a branch of the metropolitan veterans' association.

In 1952 the veterans' organization had 75,000 members dispersed over a territory of 4 million square kilometers (1,544,409 square miles). In this period veteran cards had already been distributed among World War I veterans, but the distribution for World War II veterans was just in its initial stages.[68] As the organization suffered from a shortage of staff, the mission of keeping in contact with all of its members was not realistic. It needed the help of local veterans' associations. For this purpose, the military authorities acted to encourage the establishment of veterans' associations in every administrative territory. These associations were supposed to reach every veteran and inform the military of the needs and aspirations of their members. All of these associations were supposed to be affiliated with the federal veterans' organization.[69]

Making sure that every administrative unit in the federation had its own veterans' association and that every veteran living in the area would become a member of his local association were not simple matters. Even if an association officially existed, it did not necessarily function properly, and as membership in these associations cost money, not all veterans were able to join them or were interested in doing so. In January 1951, for example, the head of the Tivaoune subdivision in Senegal reported to his district commandant in Thiès that the veterans' association in his town existed in name only. Out of the seven members who composed its committee, two had resigned, two had left town permanently, and the three who remained were fighting constantly with each other. The administrator especially noted the bitter animosity between the president of the association and his vice president. He suggested that a meeting of the branch be called immediately and be directed by an influential veteran so that the association could return to normal activity.[70]

The effective functioning of the veterans' associations was influenced not only by the hostility between the veterans who ran these associations but also by the potential members. Not all veterans could afford to pay the fees. In the above-mentioned association in Tivaoune, the veterans had not paid their membership fees for four years. This was a general problem throughout AOF, and an overall solution was required. The simplest option was to ask the military or colonial authorities to allocate more funds to associations that were not able to depend on the meager sums they managed to collect from their members. Not surprisingly, military and colonial officials were not happy with this solution and attempted to find alternative ways of keeping the veterans' associations active. In particular, the authorities attempted to advise the veterans' associations on establishing financial independence. One idea was to attract members through massive advertising. Another was to organize celebrations on holidays and memorial days that would include film screenings, dances, theatrical performances, sports competitions, and games. The idea was to spend as little as possible on these various events by asking actors to volunteer and by borrowing films from various agencies. Alongside these activities, for which the public would pay, the organizers would include a *tombola*, a lottery in which winning tickets were drawn from a revolving drum, in order to augment the revenues from these events. The idea was to find original ways to generate funds to be used for the benefit of the veterans. The president of the veterans' committee of Senegal emphasized the importance of involving veterans and their families in the organization of these celebrations.[71]

This plan to raise funds for the veterans' associations without the need to burden the colonial budget was successfully implemented. In October 1951 the president of the local veterans' committee in Senegal happily reported that in 1949 the celebrations of November 11, the date of the armistice that put an end to World War I, raised a profit of 990,235 francs which were divided among the various local associations. In 1950 the income was somewhat lower (631,268 francs), but this was still a significant sum. Not surprisingly, the president encouraged the administrators of Senegal to organize these celebrations again the following year.[72]

While it seems that the colonial and military authorities did everything they could to avoid allocating financial aid to veterans' associations, in fact the late 1940s and early 1950s saw a dramatic increase in the budget allocated to the main veterans' organization. In 1946 the budget was just over 1 million francs, while in 1955 it increased to 38 million francs.[73] At the same time, significant sums were invested in the veterans' elevated pensions and in social assistance to both soldiers and veterans. In addition, as we have seen, the army allocated the veterans' organization large sums of money, which were mostly spent on veteran loans. In 1952 the veterans' organization offered 144 loans to veterans for a total sum of 2,340,000 francs, though in fact the veterans' office in Dakar had received 25,000 letters requesting funding, mainly loans for the purchase of a house or agricultural land.[74] In September 1948 François Saiba, an ex-POW, asked for a loan based on the ordinance of October 5, 1945, regarding loans to ex-POWs. Saiba's letter is rather typical; it first describes his military service in detail and then evokes the metropolitan law in order to ask for a loan. Saiba, who was working at the time as a chauffeur for Air France in Dakar, asked for a loan of 300,000 francs. He wrote that he had volunteered for the French army while working in Paris in 1938 as the chauffeur of the then minister (later to become prime minister) Paul Reynaud. He had served in several regiments of the Tirailleurs Sénégalais and became a corporal in 1942.[75] His request was turned down at the time because the metropolitan regulations regarding the rights of veterans had not yet gone into effect. When Saiba reapplied in 1950 the request was reconsidered, as this time he was indeed entitled to the loan.[76] In a different example, Karamako Minté's request for a loan could not be approved by the veterans' organization due to lack of funds. However, the general secretary of the organization did not despair and asked the finance department in Dakar to cover this loan, stating that the veteran was a brilliant soldier, hardworking, disciplined, and honest, and it was therefore vital to offer him assistance.[77]

Apart from the allocations to the veterans' organization, considerable funding was invested in various social and medical projects in the federation aimed at benefiting veterans and serving soldiers. The budget for social assistance for soldiers and veterans in 1951 for the entire federation, for example, was over 6 million francs. This significant sum was used to establish two medical centers, one for Europeans and one for Africans, the African center designated mainly for the families of soldiers and veterans. As we shall see in the concluding part of this chapter, this continued segregation between Europeans and Africans in the sphere of social and medical assistance demonstrates that despite the military efforts to change the nature of the colonial army, paternalistic and racist approaches refused to die out. According to the annual report of 1952, in 1951 the African center treated 8,299 women and 7,030 children. Similar centers were later established in Saint Louis and Thiès. In other colonies, such as Niger and

Ivory Coast, these funds were used to open accommodation centers for soldiers and veterans, which offered lodgings for them and their families while traveling. Additional funds of almost 1 million francs were utilized that year for the purchase of Christmas trees and toys bought in France and distributed among children of African and European soldiers and veterans. The army also organized tours for families during the holidays.[78] Again, as in the case of the EMPAs, only French administrative holidays received this kind of attention.

The military authorities were aware that not all the veterans in the federation received information regarding their rights and benefits. This defeated the purpose of the financial assistance offered to veterans, as at least part of the motive for investing in veterans was to ensure their loyalty and to advertise the privileges assigned to veterans as a way to attract other Africans to enlist. The task of advertising these benefits was considered the responsibility of the veterans' associations. Veterans often wrote to the organization's office to inquire about their rights.[79] Usually these requests represented a large number of veterans who either were unaware of the military reforms and the benefits they deserved by law or were unable to access the administrative center in which they were supposed to collect their pensions. Chief Sergeant Gaudry, an NCO who was in charge of the Senegalese veterans, reported in 1957 that many of the veterans who were over sixty continued to receive their pensions according to the old sums. He warned that as some of them were very old it was essential to correct this without delay and make sure that they received their due payments. Gaudry also mentioned that some of the old or handicapped veterans were unable to travel to the administrative centers to collect their pensions. He suggested that another way be found to deliver the money to them and free them of the need to travel.[80]

The military and the colonial authorities invested much energy and significant sums of money in maintaining good relations with their veterans. Apart from taking care of veterans' material and social needs, the authorities also tried to enhance veterans' pride at having served in the French army and encouraged them to wear their medals and decorations. This reassured the military authorities that veterans were indeed proud of their service in the army and could also impress their friends and relatives and provide good publicity for the army. One of the problems with this plan was that, surprisingly enough, until the postwar military reforms, soldiers who were awarded a medal had to pay for it out of their own pocket. This strange practice was changed in 1948, when commanders were instructed to give the medals to the soldiers for free, but it was difficult for the army to buy all the medals and decorations that the veterans living in the federation were entitled to. As many of them could not afford to buy their medals, the army commander in AOF asked the high commissioner in 1953 to instruct his district commandants to buy the decorations for the veterans living in their territory.[81] As we shall see in chapter 7, the veterans' leaders took advantage of the military's attempt to enhance the veterans' pride as a form of advertising and used their massive participation in the two world wars as a major element in their continued struggle for equality.

In sum, the military authorities attempted to use veterans as a bridge to the general population of AOF. Through them the authorities tried to present an image of a new and modern army in which the principle of equality was supposedly ensured. As we shall see, the veterans and their military glory played an important part in these campaigns. These campaigns also aimed at projecting an improved image of the new colonial army to Western-educated Africans, in spite of the difficulties in their recruitment.

Presenting the New Army to the African Population:
"Bush Tours" and Urban Military Celebrations

As the efforts to reform the colonial army had specific political aims, notably to keep the federation of AOF calm and loyal despite the upheavals in other parts of the French empire, it was vital to project this new image to the general population. This was not the first time the army had attempted to improve its image among the population of AOF. By the beginning of the twentieth century, the army had worked to efface the association between slaves and soldiers that resulted from heavy recruitment among fugitive and liberated slaves in West Africa.[82] But never before had the army invested so much effort in improving the public image of its African units. The reforms were necessary to attain this goal, but if they were not made known to the general population, the army could not hope to gain any political advantage by them. The military command in AOF invested much effort in reaching as many Africans as possible and transmitting to them the image of the new army. This was done in two ways: "bush tours" (*tournées de brousse*) among Africans living in rural areas and military celebrations designated for the urban population.

After World War II and its difficult aftermath, the military authorities in AOF had two specific groups in mind that they could use as a bridge to the general population of AOF: veterans and Western-educated Africans. These two groups were an essential part of the military propaganda campaign during the postwar years. Whereas the first group knew the army well, the second was traditionally alienated from and suspicious of it. Therefore, these two groups played different roles in the presentation of France's reformed army to Africans. The veterans were seen as a means to reach wider populations, for example, relatives and neighbors of those who served France in the past, mainly through tours in rural areas and meetings with veterans. As for the Western-educated elite, its members were to be enticed by all sorts of celebrations, sports events, and artistic performances so that they realized that the army had changed so significantly that they would now find it attractive. These events were organized mainly around November 11 (Armistice Day, World War I) and May 8 (the end of World War II in Europe), which was also Army Day (Journée des Forces Armées). Activities on these days included performances; films; games; sports competitions; horse, car, and motorcycle races; concerts; military parades; and memorial ceremonies.[83] Veterans played a leading role in the last two types of events and also took part in the organization of these celebrations.

Both the bush tours and the military urban celebrations were part of a more general military policy implemented at that period, the so-called psychological operations (*action psychologique*). This policy had already been developed during the Indochina War, became official in 1953 with the establishment of the Bureau de la Guerre Psychologique, known also as the Fifth Bureau, and was finally abolished when de Gaulle returned to power in 1958. Chapters 5 and 6 will discuss this policy in depth. Here I will only focus on the military activities that reflected the army's wish to "sell" its new image to Africans in general and more specifically to those it wanted to entice into its ranks as part of its new image: Western-educated Africans.

The term *tournées de brousse* is quite old in the colonial vocabulary. It was used to describe the administrative tours that the district commandants were supposed to perform every few months in order to maintain contact with the rural population located far from the administrative center. The traditional aim of these tours was to ensure control over the rural population and remind it of the existence of the colonial power, which for most was somewhat distant and vague. District commandants were far from enthusiastic about these tours. The journey was often long, and the travel and lodging conditions were difficult. Basically, the idea of giving up the relative comfort of their home for a long period every few months was extremely unattractive to the administrators. The constant reminders of the importance of these tours demonstrate the difficulty the colonial governors had to ensure that they actually took place.

It is no wonder, then, that when military authorities offered to conduct these tours, colonial administrators were supportive and cooperative. This was a mission better suited for military personnel than for "spoiled" civilians who liked their material comforts. These military tours took place every year, beginning in the early 1950s. They lasted around eight months and encompassed even the most remote districts. According to the military authorities of AOF, the main purpose of these tours was to reinforce the friendship and trust between the French army and the African population, to establish contact with veterans all over the federation, and to demonstrate the permanence of the French presence and concern for the well-being of its veterans. The tours' secondary aims were to collect information about the districts, to train the soldiers, to habituate them to village life, and to forge team spirit among the military units.[84]

In general, the tours were aimed at local people who did not usually encounter soldiers and did not have access to military celebrations in the urban centers of the federation. The soldiers who participated in the tours were equipped with film projectors and radio transmitters in order to bring the military's messages to remote regions. In addition, photo exhibits were organized during these visits, and soldiers handed out presents to the people who came to meet them.[85]

A special service note distributed on May 9, 1955, included specific instructions for soldiers participating in these tours regarding the manner in which they were expected to behave toward the local population. Soldiers were reminded that the purpose of the tour was to reinforce the friendship between the army and the local population, and they were warned to avoid any sorts of confrontations. The population, so the document stated, should not feel that the army considered it as hostile. The French commanders of these tours were asked to show special interest in the veterans who had received decorations for their service and to show respect toward local African dignitaries. The soldiers were told not to offer payment to the village or canton chiefs in return for the food they would receive during their tour, as this might upset them. Instead, the officers leading the tours were instructed to give each chief a sum of money, saying that it was intended for the community, to construct a new mosque, for example.[86]

The tours were initially supposed to help the army present a friendly image to the rural populations of AOF. As we shall see in chapter 6, throughout the 1950s and the political developments both in other parts of the French empire and in the international arena, these contacts became even more important, and a vast propaganda system was developed in order to prevent certain "dangerous" political ideas from winning over the hearts of Africans. The tours also had another purpose, namely, to ensure constant and close contact with veterans who lived far from the administrative centers of the federation. The tours were a two-way street, as they gave these veterans access to the military authorities while allowing these authorities to affirm their control over veterans who were usually below their radar. Even the administrative civilian authorities benefited from these relatively well-organized tours, as they served to reinforce colonial power at a time of political uncertainty and rapid change. As opposed to the success of these tours, the military officials' attempts to organize military celebrations in the urban centers and attract Western-educated Africans to them did not earn the same measure of administrative cooperation.

On February 3, 1955, the high command of the army in AOF advertised the plans for the Army Day celebrations of that year. Almost three weeks later, Gen. Pierre Garbay, the superior commander of AOF, asked the high commissioner to reserve the Dakar stadium, where the event had taken place the previous year, for this date.[87] The municipality of Dakar rejected the request, saying that the football championship of Senegal and the French West Africa Cup games were already scheduled for the same time. The high commissioner offered Garbay several alternatives, such as the local stadium of Fann. Garbay responded rather furiously and maintained that the alternatives were unsatisfactory, as they lacked the right facilities, were far from the center, and were somewhat inaccessible. The general was outraged by the fact that one of the alternative stadiums was shaped like a triangle, thus rendering horse races impossible. Finally, Garbay agreed to postpone the celebrations to the second half of June on condition that the army would be allowed to use the Dakar stadium at that time. He then added that if his request was not fulfilled, the celebrations would be canceled. In case this threat did not have the desired effect on the high commissioner, Garbay warned him that the cancellation of the celebrations would severely harm the relations between the army and the population and would create an image of mediocrity and lack of professionalism.[88]

The general's suggestion was forwarded to Mr. Bonifay, the mayor of Dakar, and he agreed. However, he made sure to request that the stadium be returned to its original condition after the celebrations.[89] This remark and the scheduling of football games during the same week in which the military celebrations were known to take place annually reflect the civil authorities' lack of enthusiasm for this form of publicity activity, as well as their different priorities.

Such grand events as the one planned for the Dakar stadium were specifically intended for Western-educated Africans, as they tended to live in the capital and other urban centers. The military authorities organizing such celebrations worked hard to present an image of a highly modernized, sophisticated, and professional army that would appeal to young educated Africans. One way to do so was to promote Africans who were already part of specialized and prestigious military units. In reality, despite the upgraded military training for Africans during the 1950s, most Africans were still being recruited to the infantry and artillery brigades. The paratroopers were the only specialized unit that incorporated a growing number of African NCOs, and a special school established in Dakar began training African paratroopers in the early 1950s.[90] The army often used this prestigious combat unit as an example of the professionalization of African soldiers. Photos of African paratroopers receiving their paratroopers' wings or jumping out of airplanes above typical African landscapes decorated the stands during military celebrations.[91] During the celebrations of Army Week in 1954 African paratroopers demonstrated hand-to-hand combat.[92] The African population was also invited to watch military drills in which African paratroopers took part, such as the one executed near

FIG. 2. African paratroopers over the savanna. Courtesy Archives Nationales du Sénégal, Dakar (ANS), 5D 214.

Thiès in Senegal, in which dozens of paratroopers jumped out of airplanes and successfully "conquered" a village.[93]

Another manner of emphasizing the modernity and professionalism of the AOF army units during such events was to include exhibitions displaying the impressive military equipment used by these units. However, in this respect the reality of the armed forces in AOF was very different from the image they wished to project. The army stationed in AOF did not in fact possess new and impressive military equipment but rather old and outdated machinery. In March 1954, during the preparations for that year's celebrations of Army Day, the superior commander of the forces in AOF sent a plea to the minister of the colonies asking that he consider giving a donation for the purchase of new equipment for the celebrations.[94] One week later this request was backed by the high commissioner, who explained to the minister that these important events could not achieve their goal if the army's broken equipment was presented to the African visitors, and it was therefore essential to bring modern equipment from

France.[95] The fact that the high commissioner supported the general's request is not surprising, as two weeks earlier the army had asked the colonial administration to accord it credit of 800,000 CFA for the preparations of Army Day celebrations.[96] The high commissioner had also tried to recruit the director of civil aviation to assist the military's efforts by asking him to deliver 1,300 kilos (2,865 pounds) of equipment from Paris to Dakar for the military celebrations.[97]

Eventually, it seems that the army was forced to adopt a more economical solution. When Colonel Saquet, an officer representing the chief commander of the forces in AOF, was interviewed on a local radio station about the forthcoming military celebrations, he noted that photos of modern weaponry would be exhibited, as well as a few select models.[98] We should bear in mind that the preparations for the Army Day celebrations of 1954 began around the time when the battle of Dien Bien Phu in Indochina broke out, and the celebrations took place one day after the defeat of the French forces. Under such circumstances the army needed more than a few photographs of military equipment in order to impress young Western-educated Africans.

In addition to the mostly futile attempts to present the French forces in AOF as modern and advanced, the military authorities also tried to expose young Africans to the personal advantages of military service during such celebrations. To this end, a publicity pamphlet prepared for the celebrations of the Army Day of 1953 included information about the training of Africans as NCOs and as officers, data about military salaries, and a list of the major officers' schools in France.[99]

As noted, while military celebrations were aimed mostly at attracting Western-educated Africans, veterans also played an important role in them. In all of the major celebrations, such as those taking place on November 11 and May 8, veterans marched, laid wreathes on monuments, and served as a sympathetic audience at various performances. While the military authorities encountered difficulties during the organization of these kinds of parades and military urban celebrations, these events did have the desired effects on some of the young Africans who graduated from the colonial educational system. Niang recounts in his memoirs how deeply impressed he was by the July 14 march of 1954, which took place in front of a large crowd. He was especially drawn by the uniformed veterans with their medals covering their chests, whom he had seen participating in a ceremony by the monument for the dead. According to Niang, these veterans were so impressive that no one had dared approach them, and Niang himself was fascinated by the stories of the veterans who had fought in the Indochina war. In his account, Niang tells of the parade of the motorized unit and the cheers of the children crying "Here they are!" as they saw the soldiers marching past them. The EMPA pupils also marched proudly, carrying French flags, and the tam-tam drums did not stop beating. "It was a festival! It was joy!" he proclaimed. In fact, Niang asserted that it was his participation in these military celebrations that made him decide to join the army. According to him, after the celebrations he returned home, reread his history book from primary school, which reminded him of the glorious history of France, and decided to enlist.[100]

The military authorities in AOF invested tremendous efforts and manpower in urban celebrations and in tours to remote areas of the federation. Their aim was to extol the advantages of army service among the population and improve the image of the army in the eyes of the local population, especially the most politically aware and active segment: the Western-educated elite. After all, there was not much point in investing so much money in the improvement of service conditions for African soldiers and benefits for veterans if this image of a new, modern, and egalitarian army was not transmitted to the population of AOF. But to what extent did this image actually reflect a real transformation in the military policy in AOF? Or, in other words, was this really a new army?

How New Was the "New" Army?

In conclusion I will examine the significance of the military reforms and try to answer the question of how new the French army in AOF was and which of its old aspects refused to disappear in spite of the reforms. We have already seen that the army units in AOF were hardly as modern as the military command tried to present them to Africans. It is quite clear that the military funds were invested mainly in areas of the French empire in which hostilities were going on. The relative calm in AOF, which had always been neglected financially compared to Indochina and North Africa, did not provide cause for further investments in military equipment. But the issue of modern equipment or lack thereof is not the crucial one here.

It is obvious that military officials in the federation were interested in rendering the military forces posted there more modern and efficient, but as they depended on budgetary decisions in the metropole, this form of modernization was beyond their control. The more interesting and important question is to what extent they were actually interested in other aspects of this new army, namely, the principle of equality between metropolitan and colonial soldiers and the attempts to entice Western-educated Africans to military service.

The establishment of the French Union, which replaced the term "French empire" in 1946, was based on the theoretical notion of an enlightened new kind of French colonialism that ensured the principle of equality between the metropolitan French and the citizens of this new union, who were formally known as colonial subjects. Although the second version of the constitution, approved by the French government in October of that year, did not provide for universal suffrage or most of the demands of African politicians for real equality, the rhetoric of the French government reflected the rejection of the old colonial methods in favor of a new form of cooperation between France and its colonies.[101] As we shall see in the following chapters, this was the image France had tried to project regarding its supposedly progressive colonialism in order to countermand criticism and demands to end colonial rule raised in the international, national, and colonial arenas. The leveling of the pensions between metropolitan and African soldiers was a significant step in the direction of equality. This acceptance of the principle of equal pay for equal work was something trade unions in AOF fought for during the postwar period with only partial success. In fact, the leader of the 1947–48 railway strike (the strike lasted for five and a half months), Ibrahima Sarr, tried to rely on the veterans' discourse of equality for sacrifices in his first speech from 1946. He maintained that the role of Africans in the French military, defending French freedom, legitimated not only veterans' demands but also those of the African railway men, who demanded equality with their French coworkers.[102] This strike won African railway men major achievements, but, a decade later, the French government realized that a full acceptance of this principle of equality in the colonial sphere would put too heavy a burden on the French taxpayer and became convinced to opt for the cheaper alternative: autonomy and eventually independence.

Although the army was the only colonial institution in which this principle was at least partially applied despite the budgetary implications, this implementation was not always smooth, as we can learn from the numerous letters of complaints written by veterans who were unable to receive their due pensions. In addition, certain persisting military policies suggested that the road to full equality between metropolitan and colonial soldiers was still long. This can be best demonstrated by two such policies. The first is the continuing practice of recruiting Africans to the notorious second portion after the formal abolition of forced labor in 1946 and even after 1950, when this form of recruitment was unequivocally supposed to stop. The second is the continued segregation between French and African soldiers in the spheres of health and social assistance. As for forced labor, the army actually helped to perpetuate a policy that supposedly belonged to a different era of a repressive colonialism. The abolition of forced labor was not decided upon easily, and it took much effort on behalf of the African members of the French parliament, most notably the initiator of the law, Houphouët-Boigny. But the credit for the abolition of the practice that was most associated with French colonial brutality and injustice was soon taken by the colonial administration, which attempted to present a liberal image of its rule. The continued practice of forced labor under the cover of military recruitment undermined the army's claim for becoming an egalitarian institution.

The persisting tendency within military policy during the 1950s to differentiate between French metropolitan and African soldiers also contradicts the proclaimed transformation of such attitudes.[103] As we have seen in this chapter, reports on the establishment of lodgings and medical centers for soldiers actually referred to separate centers for Africans and Europeans. The reason for this separation is not noted, but it probably stemmed from the assumption that these two populations had different needs and habits that could not be catered to under the same roof. The insistence on creating separate spaces of recreation and health for African and metropolitan soldiers points to a certain difficulty in forsaking the old mode of thought among military officials. Statements such as the one regarding the limited intellect of the African pupils in the EMPA schools reinforce the assertion that old colonial prejudices refused to die with the military reforms.

We have seen that French commanders sometimes complained about the attitudes of the ostensibly spoiled and demanding Western-educated soldiers. There were also incidents in which French commanders mocked educated Africans for supposedly pretending to be French and insisted that African soldiers learn simplified "Tirailleur French" instead of proper French.[104] These cases show that even if the formal military policy was to treat Africans with respect and equality, commanders in the field did not always abide by that policy, and African soldiers continued to suffer from racist and derisive treatment.

The constant breaching of the principle of equality within the army and the continued contempt for the Western-educated Africans who had joined its ranks leads us to question the image the military authorities in AOF tried to project. Nevertheless, it is important to remember that it was not easy to rapidly transform modes of thought, prejudice, and conventions that had been so deeply rooted within the units of the colonial army for decades. The fact that discrimination and inequality persisted in the colonial units of the army does not mean that a real attempt to transform these units was not taking place. The frequent quarrels with the civilian administration over measures that seemed vital to the army and the genuine attempts to reach out to veterans all over AOF demonstrate the often sincere wish of certain military officials to change old colonial attitudes and create a new type of relationship with African soldiers and veterans. However, the continuing gaps between the image the army was trying to project to Africans and the actual military reality of the African soldiers rendered the preservation of their loyalty quite complicated. The challenges the army faced in Indochina and in Algeria made the maintenance of African soldiers' loyalty, as well as that of the relative political tranquility in AOF, extremely vital. The new army was now facing a different type of war, one that was fought not only on the battlefield. This was also a psychological and diplomatic war in which African soldiers played a crucial role. In the following chapters, our discussion will move its focus to Indochina and Algeria and examine the ways in which the military authorities in these regions tried to preserve the loyalty of the African soldiers within an increasingly complex political climate.

4

African Troops in the Wars of Decolonization

Indochina, 1946–1954

The extensive efforts of the military to change the nature and the image of the colonial army, described in the previous chapter, were essential in order to render the African units more professional. This was necessary so that these units could face the challenges of the new kinds of wars that broke out in the French and other colonial empires after World War II: the anticolonial wars of liberation. The French military authorities feared that this kind of war would dangerously challenge the loyalty of the African soldiers, as these soldiers were colonial subjects just like those against whom they were required to fight. To this end, the military reforms aimed to enforce the soldiers' loyalty and sense of belonging to the French army and nation. The first challenge to French colonial domination was in Vietnam, where the Japanese retreat in August 1945 created a vacuum into which Ho Chi Minh had no problem entering. The nine-year-long Indochina war began following Ho Chi Minh's declaration of Vietnamese independence in September of that year. This war ended in disaster, as far as the French military was concerned, with the humiliating defeat of Dien Bien Phu in May 1954. Only six months after this downfall a large-scale revolt erupted in Algeria, developing into another messy colonial war that lasted almost eight years.[1]

Unlike the appeal to African soldiers recruited to fight in World War II, the appeal to Africans to help the French army save the empire required a more sophisticated rhetoric. This was not the first time African soldiers participated in military campaigns aimed at maintaining the empire; the empire had been conquered in the late nineteenth century with the significant use of African troops, who were later entrusted with the preservation of order in the colonies. However, after World War II the winds of decolonization were already blowing hard over the colonial world, and it was difficult to ignore the fact that African soldiers were being sent to fight against national movements seeking to end colonial rule—the same colonial rule under which they themselves lived.

Although this book concentrates on the region of AOF, in order to understand the French army's involvement in the political processes in this federation it is essential to delve into its use of African soldiers in the vicious wars in Indochina and Algeria. The army's attempts to deal with the problems that emerged from the encounters of these soldiers with other colonial subjects and with the struggles of liberation movements reflect the army's attitude toward major issues within AOF. This is essential in order to understand the army's efforts to "protect" its population from the forces for decolonization developing in other parts of the French and other colonial empires and the alternatives the army offered to AOF's independence. This chapter and the following one deal with the participation of African soldiers in these two major colonial wars in Indochina and Algeria. In each of these chapters I will discuss the ways in which the French military command tried to prevent African soldiers from being influenced by the local anticolonial movement's propaganda and maintain their loyalty. I will open these two chapters with a general discussion of Africans' motives to serve in the French army after World War II, especially in these two wars, and will end them with a review of the African soldiers' mindset concerning their service in both wars at the time and in retrospect.

After the general introduction to both chapters, this chapter will offer a brief overview of the major stages of the long conflict in Indochina. Next I will examine the nature of the soldiers' service, including the conditions under which they served and the specific difficulties they had to endure.

I will then explore the French military concerns relating to the African soldiers' loyalty during the war. These concerns focused on three main areas: the low morale of African soldiers due to the harsh conditions under which they served; the relationships African soldiers forged with the local populations in the territories in which they served; and the potential negative influence of enemy propaganda on African soldiers due to its emphasis on the shared destiny of colonized peoples.

Before delving into the participation of African soldiers in the two major conflicts of the post–World War II years, a word must be said about another much more limited but no less vicious conflict that took place after the war: the rebellion in Madagascar, which was brutally repressed with the help of African soldiers.[2]

African Soldiers and the Repression of the Malagasy Uprising (1947–1948)

The revolt in Madagascar, which broke out on March 29, 1947, cannot be compared in its scope and implications to the two conflicts discussed below. Though it lasted until the end of 1948, this revolt gained little international attention, mostly because it was not related to the Cold War, a fact that allowed the French to repress it without much limitation. Nevertheless, it is important to discuss it here due to the important role African soldiers played in its brutal repression. In fact, as in past situations, the French used African soldiers to inflict violence when they preferred not to be associated with it themselves. Like other regions of the French empire, the island of Madagascar was conquered with the help of Africans brought from the other end of the continent. Africans were also responsible for the maintenance of order during the entire colonial period. It is no wonder, then, that they were also the main targets of the Malagasy rebels in 1947.[3]

After World War II, Malagasy political activists began to voice demands for independence. In response, in 1946 the French colonial administration approved the foundation of the Mouvement Démocratique de la Rénovation Malgache (Democratic Movement for the Renovation of Madagascar, MDRM) as a political means through which to channel and thus control these demands. The new party sent representatives to the French parliament and tried to advance its goals through political activity. Unfortunately, this did not work as planned, as the governments of the Fourth Republic, which were under pressure from the European settlers in Madagascar, were much less open to the idea of self-determination for the island than were the liberation forces right after the war. The colonial administration began to see the MDRM as its enemy. When the revolt began, the administration hurried to put the blame on the party, although its leaders had sent a telegram to all the party's sections only two days earlier, warning that a revolt was being planned. Later, the administration claimed that this telegram was actually an order to begin the revolt, and the entire leadership of the MDRM was arrested and put on trial.[4]

In fact, the rebels came from popular social groups who were hostile to the Malagasy political elites and did not believe in the parliamentary course of action. Their first attack was on a military camp in Moramona, in the eastern part of the island. This camp served as a base for solders transferring to Indochina and accommodated many African soldiers. The rebels attacked at night and managed to kill some of the African soldiers in their beds. The next day the soldiers' comrades went out to the adjacent villages to take revenge. A French agronomist who had witnessed the violence against innocent Malagasy civilians dubbed it "the Malagasy Oradour."[5] While the French authorities criticized this violent retribution, they also expressed their understanding of the soldiers' distress. The fact that the soldiers were allowed to leave the camp might suggest that these acts of brutality against civilians were very convenient for the French authorities, as they might have served to deter the rebels from continuing their attacks.

The rebels, however, were not deterred, and the revolt lasted until the end of 1948. The French brought hundreds of African soldiers to Madagascar to assist in its repression. The number of casualties, especially on the Malagasy side, is controversial. The estimations vary from the formal statistics, citing 11,342 deaths, to as many as 89,000 Malagasy victims and 2,250 soldiers, out of whom 1,990 were Africans. The violent nature of the repression of the revolt was expressed not only in the numbers of casualties but also in the interrogation methods used to extract information from Malagasy prisoners. This information was solicited with the sole purpose of using it to support the French position regarding the MDRM's culpability. African soldiers also participated in these interrogations. According to testimonies cited by Amadou Ba, whenever an African soldier appeared in the interrogation room, the prisoner knew to expect harsh treatment. The

French officer would then leave the room, locking the door behind him. This would be a sign for the African soldier to beat up the prisoner and torture him. After a while, the French officer would return and ostensibly rebuke the African for his excessive violence. In this manner, the French could transfer the responsibility for their own violent acts to the African soldiers and use the Africans' reputation as inherently brutal to attain French aims while keeping their hands clean.[6]

The repression of the revolt in Madagascar was supposedly a minor event compared to the wars in Indochina and Algeria. It was also the last time the French managed to win a colonial conflict. It is quite obvious that the way in which Africans were utilized in this process was certainly not compatible with the French declarations of a new colonial army. The highly problematic role African soldiers were assigned during this conflict raises the question of their motives to fight against anticolonial movements on the side of their own colonizer. The next section will examine this question.

Africans' Motives for Serving in the Colonial Army after World War II

First and foremost, it should be clarified that a discussion of the motives behind the African soldiers' decision to serve in France's wars of decolonization is based on the assumption that they were volunteers rather than conscripts. As we have seen in the previous chapter, soldiers could not be forced to serve in Indochina unless they had volunteered for military service. These soldiers joined the French army knowing that their main mission during their service would be to protect the empire against anticolonial movements. Even though they could not have foreseen the brutal nature of both wars, they probably had not expected their experiences to be pleasant. Why did they then choose to volunteer?

As described previously, the conditions of service in the colonial army changed significantly during the late 1940s and early 1950s. The extensive reforms the army had initiated in order to improve its relations with African soldiers and veterans not only contributed to the restoration of the soldiers' trust in the French army but also attracted volunteers who wanted to take advantage of the social and economic opportunities the "new army" offered them.[7] According to Michel Bodin, the possibility of a pilgrimage to Mecca (a practice that will be discussed in detail in the next chapter) was one of the motives for Africans to join the army voluntarily.[8]

Myron Echenberg notes that the motives of young Africans to volunteer into the army after World War II were mostly economic, resulting from unemployment in the urban sector. In addition, soldiers who managed to reach the rank of sergeant received a salary roughly ten times higher than that of urban or rural laborers.[9]

Some of the veterans confirmed that they chose to volunteer into the army even though their relatives and friends criticized this decision. Mamadou Niang volunteered to serve in Algeria and needed his mother's signature.[10] In order to attain it, he had to trick her into going to the police to sign her approval with her thumbprint without her knowing what she was signing. Niang said that when his mother found out that she had actually allowed her son to enlist, she was scared, because "people thought you go to the army to die." He, on the other hand, thought of the army as an opportunity, a gateway to social and economic advancement. His goal was to become a noncommissioned officer, and he eventually did become a paratrooper. He stated that his salary was good and allowed him to live comfortably and help his family.[11]

Papa Figaro Diagne was also attracted to the economic and social benefits associated with a military career. According to his calculations prior to volunteering for the army, at the age of thirty-two he would receive a pension from the army and be able to continue working as a civilian, receiving two salaries simultaneously. In an interview conducted in 2011, Diagne insisted that he did not see military service as an adventure. He had well-defined goals: he wanted to learn a profession that he could not have learned by staying in Senegal, and he was not really interested in fighting. Though his friends and relatives thought that he was insane and warned him that he would get himself killed, Diagne responded by telling them that they were cowards. Eventually, he said, they were all happy to receive presents from him when he returned to Senegal.[12] Another soldier, Sadibou Badji, joined the French army in 1957. His parents were not happy about it, but, being an only son, he felt that military service would help him support his family.[13]

In these three examples, the motives for enlistment were financial, and friends and relatives were not supportive. African soldiers who studied at military schools enjoyed much more family support, as they had been destined for military service from a young age. These were most often Africans who came from families with a military tradition. Such was the case of Marc Guèye, who studied in a military school and enlisted in 1948 upon graduation. He joined the army because of his passion for military professions and his wish to become an officer. When asked about his salary, Guèye said that it was low at first, but when he achieved the rank of corporal and later sergeant, his salary became satisfactory.[14]

Young men had other personal motives for volunteering to the French army, ranging from the wish to attract women to attempting to evade familial authority.[15] In general, most Africans volunteered in order to change the course of their lives for the better and gain economic and social control. It is important to bear in mind that for these soldiers, joining the French army was a career choice and not a political or ideological statement. Probably aware of this motivation, French authorities were afraid it would not provide enough support to cope with the daily hardships that awaited African soldiers in Indochina.

The Indochina War (1946–1954)

The Indochina war, which ended with a disastrous French military defeat, developed in three main stages. The first began with the Japanese surrender and Ho Chi Minh's establishment of the Democratic Republic of Vietnam (DRV) in the northern part of the country in August 1945. The Vietnamese leader demanded the unification of Vietnam and immediate self-determination under his rule. While it seemed for a while that a compromise might be reached, granting Ho Chi Minh power over part of the country while allowing the French to continue controlling southern Vietnam, the diplomatic efforts failed, mainly because of the French settlers in Vietnam and military pressure not to give up northern Vietnam. The French deadly attack on the northern port city of Haiphong on November 23, 1946, in which thousands of Vietnamese were killed, signaled the end of negotiations and the beginning of the Indochina war.[16] A few weeks after this attack, Ho Chi Minh made one last failed attempt to negotiate with the French, after which hostilities were resumed. During the first years of the war, neither side was able to achieve any substantial advantage over the other. The Vietnamese lacked equipment and ammunition. They tried to improve their position by encouraging villagers to take part in the fighting and by establishing relations with various states in the region, such as India, Burma, Indonesia, and the Philippines. French power remained limited because its soldiers were needed for the occupation of Germany and for other anticolonial struggles, such as the revolt in Madagascar. In order to countermand the situation, the French tried to win international support for what they termed "the Bao Dai solution." The idea was to recognize the politically powerless Vietnamese emperor, Bao Dai, as the head of state in the south and allow continued French control through him. The Americans and the British hesitated to endorse this solution, until the Communist victory in China in 1949 marked the beginning of a new stage in the war over Vietnam, a stage in which the war became internationalized. It was now no longer a local anticolonial struggle against the French, similar to Madagascar, but rather a part of the intensifying global Cold War. From 1949 onward, the Viet Minh enjoyed the support of Communist China and the Soviet Union. Their position was thus greatly reinforced, although relations with both countries were tense. On the other hand, this change in the state of affairs and the changing international climate drew the United States into the conflict. France now received significant financial aid to continue the struggle. In spite of the growing American and British support, by 1953 France was in a difficult situation in Indochina. Total casualties reached 150,000, and the war drew half of the country's defense budget, even with the increased American aid. A poll conducted that year in France established that 50 percent of the public favored either immediate withdrawal or negotiations, and only 15 percent demanded continuing the war until a full victory was achieved.

In early 1954, while discussions about negotiations were already in the air, the Vietnamese began moving substantial numbers of soldiers into the hills surrounding Dien Bien Phu in northern Vietnam. The French hoped that an open battle that did not conform to the Viet Minh's guerrilla methods would help them achieve a decisive victory. However, the Vietnamese two-month siege on the French forces, which isolated and trapped them, forced the French to surrender on May 7, 1954. This battle marked the final defeat of French colonialism in Vietnam, and the country was divided between the DRV in the north and Bao Dai's government in the south.[17]

The Service of African Soldiers in Indochina

Up until the beginning of the Indochina war, only *originaires* served in French Indochina. Even when the war started and the French army

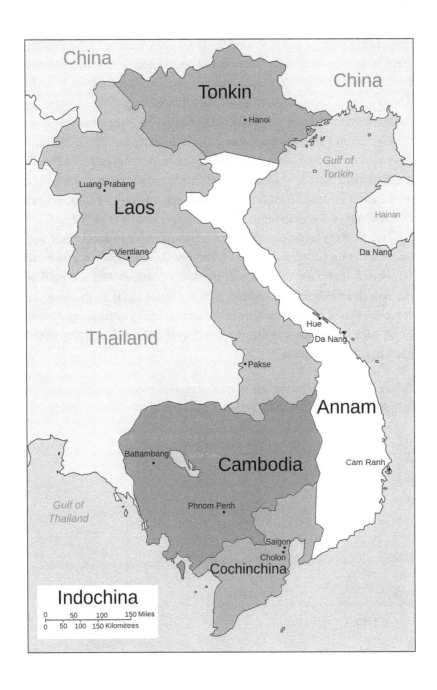

FIG. 3. Map of French Indochina. Source: Wikimedia Commons.

desperately needed reinforcements, de Gaulle objected to the deployment of African colonial soldiers in the region because he was worried that they might be affected by Vietnamese national sentiments. In addition, the French were worried about the soldiers' state of mind following the revolts that erupted at the end of World War II. Once it became clear that the conflict in Indochina was going to be long and costly and that more soldiers would have to be recruited, this policy changed. The French government's refusal to initiate a draft in France also encouraged the recruitment of colonial soldiers. With the appointment of Gen. Edgard de Larminat as commander in chief of the French forces in West Africa, the French army initiated a policy of attracting African volunteers, and recruitment for Indochina began.[18] The first African soldiers arrived in Hanoi and Haiphong in Tonkin in 1947. Sub-Saharan Africa served as the French army's human reserve, as it had since 1914. By the time the cease-fire was in place, it had supplied 60,340 soldiers to the army. Almost 3,000 Africans perished in the war, 3,706 were wounded, and 2,546 were discharged due to illness.[19]

Table 1. Number and percentage of African soldiers serving in Indochina (Fiches annuelles d'effectifs 1947–1954)

YEAR	NUMBER OF AFRICAN SOLDIERS IN INDOCHINA	PERCENTAGE OF THE FRENCH FORCES
1947	617	0.72
1948	5,094	6.9
1949	9,091	10.66
1950	13,204	12.41
1951	16,901	15.02
1952	19,195	15.57
1953	18,382	14.98
1954	18,887	15.95

Source: SHD/T 10 H 505-8.

As we have seen, with the Communist victory in China in 1949, the war in Indochina entered a new phase. The Viet Minh, who until then had conducted guerrilla actions against the French, began to receive open support from the new regime in China, and their numbers grew steadily. The French army suffered increasingly heavy casualties and loss of morale, and as a result, the presence of African soldiers in Indochina dramatically increased.[20]

The Indochina war was the first large-scale anticolonial war in which African soldiers took part. Soldiers were exposed to a new and unfamiliar culture and to a different kind of war, one that involved both guerrilla and psychological warfare. In addition, African soldiers arrived in Indochina quite unprepared for the sort of challenges that awaited them there, and most were simply not equipped to cope with these challenges. Almost all of the African soldiers who fought in Indochina were illiterate. Only 9 percent were corporals or sergeants. There were very few NCOs and even fewer officers. There was only one African officer for every battalion and sometimes none. Almost all of the regular soldiers had no chance of being promoted, because they were unable to pass the required exams.[21]

In order to prepare them for this new kind of battlefield, African recruits were sent to Fréjus, on the French Riviera, for a two-month preparatory course before arriving in Indochina. They learned how to use weapons, advance in silence, and surround a village. They were taught to fight nocturnal missions and implement maritime military actions, which were supposed to address their fear of night and water, which the French believed stemmed from ancestral beliefs about demons of the night and spirits who lived in the water. Sadly, the preparation was insufficient, resulting in a needless loss of lives, as the young recruits arrived in Indochina completely ignorant of the methods the Viet Minh were using. They often fell victim to landmines and traps, about which they had not been warned during their training.[22] In a report on African morale from July 1951, Gen. Jean de Lattre de Tassigny, France's high commissioner in Indochina and the commander of the French forces stationed there, cautioned about this situation. He remonstrated that while training in France, the soldiers were occupied in all sorts of menial labor, which did nothing to improve their military skills, while suffering terribly from the cold. When they arrived in Indochina, the soldiers were ordered to perform missions for which they were poorly prepared, putting themselves and their comrades at risk. Occasionally, the general noted, they were lucky enough to serve with Europeans from the Colonial Corps who were able to instruct them and prepare them for their missions. In other cases, the Europeans with whom they served were not used to African soldiers and were therefore not helpful in guiding them.[23]

This problematic situation was also noted in the military annual report for 1951. The report specified that 13,694 soldiers, out of whom 8,054 were career soldiers, were destined to serve in Indochina that year. This was 60 percent of the African forces. While the superior commander of the army in FWA had instructed in June 1951 that all soldiers sent to the fighting zones of Tonkin and Cochin China must complete their training before they arrived in Indochina, this was not possible due to the dire need for reinforcements. According to the report, about half of the soldiers earmarked to serve in Indochina had served for less than a year in the army, and 15 percent had only served between two and six months. The new recruits underwent five months of basic training, which was not enough to prepare them for their service in Indochina. Many of the soldiers, so the report noted, hardly understood French, a fact that made their proper training even more challenging. After November 1950, the deteriorating situation in Indochina necessitated reducing the training period even further, to only two or three months; by 1951 about half of the soldiers did not receive proper training before being sent to the battlefields of Indochina. The solution the report offered was to note in a soldier's personal service records which training he had received so that it could be completed after his arrival in Indochina. Obviously, in most cases this was not at all possible.[24]

In reviewing the veterans' recollection of their experiences during the Indochina war, it is obvious that they were not prepared for the hardships that awaited them. When recalling their service, veterans usually focused on the harsh geographical conditions. Heavy rains, floods, unfamiliar and dangerous animals all made fighting in Indochina extremely onerous. For them, the brutal and evasive character of the Viet Minh warriors was another difficulty, and the blurred borders between warriors and civilians were especially taxing.[25] Every peasant could transform into a Viet Minh warrior in a second. Even women were occasionally dangerous. Ousmane Niang recalled how in 1950 he and other soldiers captured a woman who was spying on them in Luang Prabang in Laos. When they attempted to stop her for interrogation, she pulled a hand grenade out of her hair and tried to throw it at them. Luckily, the soldiers managed to push the woman to the ground before she was able to throw the grenade.[26]

The soldiers lived in isolated outposts fortified by trenches and barbed-wire fences. The physical conditions in these posts were harsh. The soldiers slept on the ground, and each pair of soldiers shared a tent, in which they dug a hole where they could hide in case of a Viet Minh bombardment.[27] Soldiers stayed at their posts between three and six months, sometimes more, though occasionally they were awarded a leave of up to fifteen days.[28] Vacations at home were very rare; in some cases soldiers served two years in Indochina before returning home on leave.[29] A military report from May 1951 referred to these infrequent and short vacations as one of the main causes for the low morale of African troops.[30]

While African soldiers shared most of these difficulties and challenges with French metropolitan soldiers, they also had to face their own particular hardships. Even though formal racist attitudes and discrimination against African soldiers significantly decreased after World War II and the military reforms, which were geared to attract Africans to serve in the army, African soldiers often encountered racist behavior and attitudes from their French commanders and comrades, as well as the local population. Moreover, the definition of a certain act or expression as racist depended upon the social reality of the time: during the post–World War II years significant changes occurred in the colonies, and African soldiers certainly grew more impatient with racist attitudes toward them. Accordingly, they expected their commanders to practice the military egalitarian discourse. This did not always happen, as African soldiers continued to suffer from discrimination and abusive behavior at the hands of French officers, soldiers, and members of the Foreign Legion. They were verbally insulted and sometimes even physically attacked. In some cases, complaints about discrimination reached the administrative authorities in AOF, but this was mostly only when an *originaire* had been the victim of such improper behavior.[31]

Some African soldiers responded to these difficult and stressful conditions with violent acts toward their comrades and commanders. It is difficult to establish the exact frequency of these acts during the Indochina war, since they are not all documented in the archives.[32] However, between May 1953 and March 1954, African soldiers murdered at least three French commanders.[33] Investigation reports issued after these incidents pointed to the difficult emotional and psychological states characterizing the perpetrators of the crimes, which were a consequence of harsh service conditions.

Even though the African officers in charge of these investigations tried to downplay discrimination as a motive for the murders, the witness accounts and the confessions of the perpetrators themselves mention the level of frustration they felt due to the harsh treatment they received from their direct commanders.[34]

In interviews conducted in later years, some African veterans referred to the high emotional and psychological price soldiers paid for their participation in the Indochina war, even years after it ended. Veterans said that the war traumatized them. One veteran's wife recounted that after the war her husband was constantly nervous, and she was unable to understand him. Many of the soldiers had to be hospitalized for months after the war, and others had nightmares for years. Some soldiers became addicted to opium during their service in Indochina, as it was one of the few means available to them to alleviate their anxiety.[35] Military reports on African soldiers returning from Indochina to West Africa indicate a problem with alcoholism among these soldiers, a phenomenon that according to these reports did not exist previously.[36]

The fighting in Indochina presented African troops with extreme challenges for which they were not prepared. The unfamiliar territory, the determined enemy before them, and the physical and mental hardships they endured significantly harmed their morale and made them more susceptible to Viet Minh propaganda. Let us see now how the military authorities dealt with this problem.

Military Concerns Regarding African Soldiers' Morale

The harsh conditions under which African soldiers served in Indochina and their frustration from the ongoing discrimination and disdain aimed at them definitely harmed their morale. The military authorities considered low morale among soldiers in general as a serious problem. This problem became even more alarming where African soldiers were concerned, as it was combined with a general suspicion concerning their loyalty and motivation. It is not surprising, then, that the army invested great efforts in improving African soldiers' morale, efforts that were reflected in many letters and reports. As we shall see, some of the solutions to this problem actually caused new problems, especially when they involved the African soldiers' encounters with local men and women.

In order to tackle the problem of African soldiers' morale it was first essential to monitor it. In the French colonial world in general, monitoring colonial subjects' morale was an important tool of control, performed regularly on several administrative levels. Colonial administrators all over the empire published morale reports every trimester. The value of these reports, both as tools of colonial control and as sources for historians, is sometimes dubious. Most opened with the soothing sentence "In general, morale is very good" and gave the impression that French colonial rule is the best assurance for happiness. Nevertheless, when a real problem occurred requiring immediate attention, it was commonly noted in these reports, though in the least alarming way possible. In our case, morale reports were usually more instructive, as they were written in a time of war for a specific and urgent purpose.

In addition, African officers, who truly aspired to solve the problems they raised, were usually the ones who wrote the reports on African soldiers' morale in Indochina. These officers were employed by the Bureau of African Affairs (Bureau des Affaires Africaines, BAA), inaugurated in 1952 for the purpose of monitoring African soldiers' morale. A French metropolitan officer headed each bureau and supervised an African officer. The central BAA was in Saigon, and the other two branches were situated in Hanoi and Haiphong. The role of the staff was to periodically visit the troops; assess their performance, level of discipline, and morale; and investigate violent incidents. The BAA staff was also supposed to visit sick and injured soldiers and solve personal problems. Obviously, these missions were overwhelming, as problems, incidents, and grievances were constantly on the rise. The bureaus were underfunded, and their personnel lacked the necessary skills for their missions. In addition, the BAA's African personnel had no authority to deal with incidents in which metropolitan soldiers or commanders mistreated African soldiers, other than alerting their superiors.[37]

One of the main problems the BAA warned against was the discriminating and belittling treatment African soldiers received in newspapers published both locally and in France. The African officer responsible for monitoring all African soldiers stationed in southern and central Vietnam, Laos, and Cambodia, Captain Guedou, complained in one of his reports about the negative psychological effects the military journal *Caravelle*, published in Indochina, had on African soldiers. According to Guedou, unlike the North African soldiers, who had their own Arabic journal, the literate Africans knew only how to read and write in French and therefore were supposed to read general newspapers. Reading the *Caravelle*, so Guedou wrote, was a depressing experience for African soldiers, as the journal often ridiculed them and hurt their feelings. Guedou also noted that the journal intentionally ignored all African military achievements during the war. On one occasion, a battalion of African soldiers had blocked a Viet Minh attack, and the journal attributed this achievement to a Vietnamese unit of the French army. In the report, Guedou expressed his astonishment at the honorable treatment accorded to Arabs and the Vietnamese in the journal despite their revolts against France, while the loyal Africans were systematically forgotten. He even went as far as attributing the journal's attitude to a general wish to conceal the African presence in Indochina.[38]

Another report, written by Captain Keita, who was responsible for the BAA in Hanoi and Haiphong, described an incident in which an African soldier was replaced by a European one when a photographer for the metropolitan magazine *Match* was taking a photo of Paul Doumer Bridge, which connects the two parts of Hanoi (now Long Bien Bridge).[39] Military agents in Indochina regularly published such reports containing complaints about discrimination toward African soldiers. It is not clear, however, how much was done in order to solve the problems they reported.

One rather elementary yet somewhat complicated means to uplift Africans' morale was to ensure reasonable contact with their families. As we have seen, Africans who served in Indochina could spend months and even years apart from their families. The separation from their environment and the move to a foreign land were certainly difficult. According to various morale reports, African soldiers often complained about the lack of communication with their families.[40] To alleviate this situation the military authorities in Indochina notified the colonial administration in AOF of the names of these unhappy soldiers and asked that their families be located and encouraged to write to them.[41] In cases in which no one in the family was able to read or write, the district commandant was instructed to recruit letter writers and readers and ensure that they did not charge excessive fees for their services.[42]

In addition to these measures, when African soldiers arrived in Indochina, the commander of each company contacted the district commandant of each soldier in his unit through the governor of the colony so that information regarding the soldier would be passed on to his family. In October 1952 the commandant of Zinguinchor district in Senegal, for example, sent a telegram to Cor. Benoît Bamkopi, who was serving in northern Vietnam, to inform him that his family was well and was vacationing in Dakar and that one of his brothers had gone to France to continue his studies. The telegram culminated with a reminder to the soldier to fulfill his duties.[43]

Alas, these efforts were not always successful, as indicated by the ongoing complaints about the lack of communication. Moreover, ensuring that soldiers received news from home did not always help to improve their morale, as this obviously depended on the nature of the news. Military reports often complained that soldiers were upset by the letters they received from home, either because their families reported that the colonial authorities were not taking proper care of their needs or, even worse, because they had been told that their wives were tired of living alone with their families and had run away.[44] This situation, the minister claimed, was harmful both to the African soldiers' morale and to the social stability in AOF. As Gregory Mann shows, French commanders in Indochina could not persuade their African soldiers to invest their earnings in savings accounts because soldiers were so pressed to send money to their wives at home so that they would not run off. These soldiers were even willing to take the risk of transferring the money through a third party.[45]

Another means to encourage communication with home was the establishment in 1948 of an agency to aid soldiers from AOF, which, among other tasks, organized the dispatch of packages to soldiers serving in Indochina. Special radio broadcasts allowed families to deliver messages to serving soldiers, and veterans recalled how happy they were to listen to these broadcasts.[46] By 1953 a daily half-hour transmission in Indochina was dedicated to African soldiers. On one of these programs, the wife of a Senegalese *originaire* officer provided African soldiers with "feminine encouragement."[47] Radio broadcasts were also used to transfer messages from African soldiers serving in Indochina to their families in AOF. While radio transmitters were not widely accessible in AOF, the French administration used powerful transmitters in public listening posts for these broadcasts.[48]

Occasionally, photographs from home were used to boost African morale. As it was difficult to obtain specific photos of family members, in

1952 the local administrations sent over one hundred photographs to the soldiers, depicting various aspects of life in AOF. In addition, they sent over a hundred photos of governors of the various territories of the colonies and of the high commissioner.[49] While it is not known exactly how these photos influenced the soldiers' morale, it is hard to believe they made the soldiers in Indochina especially cheerful. The colonial administration in AOF also regularly sent these soldiers records of African music and recordings of radio programs from Radio Dakar so that they could listen to familiar programs and music on the local radio.[50]

Newspapers were another venue through which the military authorities hoped to encourage African soldiers. In January 1953 Gen. Raoul Salan, the commander of the French forces in Saigon, later to become a key military figure in the Algerian war, wrote to the high commissioner of AOF suggesting the publication of a special section for African soldiers in the weekly *Caravelle*. As the authors of this section had to rely on news items published in AOF, Salan asked that African newspapers be dispatched as quickly as possible to Indochina so that *Caravelle*'s editors would have the necessary material for this section.[51] A donation by the Red Cross also enabled the military authorities in Indochina to allow African soldiers to subscribe to the African illustrated journal *Bingo*, published in AOF.[52]

According to Gen. Henri Navarre, chief commander of the forces in Indochina, these measures served their purpose, especially in addition to the special packages African soldiers were receiving from AOF, as they made the soldiers feel that they were no longer the "poor relatives" of the North African soldiers serving in Indochina. The general estimated that the only problem left to be handled regarding the African soldiers' morale was their long and tedious transfer back home after the end of their service in Indochina.[53]

In addition to the their efforts to ensure reasonable contact with soldiers' families, the military authorities also attempted to take care of the soldiers' entertainment during their free time. In 1953 the army decided to construct two "African houses" (*maisons africaines*), designed to serve as cultural and social clubs for African soldiers in Saigon and Haiphong. The idea was for Africans to get together, listen to recordings of music from West Africa, and play cards and checkers. The two centers were supposed to be built in the pseudo-Sahelian architectural style, just like the African mosque in Fre, / / more a cultural and social center than a religious one.[54] However, the French defeat a year later, these centers were never actually built.[55]

While the military authorities put much effort into making the African soldiers' stay on their bases as pleasant as possible, nothing was better for their morale than going off the base, preferably into town to dance in a club or stroll along the streets. According to Christopher Goscha, although most studies on the Indochina war describe it as a rural war, the numerous rural zones under Communist control heavily depended on their connection with urban centers. Therefore, the widespread vision of the cities in Indochina as a safe haven or refuge from the horrors of the war is largely misleading.[56] It is interesting to note, then, that for the African veterans this false image of the cities, especially Saigon, as safe and relaxing havens was in fact very real. This might be because most African soldiers were assigned to rural posts and consequently enjoyed the wonders of the cities so much that they perceived them as much more peaceful than they actually were.

The attractiveness of Saigon as such a refuge can be gleaned from Marc Guèye's memoirs. Guèye describes Saigon as a beautiful city with two grand boulevards and fashionable streets. He writes that the two boulevards carry the names of two great men: Joseph Gallieni (1849–1916), the French general who was central in the colonization of what was to become the French empire, and Norodom, king of Cambodia (1860–1904). Guèye leads the reader through Catinat Street, with its magnificent shops and its photography studios, and speaks of the French and Asiatic styles of the city, the important administrative buildings, and the modern hotels, such as the Continental. Guèye specifically mentions the great number of dancing bars, such as the Lion d'Or, the Tabarin on boulevard Gallieni, and Oiseau Bleu in the Chinese quarter of Cholon, in which he had some pleasant moments. Guèye also describes the Parc à Baffles, a brothel at the heart of Saigon where more than four hundred young Vietnamese women "full of eroticism and whose physical maneuvers are exquisite" worked. This institution, according to Guèye, attracted soldiers from all the armed forces posted in Indochina and provided music and dancing along with sexual services.[57]

When African soldiers did not receive a long enough leave to be able to explore the wonders of Indochina's big cities, they settled for short outings into the nearby villages. However, these outings were severely controlled, and in some cases soldiers left their bases without authorization. Papa Figaro Diagne recalled the harsh measures taken against soldiers who left their posts without permission while describing an incident that had occurred on his post. A young soldier by the name of Ndiaye Marcelle, known as a troublemaker, went off the post into the neighboring village to see women. When Marcelle ran into a French patrol, the commander told him that he was not supposed to be there and asked for his name. Marcelle told him his name was "Do to ma guis." The commander ordered him to go back to his camp and said he would visit the camp soon in order to send Marcelle to prison. When Marcelle returned to the army camp he went to see his French commander, who, according to Diagne, "loved him like a son," and told him what had happened. His commander wanted to help him, so he told him to stay in his tent and lie low. Two days later the patrol arrived at the camp, and their commander asked for a soldier called "Do to ma guis." No one answered, and the French colonel suggested they try elsewhere. Later Marcelle's commander asked him what the name he gave meant, and Marcelle replied that in Wolof it meant "you will never see me again." The commander laughed and told him that he was clever, as the patrol really did not see him again. As we can see from this anecdote, despite military efforts to control such outings, African soldiers were not easily deterred from leaving their posts whenever possible. The problem with these outings, as far as the soldiers' commanders were concerned, was that although they certainly boosted African soldiers' morale, they also created a new kind of threat, namely, encounters with the local population.

Military Concerns Regarding African Soldiers' Contacts with the Local Population

The main motive for trying to limit and monitor such outings, whether to the big cities or the nearby villages, was the commanding officers' apprehension that the soldiers' encounters with the local population might affect their motivation and loyalty. First and foremost among these concerns were the African soldiers' relations with local women. Contact between African soldiers and local women, especially Vietnamese, was hardly a rarity. While Indochinese women were initially scared to get close to African soldiers, who seemed alien to them, soon they realized the advantages such relations could bring to them, including money and protection that would somewhat alleviate their difficult daily routine. The African soldiers, on their part, preferred to take an Indochinese woman as a mistress (*congäie*) and cater to her needs rather than go to prostitutes.[58] When interviewed, Senegalese veterans took care to distinguish between women who supported the French and accepted the Senegalese soldiers and "Giap's women," who were hostile to them and might even deliver them to assassination committees.[59] For such women, the soldiers were *tai den*, "blacks," with all the prejudice that accompanied the term, and considered as mercenaries. Despite the usually practical nature of these relations, some soldiers managed to conquer the hearts of the women and forged intimate relations with them. Some even married them and brought them to West Africa after the war.[60]

The military authorities in Indochina were extremely worried about the intimate relations African soldiers established with local women. This concern stemmed both from general colonial anxieties and from practical motives. In her article "Sexual Affronts and Racial Frontiers," Ann Stoler discusses French colonial anxieties concerning interracial relations and their consequences, mainly the creation of a *métis* community, which might challenge and blur colonial categories and boundaries.[61] Although Stoler refers only to relations between Europeans and colonial subjects, it is certainly possible to extend her conclusions to relations between colonial subjects originating from different ethnicities, such as in the situation under discussion. French colonial and military authorities were worried about the implications of sexual relations between Asian women and African men, since colonial rule depended on a certain kind of order in which various categories of colonial subjects remained separate and intact. The creation of a community of Afro-Asian children was perhaps not as disquieting as that of Euro-Asian or Euro-African children, but it was still concerning enough for the military authorities to consider it as a threat to colonial stability. In fact, this problem occupied the highest levels of government, as can be seen in a document written by the minister of defense to the commander of the French forces in the Far East, discussing a negative phenomenon related to these mixed-race children. According to the minister, Vietnamese women who gave birth to such children treated them as merchandise and sold them to their African fathers. As distressing as this practice was, he wrote, there was not much that could be done about it, as this was the only way African fathers could keep their children. The minister asked that an effort be made to establish whether these children were indeed recognized and that they be supervised after their arrival in West Africa.[62]

These relations also raised other concerns, as they probably invoked some hostility in the local men. The military authorities were also concerned that some of the women were Viet Minh agents sent to extract secret information from ostensibly gullible soldiers. Some commanders worried that these women might distract African soldiers from their duties and even entice them, either deliberately or unintentionally, to desert. The solution to this problem was the establishment of a special military brothel, called BMC (*bordel militaire de campagne*), in which Vietnamese women were employed as prostitutes. The military authorities hoped that these brothels would satisfy the soldiers' sexual needs and prevent them from forging long-term relations with the local women. The soldiers, however, preferred going to the city and choosing their own women. One veteran explained that they were not interested in prostitutes but rather in well-mannered women from good families.[63] In their attempts to minimalize relationships between soldiers and Vietnamese women, the military authorities tried to dissuade the local women by telling them about the lifestyle of the Senegalese in their homeland, their culture, and their material and social conditions. However, this was superfluous, as many of the soldiers did not wish to marry the women but rather simply to pass the time with female company.[64]

It is perhaps not surprising, then, that the relations between the African soldiers and the Vietnamese men were rather tense and that Vietnamese women were occasionally the cause of violent altercations between African soldiers and Vietnamese civilians or ex–Viet Minh who had joined the French forces. In one such incident, a dozen Vietnamese attacked an African soldier who went to the village's tailor to collect a suit. The African officer who reported this attack stated that Vietnamese commanders within the French forces had incited the locals against African soldiers. However, in another report about this same incident, Captain Keita explained that the motive was a quarrel over a woman.[65]

While the hostility between African soldiers and Vietnamese men was perhaps not as alarming to the French military authorities as the goodwill offered by Vietnamese women, it was certainly a concern for the direct commanders of the African soldiers, especially when it resulted in violent attacks. Squabbles over women were often the motive for such attacks, but they were certainly not the only one. According to a report from 1952, written by an African lieutenant to the commander of the Twenty-Sixth BMTS (Bataillon de Marche de Tirailleurs Sénégalais), at that time Vietnamese villagers and soldiers were attacking African soldiers on a daily basis. Lieutenant Ketty reported a number of incidents in which several Africans were beaten up and wounded. None of these incidents, according to Ketty, were initiated by the Africans. Ketty warned in his report that such "antiblack attacks" might have a catastrophic effect on African morale.[66]

This widespread anti-African animosity stemmed in part from uninformed prejudice, but it was also incited by rumors spread by the French military commanders. According to one interview, the French spread rumors about the Africans, saying that they could get along without food for a month and that they ate their enemies' dead bodies. These rumors, along with much ignorance regarding Africa and its inhabitants, resulted in deep fears.[67] One veteran recounted how during a visit to town a local traffic policeman panicked when he saw the veteran and his comrades and deserted his post, fleeing hysterically while followed by numerous anxious pedestrians.[68] In time, when the number of Africans in Indochina increased, these fears diminished, but from the various reports on violent incidents between African soldiers and local men, it seems that suspicion and hostility persisted to some extent until the end of the war.

As mentioned above, the French army deliberately spread frightening rumors about the African soldiers with the specific purpose of intimidating the Viet Minh. Unfortunately, one undesired consequence of these rumors was the hostility that arose among both civilians and the Vietnamese who fought for the French side. These frequent violent incidents between African troops and Vietnamese men were mainly the concern of the soldiers' direct commanders and of the African officers who monitored their morale. Interestingly, this matter was certainly far less concerning to the higher military authorities than the African soldiers' intimate relations with local women.

Military Concerns Regarding the Effects of Enemy Propaganda

The Viet Minh's anti-French propaganda campaign caused psychological and emotional difficulties among African soldiers, and consequently a significant component of the French struggle against the Viet Minh was the diffusion of pro-French counterpropaganda. The need for an efficient means of counterpropaganda became exceedingly apparent during the Indochina war, when the Viet Minh launched highly effective psychological warfare against the French, luring Vietnamese soldiers and civilians to its ranks.[69]

The initiators of this propaganda also targeted African soldiers. As we have seen, the Viet Minh had distributed two kinds of propaganda among African soldiers serving in Indochina, one aimed to frighten the soldiers and the other to persuade them to defect. Rumors were spread about planned massacres of all African soldiers in a certain post, and veterans recalled that such rumors prevented them from sleeping at night. The veterans testified that they used to sleep with their weapons, and every time they heard a noise, they jumped out of their beds, though rats were usually the source of this noise. The African soldiers constantly feared for their lives. One of the veterans said, "Every day, the soldiers saw their comrades die a catastrophic death and told themselves that they would die in the same manner."[70]

The second kind of propaganda was geared toward convincing African soldiers that they were fighting on the wrong side. Viet Minh pamphlets called Africans to join the anticolonial movement and forsake their colonial oppressors. While the Viet Minh's psychological warfare was aimed at all the soldiers serving in the French army, it regarded the African soldiers as easier targets and potential defectors, considering African soldiers as lost sheep who just had to be shown the right way. Its main argument was that Africans were colonized by the French just like the Vietnamese and therefore had no reason to fight with them. The Viet Minh even distributed pamphlets, titled *Passeports pour la liberté* (Passports for liberty), meant to convince Africans to defect.[71]

Since the soldiers' morale was already low due to the harsh physical conditions, limited supply and inferior quality of the food, and discriminatory treatment from French soldiers and commanders, such messages did occasionally manage to convince soldiers to defect. In interviews conducted by

Sarah Zimmerman, veterans reported an ambivalent approach to desertion. Some saw it as a sign of cowardice and some (mostly Guinean veterans) as a sign of courage. None of the veterans interviewed admitted to having defected, but they had heard rumors about others who had. In general, veterans claimed that only a very few African soldiers had deserted during the Indochina war.[72] According to Michel Bodin, only ninety-four African soldiers defected between 1949 and 1954. He also maintains that most of them did not defect for political or ideological reasons.[73] However, the official numbers are difficult to verify, as deserters were often mistaken for POWs. One veteran recalled that some deserters even took advantage of the chaos following the defeat of Dien Bien Phu to show up in the French ranks and be repatriated with the retreating soldiers.[74]

African soldiers were most exposed to Viet Minh propaganda when they were captured and imprisoned in POW camps. The number of African soldiers captured by the Viet Minh is not clear. The Viet Minh reported that they had captured 686 African POWs, while the French estimated the number as closer to 1,040.[75] Conditions in the Viet Minh prisoners' camps were harsh. The soldiers were detained in isolated camps and received no mail or information from the outside. There was no strict surveillance of the prisoners, as escape was impossible due to the forest surrounding the camp. The prisoners were occupied in forced labor, and all the prisoners were sick to some extent. Nutrition was bad, and fresh drinking water was almost nonexistent. However, this was not all that dissimilar to the conditions that African soldiers experienced during their army service in Indochina. In the prisoners' camps, at least, they did not have to worry about Viet Minh surprise attacks and bombardments.

One characteristic of being prisoners of a highly ideological organization was that African soldiers, together with French soldiers, were forced to listen to long lectures about Communism and the fight against imperialism. They learned about the causes of colonization and were encouraged to fight for their independence upon their return home. In the evenings, the prisoners watched theater plays conveying similar messages. One prisoner said that after watching these plays, which described all the scandals caused by French imperialism, he had asked himself why he was fighting this war.[76] According to Marc Guèye, a comrade who was a POW told him that one of the lecturers in his camp was an African who was fluent in Vietnamese.[77]

The French military authorities took the Viet Minh propaganda efforts very seriously and responded by distributing counterpropaganda attempting to limit soldiers' access to noncontrolled information sources, including metropolitan and local newspapers, and closely monitoring African soldiers released from Viet Minh captivity. They also occasionally attempted to reach African POWs through the Red Cross in order to supply them with medicines and letters from home. In September 1953, for example, the Red Cross organized a dispatch of medicines and mail to POWs in Indochina that was to be parachuted into the POW camps. The high commissioner of AOF was instructed to ask the families of African POWs to write to their loved ones in haste so that these letters could be added to the dispatch.[78] Such measures were designed to boost the POWs' morale, thus lowering the risk of their "conversion" to Viet Minh ideology. French commanders were worried, mostly in vain, that some Africans might have been enticed by this kind of tedious propaganda. For this reason, when African soldiers were released from Viet Minh captivity after the French defeat in Dien Bien Phu, the military authorities investigated each of them and drafted a report about the potential influence of captivity on the soldiers in question.

The form that was filled out after each investigation included the soldier's basic personal details and more specific information, such as the circumstances of his captivity and release, his exposure to the propaganda activity of the Viet Minh, and the opinion of the officer of African Military Affairs. In most forms, the section describing the Viet Minh propaganda included only these words: *cours politiques* or *travail et cours politiques* (political courses or labor and political courses), and no special recommendations were offered.[79] In general, these forms seem to suggest that while the military authorities were deeply concerned about the potential political influence of captivity, their concerns were usually unfounded.

In fact, the colonial authorities were still concerned about the POWs even after they returned to AOF. In a letter from the governor of Senegal to the district commanders in his colony a few months after the French defeat in Dien Bien Phu, he announced the return of forty-nine POWs to Senegal. The governor noted that the exact number might be lower, as some of the POWs might have died, but it could also be higher, as some who were considered dead might actually have been in captivity. This uncertainty about the number of POWs points to the relative disorder that existed in the French army during the Indochina war, especially in its final stages. In his letter, the governor warned the circle commanders that these POWs might have been exposed to Viet Minh propaganda and additional harsh experiences. He therefore asked the commanders to take good care of the soldiers and supervise them closely, and he even suggested that the administrators make sure they found these POWs a job, preferably in the administration. Those who lived outside the principal cities should be sent to their villages, where they would surely return to the customs of the ancestors and to their daily concerns.[80]

This plea to assist and monitor African demobilized soldiers, mainly former Viet Minh captives returning from Indochina, reflects the major concerns the colonial administration had regarding the political effect of their return after the war. The military authorities also tried to boost the morale of African veterans by offering a great number of them decorations and citations. This was supposed to compensate them for the fact that it was very difficult to promote most soldiers due to their inability to pass the necessary exams. Decorations were distributed so freely that some African soldiers found this practice grotesque. On the other hand, French metropolitan soldiers were upset by this apparent discrimination against them.[81] These tremendous efforts to keep the demobilized soldiers happy were a result of the recollection of the difficult demobilization after World War II. The turbulent return of the African soldiers from the battlefields of Europe, less than a decade before, still resonated in these administrators' minds. Unlike World War II, which ended in victory, albeit a shaky one, the Indochina war ended in a shameful defeat. This fact was of course highly significant to the colonial administration and affected their concerns regarding the returning soldiers.

As we have seen in this chapter, African soldiers endured many hardships during their service in Indochina. The military authorities monitored their morale closely and tried to keep the Viet Minh propaganda from having a negative influence on the soldiers. The commanders of the African soldiers were also deeply concerned about the relations between African soldiers and Vietnamese men and women. In spite of all these concerns, African soldiers proved in general to be loyal and were hardly seduced by Viet Minh propaganda. Even the humiliating defeat that ended the war did not seem to undermine African soldiers' willingness to continue to serve in the French army. The military authorities on their part tried to turn this defeat into a shared unifying experience for French and African troops.

On May 8, 1954, the day after the French defeat in Dien Bien Phu, perhaps the greatest defeat in French colonial history, Bernard Cornut Gentille, the high commissioner of AOF, published a formal announcement relating to the difficult events in Indochina. He first passed on a message from the Ministry of Defense, stating that the French army had been defeated the day before in Dien Bien Phu. This, so the message said, was indeed a day of mourning but not a day of humiliation. The French forces fought bravely for five months and prevented the invasion of Laos, a member of the French Union. The quoted telegram then compared the courage of the soldiers who took part in the battles to that of French soldiers who fought in famous battles during the two world wars. After quoting the telegram, the high commissioner expressed his faith in the military units of AOF. He stated that he knew that the citizens and soldiers in AOF believed in the army and its commanders and that they were saddened by this painful episode, but at the same time they were determined to continue to serve France.[82]

Only a few months after the French defeat in Dien Bien Phu, the army faced a new challenge in the most important territory of the empire, a territory considered by the French government as an integral part of the French republic: Algeria. African soldiers who had spent years in difficult conditions in Indochina and witnessed French defeat there were now to be reassigned to fight against another anticolonial movement. This time the conflict took place on African soil, and the people African soldiers had to fight were much closer to them culturally. This was a war fought close to home, a fact that shaped the military concerns and policies regarding African soldiers fighting in Algeria.

5

African Troops in the Wars of Decolonization

Algeria, 1954–1962

On November 1, 1954, barely six months after the defeat in Dien Bien Phu, a series of coordinated bomb attacks on symbols of colonial power shook the French colony of Algeria. The FLN soon claimed responsibility for organizing these attacks and called the Algerian people to revolt against French colonial rule. While at the time the French government and the army defined the conflict as an easily overcome rebellion, this was actually the opening shot of an eight-year bloody war in Algeria. In fact, even when violence escalated and French reserve soldiers had been recruited, the French government continuously avoided using the term "war" to refer to the events in Algeria. Only in 1999, forty-five years after the beginning of the conflict, was the situation finally officially acknowledged by France as a war.

This reluctance to define the events in Algeria as a war was a direct result of this territory's special status since 1848 as a *département d'outre-mer*, meaning it was under the authority of the Ministry of the Interior rather than the Ministry of the Colonies. This special status, along with the French perception of Algeria as an integral part of the single indivisible republic, made compromises in Algeria much more difficult than in Indochina. The one million European settlers who lived in Algeria when the war started (out of a population of roughly nine million), known as the *pieds noirs*, further complicated the situation and made the French colonial position even more inflexible than elsewhere. The *pieds noirs* included French, Italians, Spanish, and Maltese nationals, and they possessed great political and economic power, controlling most of the agricultural and commercial activity in Algeria. They formed a powerful pressure group both when the extension of rights to Algerians was discussed before the war and when the possibility of self-determination and independence was explored in the war's final stage.

This chapter deals with the participation of African soldiers in the eight-year conflict in Algeria and the manner in which the military authorities tried to preserve their loyalty and boost their morale. While these events will be examined in a similar manner to the Indochina war described in the previous chapter, the different nature and geographic location of these two conflicts also dictate new questions. These will deal mostly with the religious and cultural affinity between Algerians and West Africans (many of whom were Muslims) and the ways in which the army dealt with this perceived threat. I will first present an overview of the main military and political events during the Algerian war and then introduce the concept of psychological warfare. While psychological warfare was utilized in the Indochina war, it was only implemented in full force in Algeria. This type of warfare was designed mainly to win the support of the Algerian population in the battle against the FLN, but it was also linked to the army's policies toward both the African soldiers and the civilian population in AOF. Next, I will examine the propaganda diffused by different sources against the deployed African soldiers in Algeria and the measures the army took to "protect" its soldiers from the potentially damaging effects of this propaganda. As part of the propaganda efforts directed toward African soldiers, I will discuss in some detail the military use of organized pilgrimages to Mecca as a major tool of propaganda. A closing section will compare the nature of the participation of African soldiers in both wars—in Indochina and in Algeria—from the African soldiers' and from the French military's point of view.

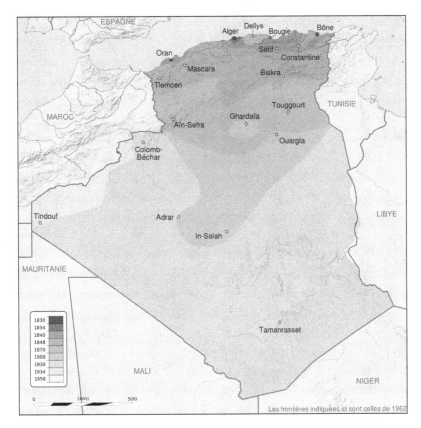

FIG. 4. Map of Algeria under French rule. Source: Wikimedia Commons.

African Soldiers in the Algerian War

When the FLN began its attacks on French targets in November 1954, the French did not take this too seriously and believed that it would be simple to crush this revolt rapidly. However, soon the FLN's attacks on government buildings, administrators, and settlers intensified, and the administration demanded more firepower. The governor, Jacques Soustelle, clarified that despite the negotiations regarding the independence of the neighboring protectorates of Morocco and Tunisia (which indeed came into effect in 1956), the French presence in Algeria was nonnegotiable: "Algeria and its inhabitants form an integral part of France, one and indivisible. All must know, here and elsewhere, that France will not leave Algeria any more than she will leave Provence and Brittany. Whatever happens, the destiny of Algeria is French."[1]

In 1956 the conflict escalated, and the French government began recruiting civilians into the army to serve as reinforcements. Unlike the Indochina war, in which only professional French soldiers and foreign and colonial forces took part, the conflict in Algeria directly involved the French public through the compulsory draft. That year also marked the beginning of what was known as the Battle of Algiers and the internationalization of the war. The FLN received support from Nasser's Egypt, the Eastern Bloc, and the Spanish dictator, Francisco Franco, who was hostile to the French policy in Morocco. The organization was also active in the United Nations, lobbying for diplomatic support. By the end of 1957, the FLN had lost the Battle of Algiers but won the more important battle over international opinion, which came to view the organization as self-sacrificing and legitimate. The military efforts were now focused on the mountainous areas of Algeria.

A new stage in the war began in May 1958 with the return of de Gaulle to power. At first it was not clear what his policy regarding Algeria might be. The settlers believed that he supported the idea of French Algeria, but they were soon to be disappointed. While the French army was winning on the ground, pushing the military section of the FLN, the Armée de Libération Nationale (Army of National Liberation, ALN), to the brink of military defeat, the French government offered the FLN a ceasefire and initiated negotiations. Several French generals saw this contradiction between the military success and the political wish to negotiate with the FLN as an act of betrayal by the political elites. Eventually, they attempted to commit a coup against the French government in April 1961. The Organisation Armée Secrète (Organization of the Secret Army, OAS), which included settlers and military commanders who refused to give up on French Algeria, intensified its violent activities against decolonization. These attacks continued throughout the negotiations, which ended in March 1962 with the Evian agreement. In spite of de Gaulle's efforts to allow the settlers to stay in Algeria, they were all forced to leave when the FLN took over the country.

The Algerian war was one of the most vicious conflicts of decolonization. It was extremely violent on both sides. At least 300,000 Algerians died in the war, and a large number of the dead were killed by fellow Algerians. Over the first three years of the war, 1,315 European civilians were killed, as well as 740 police personnel and approximately 4,000 soldiers. During the last two years of the conflict the OAS murdered approximately 3,000 Algerians and French who were considered "traitors to French Algeria." The French security forces considered the FLN fighters criminals, terrorists, or rebels. FLN detainees were tortured routinely, although this type of behavior was officially illegal. The FLN also used excessive violence, and many of its victims were Algerians who were accused of collaborating with the French. The Algerian population was thus trapped between the two forces and had to survive violent attacks from various directions.

Although officially the conflict in Algeria was not a war, the French army certainly treated it as such when it became apparent that the FLN was far more dangerous than it initially appeared. After Dien Bien Phu, the army was determined not to accept another defeat. Before the decision to recruit French soldiers in 1956 and to some extent even later, the French army in Algeria relied heavily on the soldiers of the Foreign Legion, the Harki (Algerian loyalists who served as auxiliaries in the French army during the Algerian war), and West African soldiers.

Around 25,000 African soldiers were serving in Algeria by 1956.[2] Some arrived directly from Indochina, and their commanders were concerned about the effect of this transfer from one battle zone to the other on their morale and motivation.[3] Until the defeat of the FLN in Algiers in 1957, African soldiers mainly experienced an urban guerrilla war. Later, the main action was in the mountainous rural area into which the French army had pushed the FLN. Both kinds of warfare were psychologically difficult for African troops. In addition, the French assigned the dirtiest tasks of the war to the African soldiers, even ordering them to take part in torturing FLN prisoners.[4]

Unlike Indochina, Algeria was supposedly less foreign and strange to African soldiers. This did not mean that it was like fighting at home. Archival sources do not provide much evidence describing African soldiers' experiences in Algeria, but we can get a glimpse at the challenges they faced from Niang's memoirs. Niang arrived in Algeria in June 1956 and was stationed with his paratrooper unit in Tebessa, near the Tunisian border. He describes the heat as unbearable, a genuine "Dante's inferno," as he labeled it. Wind was rare, and nothing moved. The terrain was treacherous and full of natural obstacles. The fear of civilians who might turn into warriors unexpectedly was as vivid in the mountains of Algeria as it was in the forests of Vietnam. According to Niang, anyone could be the enemy: "This old man crouching at the foot of his hut; this old woman looking after her distaff; this young shepherd with his sheep." Every civilian was linked in one way or another to this war of independence that the Algerians, who were considered rebels at the time by Niang and his comrades, were fighting. All the people they encountered were distressed by the soldiers' presence in their country. Niang describes the long marches in the desert with insufficient water futilely searching for FLN fighters. When his unit finally encountered the fighters the ensuing battles were extremely vicious and bloody. The FLN fighters had sophisticated weapons and used their knowledge of the terrain to their advantage. They often blocked the roads using trees and rocks and could hide well. These fighters sometimes left notes for the French soldiers such as the one Niang quotes: "Go eat your sardines elsewhere you miserable colonizers." The paratroopers occasionally called the commando for backup, as the dead and wounded were not replaced, and they soon became outnumbered by the FLN members. After numerous sleepless nights and violent battles, Niang and his comrades clung to the thought of their next vacation in order to keep their minds on their missions and perform them successfully. They often spoke of their comrades who lost their lives at the young age of twenty and were deeply worried about their own fate.[5]

This vivid description of the difficult service in the Algerian war is not unique to African soldiers. Niang, who held French citizenship, was in fact one of the few Africans in his unit. In addition to these difficulties he shared with his metropolitan comrades, Niang was aware that his color required him to work harder continuously in order to earn the esteem of his platoon's staff, who regarded honor and sense of duty more highly than rights.[6] Such challenges, along with the day-to-day hardships of the war, could very easily lower African soldiers' morale.

As we shall see in this chapter, many of the concerns of French military commanders regarding the morale of the African soldiers who served in Indochina were also relevant during the Algerian war. However, these concerns were much graver. After all, this was a war fought on the African continent and against people who had long political, cultural, and religious connections with the regions from which most African soldiers originated.

As I will demonstrate later in this chapter, the religious component, which became more and more worrisome for the French in the second half of that decade, played a major role both in the French military concerns regarding the African soldiers' state of mind and in the solutions they sought.

Before we examine the military policy regarding the Africans serving in Algeria, it is vital to discuss the concept of psychological warfare, which was officially adopted by the French army during the Algerian war and implemented, as we shall see in the next chapter, also in AOF. The use of psychological warfare as a weapon was crucial in Algeria and also influenced the military policy toward African soldiers and the FLN's attempts to lure them to defect to their camp.

Psychological Warfare: The Origins of the Idea and Its Implementation in Algeria

Prior to the Algerian war, psychological warfare played only a very marginal part in the military practices of the French army. While the term *action psychologique* (psychological operations) was first mentioned in a decree from April 1, 1950, concerning national defense, no one within the military seemed interested in the significance of this term. The first official plan that was related to psychological warfare was developed at the beginning of 1955 and was aimed against the FLN in Algeria.[7] Although the notion of psychological warfare is quite ancient, only in the mid-1950s was this tool formally adopted by the French army.

Defining psychological warfare is not simple. On the one hand, this is a modern concept related to the development of the discipline of psychology in the nineteenth and twentieth centuries. On the other hand, we can find many examples of military actions in descriptions of biblical battles, as well as in antiquity, that are quite similar to what we perceive today as psychological warfare. The idea of psychological warfare is based on the assumption that soldiers will perform better when their morale is high and when they are convinced of both the justness of their cause and their ability to defeat the enemy. Thus, the outcome of a battle can be determined not only by the use of military force but also by actions aimed at lowering the enemy soldiers' morale. In the case of colonial wars, during both colonization and decolonization, the civilian population was also a crucial factor in the extent of the military success, as its support was vital to movements that resisted colonization or attempted to overthrow the colonial regimes. The civilian population thus became a legitimate target for these psychological operations. In fact, when French senior officers decided to officially implement psychological warfare in Algeria, they relied on techniques used by the first French colonizers. Thomas Robert Bugeaud in Algeria, Joseph Gallieni in Tonkin and Madagascar, and Hubert Lyautey in Morocco had all attempted to entice the local population in the regions they conquered, along with the use of extreme violence.[8]

A major incentive to adopt psychological warfare was the French military experience in Indochina and the context of the Cold War. When Charles Lacheroy, the main architect of the psychological warfare in Algeria, visited Indochina in 1951, he searched for a solution to a mystery that French military commanders could not unravel: the French army was superior to its adversary, the Viet Minh, but it still watched victory slipping out of its reach. Lacheroy examined the Viet Minh's control over the social structure of Vietnamese society and realized that this was the decisive factor that prevented the French from winning. The success of the Viet Minh in controlling the minds of the civilian population and even in converting French POWs to Communism was thus seen as the explanation for their victory over the more powerful French.[9] The French army faced an enemy that did not fight in the same way and did not follow the same rules. Giap's comment that France was defeated in Indochina because the army did not engage enough in politics was taken very seriously by some of the French commanders.[10] This war and the successful techniques of the Viet Minh persuaded French officers, most notably Colonel Lacheroy, that the French army must adopt the use of psychological warfare. In August 1954 he published two articles regarding this concept, though it took several months until his motion was adopted. Only the intensification of the Algerian conflict finally pushed the army to study the concept of psychological warfare, and on January 1, 1955, the Bureau de la Guerre Psychologique, known also as the Fifth Bureau, was formally established.[11] The bureau was responsible for supporting French soldiers' morale; encouraging the Muslim populations in the countryside to trust France and reject the rebels; and demoralize FLN fighters by "surprise attacks" (*actions de choc*), causing them to doubt the dogma that influenced them and return to the so-called Franco-Muslim community.[12] In practice, French soldiers' morale in Algeria was boosted by providing them with good news and reinforcing their patriotism. As for the Algerian Muslim population, the bureau's activities included broadcasting positive messages about the French regime and its military successes and negative messages regarding the rebels and their aims. This was done by various means of communication, such as the use of mobile loudspeakers in urban areas and air-dropping leaflets in rural regions. It also included inviting journalists to the openings of new schools and hospitals while also exposing them to the damage caused by FLN members. In this manner, the bureau created a media war struggling over public opinion in both France and Algeria, demonstrating the benefits of French rule and its commitment to the idea of the "civilizing mission," in contrast to the "backwardness" and "barbarism" of France's enemies.[13]

Although the psychological operations in Algeria proved quite successful and received partial credit for the army's victory in the Battle of Algiers, there was growing objection to these actions among the military and political elites. Eric Ouellet and Pierre Pahlavi explain the objection within the army by contrasting the idea of psychological warfare and the norms of the French military institution. While officers who served in Indochina and young officers trained in the merits of psychological warfare continued to support it, French conscripted and reserve soldiers could not understand its rationale. Many of the French senior officers also could not grasp why the army had to take care of issues such as psychology, education, and social welfare instead of focusing on its main purpose: fighting the enemy. It was this aspect of psychological warfare—turning the army into a state within a state by delegating to it many of the responsibilities of the civilian authorities in Algeria—that caused French politicians, and especially de Gaulle after his return to power in 1958, to reject the notion of psychological warfare. In fact, before de Gaulle's comeback and the establishment of the Fifth Republic, the army was dissatisfied by the feeling that no clear guidelines were being issued by the successive governments of the Fourth Republic and initiated its own political plan in Algeria. This plan was based on three basic aims: preserving French sovereignty in Algeria, providing Muslims with full civil equality, and encouraging economic and social progress. The army's social activities in Algeria, its control over the media and the "proper" messages for civilians, and its political agenda for the future of the region made it a dangerous institution in de Gaulle's eyes. Thus, when he took power he immediately declared that the army must understand that its role was purely technical: it was there to carry out orders.[14] In early 1960 after the repression of a settlers' rebellion, which some military figures supported (known as "the week of the barricades"), de Gaulle appeared on television in full uniform and called the army to order: "I am speaking to the Army, who is winning in Algeria through brilliant efforts. Some of its elements, however, are ready to believe that the war is their war and not France's. Let me say this to all our soldiers: Your mission is not equivocal, nor does it require an interpretation."[15]

About two weeks later de Gaulle decided to dissolve the Fifth Bureau. This officially ended psychological warfare. Nevertheless, up until 1960 it was a vital element of French military policy in Algeria, as well as in AOF. Understanding the importance of the psychological operations within the army in both regions is vital. These operations dictated the military policy regarding African soldiers serving in Algeria and their exposure to FLN messages and anticolonial views among partisans of West African political movements. The French military command in Algeria used this measure to "protect" African soldiers from the negative influence of such messages.

Anti-French Propaganda Aimed at African Soldiers Serving in Algeria

One of the most important aspects of the psychological warfare used in Algeria was the counterpropaganda. The idea that the Viet Minh defeated the French army with the assistance of mind-controlling tactics made the French military authorities vigilant in order to ensure that the FLN did not attempt to do the same in Algeria. The population under examination here, the soldiers originating from AOF, was one of the FLN's preferred targets for this form of warfare.

Unlike the Viet Minh, the FLN could base the propaganda aimed at African soldiers on the common continent shared by Algerians and West Africans and on the common religion—Islam—that some of the African soldiers shared with their alleged enemies. In this case, the claim that African soldiers were subject to the same oppression as Algerians and therefore should fight with them and not against them had the potential to sound even more convincing than in the Indochinese case.

The FLN distributed its propaganda to the African soldiers mainly in pamphlets and through the radio. This propaganda contained three main messages that were supposed to encourage African soldiers to defect from the French army and join the FLN, or at least return to AOF with the movement's help. The first message emphasized the shared suffering of France's colonial subjects and their common destiny. The FLN, so one of the pamphlets noted, did not distinguish between the different struggles against French colonialism and was convinced that all of the colonized peoples had but one enemy and one aim.

The second message referred to the ingratitude of the French commanders toward African soldiers and their sacrifices. The only compensation the soldiers would receive upon their return to their villages, so one pamphlet warned, was the contempt and racist attitude of the administration. In another pamphlet, an African soldier who had decided to desert and join the FLN encouraged his brothers to join him. Since June 1, 1956, so he wrote, he had been living as a free man. He was waiting for his brothers to understand that nothing would work with those "civilizers" who stupidly risked the lives of their African soldiers and did not care at all about their fate. The French, so the soldier said, only wanted to benefit at the African soldiers' expense.

The third message regarded the specific French colonial policy in West Africa. Here it seems that the FLN had a problem. It was clear to its leaders, mainly after the political reforms of 1956, that the colonial situation in AOF was essentially different from that in Algeria. AOF had a different status, most of the population had the right to vote, and African local governments enjoyed some autonomy. The FLN leaders were also aware of the fact that most African politicians called for equality and not for independence. The formulation of the FLN attacks on the nature of French colonialism in AOF is interesting, as it focused on the colonial policies of the past and not of the present. For example, one pamphlet reminded the soldiers that just a short time before they had been subject to forced labor and barbaric laws. They were also reminded of their massacred brothers, who were killed by the French colonizers, and of the racism and hate of the French colonizers. While all this, so the text continued, was in the past, it was a cumbersome past. This sentence is based on two interesting assumptions. One is that all French colonial injustices in AOF were in the past. The second is that the soldiers actually needed to be convinced that French colonialism was negative by nature. In another pamphlet, the soldiers were asked to understand that a regime that had been enslaving them for a hundred years could not change overnight. Here again it seems that the FLN was aware of the French attempts to reform its colonial rule in West Africa and of the military reforms that significantly improved the service conditions of African soldiers. The fact that this propaganda was based on past events rather than on the present in order to convince African soldiers to desert the colonial regime shows how difficult it was to equate the Algerians' situation with that of West Africans, despite obvious similarities.[16]

Another way the FLN used to delegitimize any kind of alternatives to independence was to publicize the list of all those countries that were already liberated from the French yoke. The list included Syria, Lebanon, Indochina, Tunisia, and Morocco. In 1957 another African country was added to this list, though it had not been under French rule: the Gold Coast, a former British colony. The fact that this country changed its name to Ghana apparently helped enhance the list even further, as in one of the texts Ghana and the Gold Coast were mentioned as two separate states. The same text also mentioned Guinea, although this country gained its independence only a year after the text's publication.[17] It is clear that the FLN believed that the longer the list was and the more African states were included in it, the more persuasive its message would be.

What is also interesting in the FLN messages is the rare reference to Islam as a common religion shared by North and West Africans. The language these texts used is mainly political—a call for a common struggle against a criminalized enemy. In some texts it is implied that by serving in what the FLN defined as "the most barbaric among the criminal armies in the world," African soldiers were turning themselves into criminals who shed the blood of their brothers.[18]

The FLN was not the only movement to target African soldiers in its propaganda. The French authorities were even more worried about the propaganda emanating from West African origins. The Algerian war was a crucial factor in the radicalization of West African trade unions and the student movements. The military authorities were aware of this influence and followed with concern any criticism of the French deployment of African soldiers in Algeria.

According to military reports, it seems that the danger came from three main directions: workers' unions, student movements, and occasionally certain African politicians. In order to understand the reason for the French concern regarding the impact of these three elements on African soldiers' motivation, it is necessary to understand the political discourse of these factors in AOF at the time. As we saw in chapter 1, independence was not on the agenda of most African political parties in the federation until a very late stage, when the alternative political solution—equality within a French framework (the French Union and later the Franco-African community)—reached a dead end. In fact, the question of independence was not the main political issue in the federation for most of this period.

One main question that was under debate at the time was the structure in which political action should be taken, namely, federal or territorial. Another issue was the strategy that should be used to gain equality: through opposition and alignment with anti-imperialist international movements such as the French Communist Party, or cooperation with the French colonial authorities and affiliation of West African political parties, student movements, and trade unions with their metropolitan counterparts.[19]

Among workers, the French universalist discourse of assimilation was strategically used to demand equal pay for equal work. This was the principle behind all the strikes during that period, while no call to overthrow the colonial system was heard.[20] Nevertheless, here too there was disagreement regarding the affiliation with the French Confédération Générale du Travail (General Confederation of Labor, CGT). Finally, in 1957, the five worker organizations existing in AOF at the time were united under the Union Générale des Travailleurs d'Afrique Noire (General Union of the Workers of Black Africa, UGTAN), which was not affiliated with the CGT. The French colonial administration encouraged this at first, as it feared the Communist influence of the CGT over African workers. The administration soon found out that this decision to disaffiliate from the CGT and the man behind it, Sekou Touré, would lead African workers to question the option of equality within the French system and demand independence.[21]

As for the students, their young age and exposure to anticolonial ideas and movements in the metropole made them the representatives of the most radical political claims. African students first organized in France. While the initial purpose of the establishment of a students' organization was to protect their interests as students, soon their organization became politicized. Many African students in France opposed the RDA's decision to disaffiliate from the PCF and established a new organization, the Association des Étudiants RDA (Students' Association of the RDA, AERDA), which supported the previous line of the RDA. In March 1951 the great majority of African students in France were brought together into a single union, Fédération des Étudiants d'Afrique Noire en France (Federation of the Students of Black Africa in France, FEANF). This organization was engaged in politics from the start, and its policy was influenced by a notable struggle between the AERDA, which accepted the RDA strategy of demanding equal rights within the framework of the French Union, and another group, Groupement Africain de Recherches Économiques et Politiques (African Group of Economic and Political Studies, GAREP), which was influenced by Kwame Nkrumah, the leader of the Gold Coast, and called for full independence from France.[22]

The organization of students in AOF was slower, as the first institution of higher education was established there only in 1950 (Institut des Hautes Études de Dakar) and the first university, the University of Dakar (today Cheick Anta Diop University), in 1957. The General Association of Students of Dakar (AGED) was established in December 1950 and focused mainly on student issues. It was soon influenced by the politicized FEANF and in 1954 refused to become affiliated with the French students' union (Union Nationale des Étudiants de France, UNEF). This refusal led to an outright conflict with the organization's French members, who left it in protest. Apart from FEANF influence, international developments and especially the situation in Algeria made an impact as well. In 1954 Muslim students in Dakar established their own union, Association Musulmane des Étudiants Africains (AMEA), and began to publish a newsletter, *Vers l'Islam* (Toward Islam). By 1956 the FEANF had pushed students in Dakar toward adopting more radical positions. In that year the AGED changed its name to Union Générale des Étudiants d'Afrique Occidentale (UGEAO), leaving the word "Française" out. The events in North Africa caused it to begin calling for outright independence and criticizing African deputies in the French parliament for detaching themselves from the wishes of Africans.[23]

Both West African trade unions and student leaders had criticized the French deployment of African troops in Algeria. On June 3, 1957, Radio Tangier (Morocco) interviewed a representative of UGTAN about the conflict in Algeria. In this interview, the representative stated that the

Algerian war was proof that French colonialism had failed. The peoples of sub-Saharan Africa supported the Algerian cause but could only offer moral rather than any material support. In spite of that, so the representative emphasized, the organization helped the FLN by the messages it sent to African soldiers who served in Algeria, as they comprised most of the French forces there. The African UGTAN member seemed defensive regarding the participation of African soldiers fighting for the French side in the Algerian war, as he inaccurately added that these soldiers were forcibly recruited and that many of them were in jail for refusing to fight against Algerian freedom.[24]

Similar messages came from African students studying in France. In July 1956 an intelligence report examined what was defined as "Islamic propaganda among young students." The report noted that African students in France were escalating their lobby for the withdrawal of African soldiers from North Africa. The directing committee of FEANF, so the report warned, increased its calls to return the soldiers to their countries of origin. In addition, the leader of the Amicale des Musulmans de l'Afrique Noire en France, Ly Cire, was described in the report as a Francophobic medical student who had arrived in France a few months previously. He was responsible for distributing pamphlets that glorified Islam and called for the end of colonialism. The report also referred to the negative influence of North African students in France over their African friends. Here again we can see the paternalistic view of the military authorities, who saw any African politicization as being necessarily the influence of other, more sophisticated colonial people. The report linked this supposed influence specifically to the events in the University of Montpellier in January 1956, when Muslim students studying in France, mostly originating from French North Africa, called for a nationwide strike in all universities to protest the ongoing war in Algeria. Montpellier is located in the Languedoc region in southern France, which was very supportive of the war and the concept of French Algeria. Therefore, this city's university firmly opposed the strike, and a right-wing organization took violent action against the striking Muslim students.[25] Another strike was planned for June 14, and the French report discussing these developments raised the concern that North African students were encouraging their West African friends to take an active part in this strike as revenge for Montpellier. In addition, the report mentioned that there were rumors being spread regarding planned physical attacks on American tourists in Paris and joint protests with African workers.[26] As we can deduce from the rumors the writer of the report chose to mention, the cooperation between workers and students was seen as especially menacing to the French authorities.

The military authorities also monitored references made by African politicians mentioning the service of African soldiers in Algeria. One report commented on a speech given by Ali Jellu, the representative of French Sudan, at the Afro-Asian People's Solidarity Organization's conference in Cairo in December 1957.[27] In this case, the delegate did not refer to the immorality of the army service but rather to the suffering it caused the African soldiers. He spoke of widows and orphans in West Africa and reminded listeners that the soldiers left behind their jobs and studies in order to fight for the French in Algeria. Jellu explained that this was the motive for the African support of the Algerian people.[28] This argument explaining the problematic aspects of Africans fighting in Algeria seems to be more moderate than that of the workers and students, as it does not refer to the justness of the FLN's cause or reject French colonialism altogether. The relations between African politicians, African veterans, and the military authorities will be discussed in the next chapter. Suffice it to say here that although the army was especially worried about what it saw as "radical" African activists, the position of all African political parties and their representatives in the French parliament regarding the service of Africans in Algeria was closely monitored.

Consequently, African soldiers had to be "protected" from anticolonial messages coming from West Africans in the federation and in France and from protests against their service in Algeria. As we have seen, African students and workers were the main groups that caused the army concern. Occasionally, though, such protest emanated from unexpected sources. Such was the case of Father Berlier, a French priest from Niamy, the capital of Niger, who in March 1957 wrote a letter to an unnamed African soldier serving in Algeria. Military censorship had confiscated the letter and reported its contents, emphasizing the last paragraph and noting that it might cause trouble among the soldiers. The priest, with whom the soldier (referred to by the priest as "Cher Ami") trusted his military salary, wrote to the letter's recipient about the political situation in Niger in a manner that revealed his sympathy with the RDA and with African political autonomy. He was excited about Houphouët-Boigny's visit to the region, during which he had been received with respect. He was also happy to report that an African won the municipal elections in the city of Zinder, in the southeastern part of the colony, and added that it was great to have a "real" Nigerian as a mayor. He then told his friend that the colony's governor had been replaced and that the new governor was a simple thirty-five-year-old man who was married to a woman from Martinique and had three beautiful children. This part of the letter was probably enough to raise serious concerns among the military and the colonial authorities, as the information that could be inferred from the contents of the letter was quite worrisome: the priest was excited about the political support of the RDA, believed that Africans were best suited to run their own affairs, condoned mix-raced marriages, and was even pleased with the beauty of the children who were the result of such marriages. The most problematic paragraph as far as the military censor was concerned came at the end of the letter: "Let us hope that the war in Algeria is soon over. God does not want war. It brings only suffering. *God wants people to be free*, no matter which race they belong to, and he asks us to love and help each other truly like brothers. I pray to God that he brings health and peace to your body and to your soul. Give my regards to all the Nigerians" (emphasis in the original censored text).[29]

This letter seems to have worried the military authorities, especially due to its unexpected writer—a French priest who obviously objected to the French policy in Algeria and in AOF. This kind of criticism from a man who was not African, Muslim, or Communist was obviously rare, but like all other anticolonial messages directed at Africans serving in Algeria, the military authorities took it very seriously and took measures to reduce the potential damages of an ongoing protest against the deployment of Africans in Algeria.

As the African soldiers serving in Algeria were constantly faced with antiwar propaganda, the military command attempted to preserve their loyalty in several ways. These included monitoring morale, boosting morale through social assistance and taking care of financial needs when required, preventing close contact between African soldiers and Algerian civilians, and distributing counterpropaganda.

Monitoring African Morale

The first step the army took in order to estimate the necessary measures required to ensure African soldiers' loyalty was monitoring their morale. A report from 1956, for example, noted soldiers' lack of enthusiasm to be sent to Algeria, specifically mentioning four African officers who were supposed to leave for Algeria. One took advantage of his right to retire, and the other three postponed their departure for health reasons. Shortly afterward, they asked to be sent to Madagascar. The writer of this report suggested two reasons for this apparent reluctance to serve in Algeria. One was the low salaries of career soldiers in North Africa compared to those that their comrades were accustomed to in Indochina. The second was the short time soldiers were allowed to spend in AOF after they returned from a service period abroad. This was especially problematic for soldiers returning from Indochina. Soldiers were often sent on to Algeria before they had the opportunity to establish a family.[30]

Although these two explanations refer only to the material and practical motives of soldiers, the example presented in the report seems to contradict these conclusions. If the reason for not wanting to serve in Algeria was not political and had no connection to this specific location, why then did the three African officers who did not have the option to retire prefer to be sent to Madagascar? Later in the report, we can see that the political factor was not totally ruled out. The report mentioned that the African rank and file began to be affected by what is referred to as the *maturité politique* (political maturity) of the African civilian elites. The African *tirailleur*, it seems, could no longer ignore the political agitation and was slowly starting to develop an opinion and a desire to participate in politics.[31] Despite the paternalistic language of the report, we can surmise that the military authorities finally began to recognize that African soldiers might be interested in the political purpose of their service in Algeria and not only in material issues. This recognition led the military authorities to take special precautions to isolate their African soldiers from external political influences.

Social Assistance

In order to contend with the material and political causes of low African morale, the military authorities had to initiate different measures. One remedy the military authorities tried to apply to boost the morale of soldiers was social assistance. As we have seen in chapter 3, one of the facets of the military reforms was the military authorities' involvement in the social and medical aspects of African soldiers and veterans. This social assistance was also accorded to soldiers during their active service in Algeria with the aim of uplifting their morale and alleviating their worries about the families they had left behind, allowing them to focus entirely on their military missions. It also attempted to highlight the army's concern for its soldiers' welfare. A special social worker was assigned to North Africa to take care of the soldiers' social and financial needs. Mademoiselle Ruellan, who served in this capacity in 1956, was assigned to report on soldiers whose families were in a difficult financial situation. After submitting her recommendations, she received a detailed table of allocations for these families from her superior, Mademoiselle Ploix, who was in charge of the colonies within the army. The sum was determined according to the number of children in each family. However, as only one wife was recognized as the legitimate wife of the serving soldier, in cases of soldiers having more than one wife, only the children of the so-called legitimate, meaning the first, wife were included in the calculation.[32] Occasionally, loans were also available to African soldiers who were not in dire need but wished to invest in their future. Such a loan was granted to an African officer serving in the Fifth Bureau. The officer requested the loan because he wished to buy land in Bamako. In the letter approving the loan, General Missionier, the director of military affairs, expressed his concern that granting this approval might create a precedent and that his office would soon be swamped with similar requests.[33] The loan was approved despite this concern, probably because this was an officer who served in one of the most sensitive units in Algeria—a unit assigned, among other missions, to maintain the loyalty of all African soldiers serving in this territory.

Separating the Soldiers from Algerians

In Algeria, as in Indochina, Africans were hardly isolated from the local population, and contact with Algerian subjects was rather frequent. Concerns about such contacts were even graver than in Indochina due to the common religious factor. Most African soldiers were Muslims, and the fact that they shared their religion with the Algerians was a major concern for their French commanders, who were worried that the common beliefs might draw Africans closer to the people against whom they were supposed to fight. It is interesting to note that, unlike the reports from Indochina, the military authorities did not refer to encounters between African soldiers and Algerian women, and it seems that this was certainly not one of their primary concerns, suggesting that such relations were rare. This might be a result of the Islamic norms, which limited women severely. Alternatively, it can point to the French assumption that similar relations could not exist in Muslim societies.

One recurring theme in some of the reports on the soldiers' morale was the insistence that Arabs and Africans shared a mutual "instinctive repulsion," and it is possible that this actually points to a deep apprehension that the opposite was true.[34] In fact, other reports often mentioned cases of fraternization between African soldiers and Algerian civilians. In one case, it was reported that a soldier by the name of Saadou Diaouga asked for a copy of the Koran from a pious Algerian.[35] In other cases, the relations were less spiritual and were expressed by joint games in the evenings and joint outings to town.[36]

In September 1956 the army in Algeria published military recommendations suggesting that several measures be implemented in order to prevent or at least limit contact between the two groups. These recommendations serve as additional evidence that Africans were hardly deterred from forging friendly relations with Algerians. Among the restrictions, it was forbidden to post African soldiers in the same units as the Harki, Algerian peddlers were not allowed to sell their merchandise near bases where African soldiers were serving, and African soldiers were prohibited from guarding Algerian prisoners.[37]

When dealing with "dangerous encounters" between African soldiers and Algerian civilians, the military authorities attributed tremendous importance to the religious component. The more pious the soldiers in question, the more alarming were relations between them and the Algerians. Therefore, the army closely surveyed the soldiers' level of devoutness. In every census the military authorities took, Muslim soldiers were divided into three categories: extremely religious (*marabouts et fanatiques*), practicing Muslims (*musulmanes pratiquants*), and indifferent (*indifférents*). In a census of the Twenty-Second Regiment of Colonial Infantry, for example,

55 *fanatiques* were found, 439 practicing Muslims, and 299 indifferent soldiers. In another regiment, only 2 *fanatiques* were spotted, 29 were described as practicing Muslims, and 76 were indifferent.[38] The criteria for this categorization were the measure and zeal with which soldiers followed the commands of Islam, mainly the observance of the Ramadan fast.[39]

Even though it seems from this report that the military authorities were hostile toward Muslims and suspected African soldiers who were too devout to the military authorities' taste, their attitude to Islam, a religion shared by many of France's other colonial subjects, was rather ambivalent. In fact, the military authorities often saw Islam as an efficient tool of propaganda, albeit only if used with caution and under tight control. One of the most important propaganda activities the army implemented among African soldiers took advantage of African Islam and included monitoring and supporting African soldiers' pilgrimages to Mecca and Medina, known as the hajj, a religious duty incumbent on all Muslims.

Islam as a Military Tool of Propaganda: The Benefits and Dangers of the Organized Hajj

As we have seen, the potential religious link between many of the West African soldiers and the Algerians they encountered was a major reason for concern among the military authorities. The army attempted to counter this potential threat by paying special attention to Islam and using this religious affiliation to its advantage. One of the main ways of doing so was through the organization of well-monitored pilgrimage trips for African soldiers, as well as military involvement in hajj trips initiated by the civilian administration in AOF.

In order to understand the French military policy regarding African Muslim soldiers, their relations with North Africans, and the dilemmas around the hajj, it is necessary to examine the colonial perception of African Islam and its particular characteristics. West African Islam is mostly influenced by Sufi orders. These orders appealed to their audiences by emphasizing feelings rather than practice and by making the rigid laws of Islam more flexible. The main Sufi orders in AOF were the Quadiriyya, the Tijaniyya, and the Muridiyya (the only order that originated in sub-Saharan Africa, specifically in Senegal). When the French attempted to conquer the vast territory that was later to become AOF, they encountered diverse and numerous Muslim societies that were eventually added to the already large Muslim population the French ruled in Algeria. By the early twentieth century, according to David Robinson, France presented itself as a "Muslim power," meaning an imperial power with Muslim subjects who were under its protection, and therefore attempted to forge an "Islamic policy." During the process of colonization the French tried to understand local Muslim societies, divide them into various categories, find potential allies, and isolate enemies.[40]

Around that time, the French had begun to develop the concept of *islam noir* (black Islam), which was supposedly completely different from and even alien to Arab Islam. According to French thought, black Islam was based on two principles. One affirmed that "African Islam" was an original religion that was distanced from the alleged pure and original Islam practiced by the Arabs and adopted pre-Islamic practices. The second principle, originating from the first, saw black Islam as simplistic and inferior to Arab Islam. After World War II, when nationalism and anticolonialism characterized Arab Islam, the French colonial administrations intensified their efforts to "protect" black Islam from the dangerous effects of Arab Islam.[41] It was this fear of the negative influence of Arab Islam on Africans that was further developed by the military ethnographer Capt. Marcel Cardaire. Cardaire warned the military and colonial authorities not to ignore the fact that the supposedly apolitical and moderate black Islam could easily turn into a reformist, potentially nationalist ideology, as African Muslims were beginning to adopt this kind of Islam following their presence in Arab countries either during their studies or during the hajj. Captain Cardaire believed that the Saudis were determined to challenge the French presence in West Africa. During the early 1950s, colonial administrators, military officers, and bureaucrats in the Overseas Ministry were influenced by these views. The war in Algeria only intensified these fears and demanded measures to prevent this phenomenon.[42]

As the colonial authorities' main concern was that Africans would be influenced by Arab Islam through their direct contacts with Arab Muslims, it seems quite surprising at first glance that the main measure chosen to deal with the problem was organizing pilgrimages to Mecca, thus helping to establish these feared contacts in a highly religious context. This choice is made clearer, though, when one considers that hundreds of Africans were going on the hajj every year in any case, and therefore the idea of facilitating this trip for them while closely monitoring their actions and encounters during the voyage seems far more logical.

Nevertheless, as the 1950s progressed, military commanders were becoming more and more skeptical regarding the organized pilgrimages for soldiers and were worried that this tool of propaganda might turn into a double-edged sword. The compromise was to continue the practice while taking several precautions. The army carefully selected the candidates for the pilgrimage, the chosen pilgrims had to swear an oath of loyalty to France, and returning pilgrims were kept under the surveillance of the Bureau of Muslim Affairs long after they had performed their pilgrimage. The bureau had taken these measures when it became evident that FLN supporters were trying to distribute their propaganda among African pilgrims either in the holy cities of Hejaz or on route when traveling through Arab independent countries.[43]

The idea of organized hajj trips was not essentially military. As Gregory Mann and Baz Lecocq note, this was part of the colonial policy of the French Union in its attempt to render the newly established union more attractive to its Muslim inhabitants. In the atmosphere of protest that had developed after World War II, the support of the hajj gave the French the opportunity to present their rule in a more positive way.[44] Not surprisingly, the army was dominant in this enterprise. Apart from conducting special pilgrimages for African soldiers, from 1953 on the army was deeply involved in the organization of civilian pilgrimages, and military commanders began leading the civilian pilgrimages. In addition, most of the participants in these pilgrimages were either soldiers or veterans. The only group of pilgrims that was not necessarily connected to the army was that of African functionaries.[45]

It is important to remember that in spite of the attempt to create an official framework for the hajj, most of the pilgrims conducted the holy trip independently. There were two main reasons for this. First, the pilgrimages organized by the military were rather selective, and not everyone could join them. Second, many of the pilgrims preferred to evade the close supervision that took place during the organized hajj. The downside of going on a hajj independently was that the trip took much longer, in some cases even several years. In the organized trips, the army used better means of transportation, and all passports and visas were arranged by the authorities, so that the entire trip took less than two months.[46]

During the 1950s the military authorities began to organize hajj trips for African soldiers who had served in Indochina and were on their way back home. Even in 1952, for example, a troop of soldiers that returned from Southeast Asia via Mecca was led by Lt. Mamadou Oumar Sy.[47] I would like to focus here, though, on the later pilgrimage trips, one that took place shortly after the French defeat in Dien Bien Phu and the other organized in 1956, two years after the outbreak of the Algerian war. The colonial administration decided to transfer the organization of the civilian pilgrimage trips to the army right before the 1954 trip left for Mecca. This practice continued for three consecutive years, from 1954 to 1956. After the Suez crisis of October 1956, in which France was deeply involved, Saudi Arabia refused to allow official French delegations to enter its territory, and the practice had to be stopped for two years. By the time it was resumed in 1959, the political situation in AOF and in Algeria was already very different.[48]

The first two pilgrimage trips during this period—in 1954 and 1955—were led by Chef de Batallion Amadou Fall, and the third one, in 1956, was supervised by Lt. Tiemoko Konaté. Both were African officers whom the Bureau of Muslim Affairs "borrowed" from the army. At the end of their trips they wrote detailed reports, leaving behind much information on the use of the hajj as a tool of propaganda.

The main message these officers tried to convey both to the pilgrims and to the Arabs they met on their way was that the French Union was, in fact, a new form of progressive and liberal colonial rule. Thus, any rejection of colonialism should not include the French territories of sub-Saharan Africa. It is interesting that although the officers mentioned in their reports that they also defended France's policy in North Africa, this defense was mostly comprised of assuring interested listeners that France would be able to solve the problems there. In one case, the African officer mentioned that even the Prophet was occasionally criticized, admitting in his own way that French colonial rule in North Africa was not above criticism. Information gathered from the reports of the 1954 and 1956 hajj trips will best demonstrate how this message was conveyed.

Although only two years divide these two journeys, the political circumstances were significantly different. The first hajj, led by Fall, took place in the summer of 1954, only two months after the French defeat in Dien Bien Phu but before the outbreak of the Algerian war in November that year. The second hajj discussed here, led by Konaté, was initiated in the summer of 1956, when the Battle of Algiers had begun. Nevertheless, despite these different circumstances, the main issues that are raised in both reports are similar and can demonstrate the military policy regarding the use of the hajj as a tool of propaganda. Three issues repeat themselves in the two reports:

1. The merits of French colonialism and the attempts of the African officers who led the two hajj trips to convince Arabs they met during their travels of the liberal nature of the French Union.

2. The contrast between regions that were under French rule at the time of the report or in the past and those Arab independent countries that were not.

3. Dividing factors between West Africans and Arabs despite their common religion. Paradoxically, although the French military authorities accepted the fact that the hajj was a commandment common to all Muslims, whether they were Arab or Africans, the military used these trips to emphasize the difference and hostility between Arab and African Islam.

Defending French Colonialism

Both reports were written in the form of a journal. At each stop along the way, the author described different encounters he or the pilgrims had with locals. The officers also described in detail the cities in which they stayed and the ways in which they handled the obstacles and dangers during the trip. The reports also contain abundant examples of the merits of French colonialism. Fall, for example, looked for signs of French influence wherever he went. In Fez he described the beautiful road with trees planted along its sides and the effective police services. In Beirut he and the pilgrims were impressed by French architecture and by the dominance of the French language. Even in Damascus, which he deemed more Oriental than Beirut, he managed to note a vague similarity between its main boulevard and the Champs-Élysées. The advantages of the French civilizing mission are even manifested in the Lebanese doctor who performed the obligatory sanitary examinations of the pilgrims in Jeddah, the main Saudi harbor serving coming pilgrims, as this doctor had attained his degree from the University of Montpellier.

Fall was not satisfied with presenting the advantages of French colonial rule to the pilgrims but also engaged in arguments each time French colonialism was criticized. During the stay in Fez, for example, when the pilgrims had expressed to some Moroccans they had met their impression of the beautiful fields they had seen near the city, some of their interlocutors mentioned that these fields belonged to French settlers who had stolen them from the locals. Fall hurried to explain to the pilgrims that Morocco was a large country with room for everyone, but, evidently, the advanced French agricultural methods made these specific fields look more impressive than others. A more serious challenge to Fall's presentation of French colonialism as enlightened came from two unnamed Egyptian ministers he had met in Saudi Arabia. When they asked him why Africans did not try to overthrow French colonial rule he explained that his country enjoyed liberty and equal rights and that it sent representatives to the French parliament. They then asked him how it was possible for Africans to preserve their culture under French rule and whether he would ever be able to become a minister. Fall assured the ministers that his culture, which was oral, benefited from French rule because it was now preserved by means of the French language. As for becoming a minister or even the president of the republic, this was indeed possible, as a colored man, in Fall's words, had been appointed as the president of the French Senate.[49] The two ministers seemed to be content with this explanation and immediately began to ask the lieutenant questions regarding the positions of French units in AOF and their equipment. Curiously enough, Fall did not seem suspicious of the military nature of these questions but did not mention in his report whether he provided the inquisitive ministers with any kind of answers. Fall also mentioned several other arguments he had with Arab people he met on his way, such as a polyglot Mufti from Aleppo and a Syrian whom Fall had mistaken for an Algerian. All of them were hostile to French colonialism, but after Fall supposedly proved them wrong they moved to criticize Britain and the United States for establishing the state of Israel. One can assume that this was done out of courtesy more than any kind of conviction of the progressiveness of French colonialism. Fall also used the platform of a Saudi radio station, Radio Royal, which conducted an interview with him. He summed up this interview by saying that in AOF peace reigned everywhere and full equality existed between blacks and whites.

Two years later, Konaté described similar success in arguments with a Moroccan pilgrim, a member of the Istiqlal movement, which Konaté discovered meant "independence." The man tried to convince African NCOs on board the ship of the merits of overthrowing French rule and seeking independence. Although the soldiers assured Konaté that they were not going to be influenced by his proselytizing, Konaté insisted on debating the issue with the Moroccan until the latter's eyes opened to see the marvels of French colonialism. He talked about the hospitals, dispensaries, and schools France had built in Morocco, as well as the modern transportation. Finally, his opponent gave in and admitted to Konaté that since the French left Morocco he had encountered many commercial difficulties and that not all Moroccans were anti-French. Konaté told him that this was understandable, because in all of the new countries the innocent masses served the interests of a few lunatics, not to say bandits, who wanted independence.

The Ostensible Backwardness of the Arab Independent States

One of the declared aims of the organized hajj trips was to make pilgrims aware of the contrast between lands ruled by the French and those Arab countries visited along the journey that were independent. Both hajj leaders emphasized to the pilgrims the backwardness of those countries, specifically Saudi Arabia and, in the later trip, also Egypt. This backwardness was not only material but also moral.

In his concluding speech at the end of the trip, Fall summed up for the pilgrims what they had seen and how it should be interpreted. He reminded the pilgrims of the huge gap between regions that were under French control in the past or present and Saudi Arabia, with its bad hygiene. He also noted in his report that the pilgrims felt how the notion of liberty was very limited in Hejaz. They were shocked by the swindlers they had met and by the police brutality. In the section in which Fall noted the conclusions that the colonial and military authorities should draw from the organized hajj, he claimed that these trips must continue not only because they highlighted France's obligation to Islam but also because they demonstrated to the pilgrims what he referred to as the problematic character of the Arab states. Two years later, Konaté was more specific about the nature of this problematic character. He emphasized the backwardness of the Islamic legal system by mentioning the repulsion some pilgrims felt while witnessing thieves having their hand amputated. He also lamented the inferior status of Saudi women and the vicious treatment they received from the local men, who also despised strangers, especially blacks. Finally, Konaté went as far as denouncing all Arabs as savages. Interestingly enough, Konaté also mentioned his criticism of the Saudi consumption of American soft drinks such as Coca-Cola and Pepsi. One can only assume that this was done under the influence of the French anti-Americanization atmosphere of the 1950s.[50] Both Fall and Konaté described the Saudi cities in the manner a tourist from a Western country who had never traveled outside of Western Europe or North America might respond to a first visit in the "Third World." Fall's reference to the water in that country, which was unsuitable for drinking, and Konaté's description of the crowds of miserable beggars in Medina who touched him incessantly might lead the reader to think that the two had never visited an African country, let alone been born in one. The entire reports seem as if they were written by a French colonial administrator who described what he saw in a paternalistic manner and with somewhat amused detachment.

The difference between the two reports in this context is that Konaté was much more critical toward the moral aspect of the so-called Arab backwardness. While Fall related mainly to the lack of modernity, Konaté spoke of the barbarity of Islamic legal norms and racism toward Africans. This difference can be explained by the changing circumstances, specifically the Algerian war, which, unlike the Indochina war, involved other Muslims. It was necessary, then, to emphasize to African soldiers the barbaric nature of the enemies who had claimed to be their brothers.

Dividing Factors between West Africans and Arabs

One purpose of the expression of disdain toward Arab independent countries was to make the African pilgrims appreciate the benefits of French colonial rule, which supposedly offered them all those advantages that were absent in Saudi Arabia: progress, modernity, order, hygiene, and a humanitarian legal system. But that was not the only purpose of this comparison. Muslim Africans who performed the hajj had a religious affinity with the Arabs they had met in Islam's holy places. Some of these Arabs were North Africans fighting for their independence from the French.

ɔnaté described the pressure Algerian pilgrims put on some of the sol-
ᴅɪᴇʀs in his group, saying, "We have a common religion" or "Between our countries there is no sea. We live on the same land." He noted that it was therefore vital to explain to the pilgrims, particularly the soldiers, that black Islam was completely different from the Islam of the Arabs and Berbers and that there was no reason to envy them. Konaté hurried to discuss with these soldiers the historical Arab treatment of the African as a slave, and the subject of slavery was also evident in Fall's report. Fall dedicated a section in his report to the continued practice of the slave trade in Saudi Arabia. He also reported meeting pilgrims from AOF who had arrived in Mecca on their own initiative and found themselves stuck there with no money. According to Fall, all they wanted was to leave that ungrateful country in which the rich trample over the poor and money is king. Some looked for a job to earn enough money so that they could leave but were then told that they had in fact been bought and therefore were now slaves. Fall arranged through the French ambassador for 210 of them to board the ship and go back home with his group.

Konaté told horrifying stories about Gamal Abdul Nasser, the incumbent Egyptian president, and Egyptian racism toward blacks, finally remarking that it was a monumental mistake to see the Islamic religion as a unifying factor among believers of different races and ethnicities. At the end of his report, Konaté described the joy of the African pilgrims at going back home after becoming tired of the climate and irritated by the treatment they received. Stating that he had no interest in glorifying France but only in describing what he had seen and heard, he quoted a Guinean pilgrim as saying: "France is the only country with which the black man can live."[51]

As can be seen from the two reports, the hajj trips served as a vital propaganda tool for the military authorities. As mentioned before, in 1953 the military began organizing hajj trips not only for soldiers and veterans but also for civilians. The idea that a military officer would be in charge of the pilgrimage ensured that order and discipline would be maintained and that the monitoring would be professional. The officer could also demonstrate the army's commitment to its African soldiers. While in 1953 an Algerian officer, Lt. Col. Daudi Abdeslam, was chosen for the job, in later hajj trips two West Africans led the groups. According to Mann and Lecocq, the

1953 trip was disastrous for all sorts of reasons beyond the lieutenant's control.[52] It is difficult to tell whether this was the reason the hajj trips were transferred to the responsibility of West African officers, but in any case this was a choice that exemplifies the greater trust the military authorities accorded to West Africans.

Both officers found it difficult to maintain discipline during the hajj. In fact, Fall complained in his report about the excessive shopping African pilgrims did during the trip, which made their suitcases too large and heavy for the vehicles assigned to them in Jeddah. What Fall neglected to mention in his rebuke was that the pilgrims on the organized hajj trips were supposed to pay for their lodging and food while in Saudi Arabia. They therefore needed to purchase merchandise in Saudi Arabia that they could sell later in AOF and so pay back loans they had taken for the voyage.[53] Overall, Fall was deeply upset by the pilgrims' behavior. In his concluding speech before the pilgrims were sent home, Fall disappointedly remarked that each time they boarded or disembarked a ship or a vehicle, the pilgrims did not do so in an orderly manner but pushed their way impolitely. Fall explained to the pilgrims the importance of discipline and that Africa would not progress if everyone did whatever they pleased.

Indeed, it is interesting to note the persistence of the administration's concern regarding this problem even today, after more than fifty years of independence. The current problem of the lack of discipline and disorder during hajj trips from Senegal recently aroused a debate in that country regarding the question of whether the army should again take over these trips. Cheick Bamba Dioum, who discussed this option in his blog, even referred to Amadou Fall's organized hajj in 1954 in order to demonstrate that historically the military had been responsible for hajj trips from the region.[54]

The story of the military-run hajj exemplifies the new world with which French colonialism had to deal—a world in which mobility of people and ideas was easier and anticolonialism and Islam went hand in hand. International events such as the Suez crisis demonstrated that the days of colonialism and the dominance of the two great colonial powers—Britain and France—were almost over. The French army tried to present the French Union as a new, rejuvenated form of colonialism different from that of other powers and therefore legitimate. From the reports examined here, one can feel a certain confidence in the righteousness of the writers' position and their success in "converting" every anticolonialist they met during their travels. This supposed confidence masked a sense of deep concern and suspicion. In 1954 Fall recounted that Cheick Ibrahima Niasse, an important Tidjani Sufi leader from Senegal, had accompanied him on the hajj. Niasse spoke to his African supporters and followed Fall in most of his encounters.[55] In Algiers he gave a sermon before the Friday prayer and talked favorably about how France had facilitated Muslims in fulfilling their religious duties. Two years later, however, in a report on Muslim propaganda, the same Cheick Niasse was accused of establishing contact with a member of the Istiqlal movement in Casablanca during that trip and for establishing ties with an anti-French head of a madrassa (religious school) in Kayes (French Sudan).[56] It seems, then, that even the military-organized pilgrimage could not eliminate the dangers of facilitating the access of West African Muslims to the wider Islamic and mostly anticolonial world.

It is difficult to assess whether the benefits of the hajj as a tool of propaganda surpassed the dangers it held for French colonial stability. But in any case, the Saudi refusal to allow the continuation of the trips after the Suez crisis showed that this new world, in which colonialism was rapidly losing legitimacy and leverage, was definitely beyond French military control.

African Soldiers and the Wars of Decolonization: Indochina and Algeria

France's wars in Indochina and Algeria presented for African soldiers a new set of challenges that they had never experienced before. The two world wars were harrowing, of course, but the anticolonial wars involved guerrilla fighting and blurred the boundaries between the civilian and the military spheres. They also involved a war of ideas that was much more complex and challenging than that of World War II. Nazi propaganda, which was based on racist notions, even if it also used a supposedly pro-Islamic and anticolonial rhetoric, could hardly have won the hearts of Africans. The propaganda of the Viet Minh and the FLN, on the other hand, spoke in a language they could sympathize with. In the Algerian case, the common cultural and geographical space made this propaganda even more potentially persuasive.

The subject of African participation in the wars of decolonization waged by movements that demanded self-determination, along with the end of

French colonial rule, is seldom tackled in studies on African soldiers. As I mentioned in the introduction, most studies to date, as well as most public events and cultural products regarding the soldiers, focus on their participation in the two world wars. When dealing with these soldiers' experiences in the Indochina and Algerian wars one cannot avoid considering the accusation that anticolonial movements were often directed at the soldiers for siding with the colonizers against their colonized and repressed "brothers." Anticolonial thinkers such as Franz Fanon and Octave Mannoni debated the figure of the *tirailleur*, used as a tool in the hands of French colonialism to inflict violence and arouse fear among colonial subjects.[57] As interesting as these debates might be, they tend to ignore the agency of these soldiers and examine them only as tools in the hands of colonial power.

To conclude the two chapters on the African troops who fought in the Indochina and the Algerian wars, I would like to focus on how these soldiers perceived their participation in these wars. Although African soldiers were also deployed in the colonization of the French empire, the wars of decolonization took place in a different historical period, in which Africans were much more aware of global politics and the international criticism against colonialism. My intention here is not to serve as an advocate for the African soldiers who, as we have seen, joined the army in the 1950s mainly for economic motives. Rather, I would like to claim that the answer to this "moral" question lies in the problematic assumptions on which it is based. Accusing African soldiers of collaborating with the colonial power against their "brothers" is based on several basic assumptions: first, that Africans at the time actually considered other colonial people as their brothers; second, that they viewed independence as a common goal of all colonized people; and third, that they gave their military service the same meaning as those who criticized them at the time. These assumptions stem from a view of decolonization as a process that must inevitably lead to national independence.

In order to clarify this point, I would like to present the story of one African soldier who served in the French army between the beginning of World War II in 1939 and the beginning of the Algerian war in 1954. Sall, born in 1921, belonged to the Tukolor ethnic group and was in fact the grandson of the king of the Toro Kingdom in northern Senegal. When his grandfather tried to resist French occupation in 1890, he was captured and beheaded.

As was the custom in such cases, the defeated king's head was displayed on a pole for a few days to deter others. When Sall was twelve, the French administration demanded that his uncle, who was a traditional chief, send one of his children to the special school the French had established for chiefs' sons. As Sall's uncle only had daughters, Sall's father was asked to send Sall instead. Upon graduation the next natural choice for Sall was the school for soldiers' sons—the EET (discussed in chapter 3), to which the French accepted sons of chiefs, as well as sons of soldiers. Sall studied at the EET with Charles N'Tchoreré, who became famous when he was executed by the Germans in World War II because, being an officer, he refused to be separated from the other French officers after being taken prisoner. Sall was recruited into the army at the age of eighteen. He served for fifteen years, but not because he enjoyed his military service. In fact, he hated it. He stayed in the army ten years more than he had to because doing so ensured him a good pension after his demobilization. After World War II he served in Morocco and briefly in Algeria (before the Algerian war) and later was sent to Indochina. When I asked Sall's son what his father thought about the FLN, he told me that he simply saw them as rebels who were justifiably repressed by the army. He certainly never considered them as brothers, sharing common interests and goals. According to his son's testimony, Sall's self-identity was much more localized. He felt allegiance mainly to his extended family. He had no national sentiments and did not engage directly in politics. Nevertheless, he supported his Communist uncle, who held radical national views, simply because Sall did not like the French. When his son wanted to join the army of the newly independent Senegal, his father dissuaded him, saying that he did not want his children to have a military career.[58]

Sall's story demonstrates the difficulty inherent in examining the service of Africans in France's wars of decolonization according to simple categories such as "nationalism," "anticolonialism," or "collaboration." Here we have a man who had good personal reasons to hate the French. He had not chosen a military career but was dragged into it by pure chance at first, later staying on course because of financial considerations. Despite his hate for the French he did not support the Algerian cause and did not make the connection between his destiny and theirs. He also did not see the national cause in his own country as particularly important and was loyal mainly to his extended family. In short, he was a soldier performing his duty, a duty that held no political or moral significance as far as he was concerned.

This point can also be understood from the current views of some African veterans regarding their participation in these wars. Veterans who either wrote about their experiences or discussed them with various scholars described the Indochina war as a classic ideological struggle between the West and the Communist world. Marc Guèye, for example, emphasized in his memoirs Ho Chi Minh's Communist convictions and the training he received in Moscow and did not mention the anticolonial motives of the war.[59] Many veterans do not feel a need to apologize for their participation in this war, and although they have expressed their respect for the Vietnamese who fought against them, they did not consider them as "brothers." Their emphasis instead has been on the difficult nature of this war and the great distance and isolation from home.

Generally speaking, veterans remembered the Algerian war in an essentially different manner. This was a war that could not disguise itself as an anti-Communist war. The FLN fought for an independent Algeria—an aim that is now hard to refute. This war was fought on African soil against people who shared the African soldiers' history and, to a large extent, their religion. The best illustration of this very different approach to the Algerian war can be deduced from an interview with Mamadou Niang that was conducted during a workshop in Dakar in April 2010. Niang, whose memoirs I have referred to in this chapter and in chapter 3, joined the French army in 1955. He was trained in France and became a paratrooper, was wounded during a battle in the mountainous area of Algeria in November 1958, and was released from service shortly thereafter. Two years later, in 1960, he joined the Senegalese army, following this country's independence. Even before being asked, Niang explained that he and his comrades had fought against soldiers whom he called "our Algerian brothers," because during that time they considered themselves as French. Fifty years after the end of the Algerian war, he tried to explain the different view he had at the time, being a French soldier (he was indeed a French citizen) in the French army, fighting to keep Algeria French. However, he emphasized that he now saw things quite differently. The Algerians were fighting for an acceptable cause—liberation. They were brave and fought well, even though they had inferior weapons. Through their bravery, he said, the

Algerians proved to the world the value of the Arab, who preferred to die rather than surrender.[60]

It is clear that even if at the time the participation in both wars seemed quite acceptable to African soldiers who enlisted in the French army, in retrospect this is only true for the Indochina war. Their participation in the Algerian war seems, at least to some of the African soldiers, something that requires an explanation.

As for the attitudes of the French army apropos the African participation in these two wars and the problems it created, one can note great similarities, as well as some major differences. Chapters 4 and 5 examined military policy during both wars in three specific domains: African soldiers' morale and the attempts to uplift it, African soldiers' encounters with the local population and the dangers these encounters created, and enemy propaganda aimed at African soldiers and the military efforts to reduce its effects. The first sphere, uplifting African morale, was similar in both wars. The military command attempted, not always successfully, to ensure that soldiers communicated with their families, to entertain the soldiers, and to attend to their cultural and social needs. In the two other spheres, the encounters with the local population and management of enemy propaganda, there is a clear difference in the military policy in both wars. While in Indochina the main concern was the violence and hostility of the local men toward the soldiers, in Algeria friendly relations were considered the main threat. Assumed Arab hostility against Africans was actually seen as a valuable tool of propaganda, while close contacts, always attributed to the common religion, were considered as a potential danger. This somewhat paradoxical situation arose because of the cultural and geographical affinity between Africans and Algerians. For the same reason, the military authorities also saw FLN propaganda aimed at African soldiers as much more dangerous than that of the Viet Minh. As any expert on propaganda knows, the more the target audience has in common with the distributors of the propaganda, the more chance the message they convey will be accepted favorably.

Despite this important difference, there is one feature that is common to the military policy in both cases. The French military approach to these problems in Indochina and in Algeria demonstrates that even though the army made efforts to professionalize and modernize its African units, old colonial concerns and perceptions still survived. Africans were still considered as naive and easily influenced by ostensibly more sophisticated colonial peoples. In both cases examined here, the African soldiers represented for the French military authorities a space in which French colonialism could still hope for support if they only managed to protect it from external hostile influences. Their major assumption was still that decolonization could and should be avoided in AOF.

From the beginning of the war in Indochina up to the return of de Gaulle to power, the world as the French military authorities knew it was changing rapidly. International events that threatened to end the colonial era followed one another quickly. In retrospect, it seems that the writing was already on the wall. When we read the reports of the two African officers who monitored the hajj trips in the mid-1950s, we may smile at their efforts to dismiss the critical views they heard about French colonial rule, which now seem pathetic. We might wonder whether they really believed their own speeches about equality between blacks and whites and the so-called benefits of French colonial rule and its proclaimed liberal aspects. But in the mid-1950s the military authorities, and we must remember that these two officers were part of this system, did not yet see the end of colonial rule. Their investment in the military hajj trips and their control over those designated for civilians demonstrate their determination to protect what was left of the French empire after the defeat in Indochina. While the main aim of the organized hajj was to boost African soldiers' morale and loyalty, these trips were also meant to prevent militant anticolonial views from influencing African pilgrims and thus the areas from which they originated. As we shall see in the next chapter, although it seems that at the time the main battlefield against those who challenged French colonialism was in Algeria, the army regarded AOF as a bastion that should be protected as well.

6

Alternatives to Independence

The Army's Colonial Vision in French West Africa

Unlike other parts of the French empire in the post–World War II era, AOF enjoyed a relative calm. Although violence had characterized the political struggle in Cameroon between 1956 and 1958, this territory was a mandate that belonged to the federation of Equatorial French Africa, and the violence there was an exception rather than the rule.[1] The political struggles in AOF were mostly nonviolent, except for a brief stage of protest in the Ivory Coast during a short-lived practical and nonideological allegiance between the RDA and the French Communist Party (PCF). This does not mean, however, that the French did not impose violence at all during the postwar years, but it did not come close to the violence taking place in other parts of the empire. Although the army had no war to fight in AOF, it still played a central role in the political processes in the federation and, as in Algeria, often stepped out of the military domain in order to ensure that the civilian administration did not lose control over the population. Moreover, major challenges for colonial control were not absent in AOF, and soon the army realized that protecting even this supposedly calm territory from the winds of decolonization would not be an easy task.

This chapter takes us back to the territory from which most African soldiers originated to discuss the French army's understanding of the future of the colonial project in AOF. My main argument is that the army had its own very distinct vision of "decolonization." In the immediate post–World War II period, this vision was rather similar to that of the civilian administration and the French government at the time. After the defeat in Indochina and the escalation of the struggle in Algeria, the army refused to abandon the idea that France could continue to rule AOF in spite of what was happening elsewhere. The army thus saw the rapid political reforms after 1956 as a disaster and was concerned that they would eventually lead to the separation of France from its West African territories. The military authorities in AOF saw their own transformed relations with African soldiers and veterans as a model for a valid alternative to independence that would satisfy most Africans and keep AOF French. This vision of the political future of AOF was expressed in military rhetoric and even in actual measures such as the distribution of propaganda. The objection to independence and the criticism of the political reforms in AOF also intensified the army's encroachment on the civilian authorities.

The military authorities in the federation were concerned not only by the prospect of future independence but also by the negative influence of the political reforms and the changing attitude of the French government to AOF on the army's position in this federation. The French colonial project in AOF became a topic of discussion, and the army played a major role in this debate. Nothing was certain anymore, and this precarious situation reflected on the colonial army as well. I shall first examine the shaky position of the French colonial army in this region: its low budget, the shortage of skilled personnel, the threat of the Moroccan forces to the integrity of Mauritania after 1956, and finally the proposal to dismantle the colonial army, suggested by a French general in 1955. The heated responses to this proposal by two other generals of the colonial army reflect to a large extent the military position regarding the form French colonialism should take and the army's vision regarding the political future of AOF. I will then examine the military involvement in the distribution of colonial propaganda in AOF, which aimed at "protecting" Africans from being influenced by the struggles for independence in North Africa and in neighboring British colonies, especially the Gold Coast, which gained its independence in 1957.

I will examine these propaganda efforts through two examples. The first is the use of films to disseminate desired messages among the population of the federation. The second is the celebrations marking the centennial of the African units' establishment in AOF in 1857.

Propaganda was one way of acquiring control and influence. Another was the army's careful monitoring of political activity in the federation in order to prevent African soldiers and veterans from being influenced by what the army considered radical and foreign ideologies, that is, any demand for self-rule and independence. The military engagement with politically active civilians reflected the army's lack of confidence in the civilian administration's ability to control the population. This mistrust was translated into military attempts to get involved in the day-to-day administration of the federation. I will conclude this chapter by examining two examples of the military attempts to take over the responsibilities of the colonial administration. One is the establishment of the system of Officers of African Affairs, which was affiliated with the colonial administration. The other is the struggle between the military and the civilian authorities over the control of the District guards, the forces that were responsible for maintaining order in the federation. By examining these aspects of military activity in AOF, this chapter aims to demonstrate the army's deep involvement in the political life of the federation and its attempts to take over at least some of the areas that were under civilian authority.

The Precarious Situation of the Colonial Army in AOF:
Military Challenges and Financial Limitations

Although the military missions in AOF were much less complicated than those in Algeria due to the absence of violence, this apparent lack of urgency was also a source of weakness for the military command in AOF. The budget allocated to the military units in the federation was much lower than that in other parts of the empire. Despite its obvious downsides, violence certainly ensured that a more generous budget was allocated to the military. In addition, the increasing need for soldiers in Algeria left no choice but to send a great number of African soldiers from AOF to the battlefields of the lingering war. This meant that the West African units had to let go of vital manpower, which they actually desperately needed. The units based in AOF had to maintain order in the federation at a time when real and assumed threats to the colonial power were on the rise. These forces were also needed to protect the northern borders of the federation, especially in Mauritania, from the infiltration of North African insurgents and the nomadic groups that assisted them.

The problems in Mauritania started in 1956, following the independence of Morocco. This was a difficult year for the French army in general. The escalation in Algeria, the failed Suez operation, and the government's decision to accord autonomy to the territories of sub-Saharan Africa forced the army to adjust to a rapidly changing reality. From the military point of view, the independence of Morocco and Tunisia that year only made matters worse, as these newly independent countries were able to offer assistance to the FLN fighters. To add insult to injury, the Istiqlal, the party that had led Morocco to independence, claimed Mauritanian territory as part of independent Morocco. The party's claim was based on political and cultural affinity, but it was also aimed at preventing the establishment of a puppet state on the northern border of Morocco that would serve French ambitions in the region. Allal el Fassi, one of Istiqlal's leaders, expressed this claim in a speech he delivered in the spring of 1956. Although the monarchy did not officially support the claim, it soon led to military struggles in the region, and the French colonial army had to reinforce its units in Mauritania. Only in 1958, after launching a military operation, did the French succeed in pushing back the Moroccans, but the border areas remained under surveillance for many years.[2]

The Moroccan threat on the region of Mauritania, combined with the political implications of the Loi-Cadre, which were discussed in chapter 1, led the superior commander of the French forces in AOF, Gen. Gabriel Bourgund, to send a letter to the minister of overseas France complaining about the situation. He resented the contrast between what he termed "favored Mediterranean territories" (meaning French North Africa) and "neglected African territories." The general noted that Algeria had 350,000 men in active service, and independent Morocco still had a French presence of 80,000 men. Only 20,000 soldiers were posted in AOF, though they were entrusted with keeping the peace in a region seven and a half times larger than France. He complained about this disproportion and his feeling that AOF had turned into a training depot and transit center for African reinforcements heading first to Indochina and then to North Africa.[3]

In a military report covering the period from 1956 to 1958, Bourgund also described in further detail the difficulties faced by the army. His report pointed to three main problems. The first was the previously mentioned threat from the Arab-Islamic north. The second, related to the first, was the need to keep a balance between the forces responsible for maintaining order in AOF and those that were sent to protect the federation from the north. The army's third preoccupation was the need to adjust military policy to the new political reality in AOF, which emerged following the Loi-Cadre.

Regarding the first problem, Bourgund explained that the FLN and groups from Morocco were penetrating into Mauritania and gaining influence among the nomad population. African soldiers were being sent to protect the border, but they did not manage to block these forces altogether. The general noted that it was important to act swiftly and deliver a blow to the North African fighters and especially to nullify their influence over the local population, since their support was essential for the rebels.

As for the problem of balancing the forces so as to maintain order in AOF while guarding its borders with the newly independent countries, the general noted that this was a very difficult task because of the increasing need for soldiers in North Africa. According to the general, the army needed 50,000 more men in order to fulfill all of its missions. He wrote that the forces in AOF were actually nonexistent and that dispatching an additional 10,000 soldiers to North Africa was disastrous. To emphasize these difficulties, Bourgund referred to the shortage of trained drivers in the AOF units. Following the efforts to modernize these units, they received a large number of new vehicles. However, there were not enough soldiers who were able to drive these vehicles, rendering many of them useless. This situation was also very bad for the army's image and its ability to keep the African population loyal to French colonial rule, as soldiers who returned to the villages told their friends and relatives embarrassing stories about this miserable situation. The general warned that if this situation was not remedied, the army would not be able to attain its aims in AOF.

Referring to the Loi-Cadre vote on June 19, 1956, giving autonomy to the territories in internal affairs, Bourgund complained that no one took into consideration that military policy would have to be adjusted to this new reality. The general concluded that it was essential that no more soldiers from AOF be sent to Algeria. If this was inevitable, then at least there should be an effort to do this without destroying the forces in AOF. He accepted that it was not probable in the current situation to accord preference to AOF and to take care of all of its needs but insisted that the minimum should be done.[4]

The precarious situation of the French colonial units did not stem only from the difficulties raised in Bourgund's report. In fact, just a year before the political upheavals of 1956, the entire existence of these units was under debate following a proposal to eliminate the colonial army, incorporate its European units into the metropolitan forces, and create "national" armies in some of the territories of the French Union supervised by a committee of the Union. This rather surprising proposal, which enraged several generals in the colonial army, came from Gen. Jean-Étienne Valluy, who served at the time as the army's representative in Washington DC. Valluy was the commander of the forces in Indochina during the initial stages of the war and was held in great esteem as an expert on the colonial army.

Valluy's proposal derived from his experience in the colonial army, lessons from the wars in Indochina and Algeria, and the growing international hostility toward the French Union and French colonial rule. He maintained that the autonomy of the military units would satisfy nationalist wishes and largely reduce international criticism. In fact, Valluy suggested that France transfer to African control a domain that was significantly symbolic for a sovereign state—the area of defense. It is rather surprising that such a proposal would come from a military figure a year before the National Assembly approved the Loi-Cadre, which offered autonomy to the African territories of AOF but did not allow them to establish their own armies. This happened only with the establishment of the Franco-African Community, three years after Valluy's proposal.

After this proposal was submitted to the French chief of staff, the latter asked two distinguished generals of the colonial army, Henri Gustave-André Borgnis-Debordres and Georges Yves-Marie Nyo, to express their opinion of it. Their two extremely negative responses deserve further attention, as they reflect the military perception of French colonialism and its desired future at a time when it was under severe international criticism.

One of the generals, Borgnis-Debordres, did not deny Valluy's experience but reminded the chief of staff that Valluy was a representative of the French army in Washington, a fact, he reasoned, that had probably influenced Valluy's judgment. Borgnis-Debordres assured the chief of staff that all the principal generals affiliated with the colonial forces objected to their suppression and that Valluy was the only one who supported this idea. Borgnis-Debordres's tactic was to attack the premises on which Valluy's conclusions were based. He noted that the conclusions Valluy drew from the Indochina war were rather simplistic. Valluy had suggested that the colonial troops were not professional enough, and metropolitan soldiers had to be brought in to assist them. Borgnis-Debordres clarified that the need to bring in metropolitan soldiers had nothing to do with the performance of the colonial troops but with the personnel shortage caused by the defeat of 1940 and the entrance of the Japanese into Indochina. This claim, so he maintained, was not logical at all, because at the time, colonial soldiers had been brought in to help metropolitan soldiers liberate France, and no one had suggested then that this was due to the inferiority of the metropolitan soldiers. The general then continued to criticize Valluy's submission to the American perspective of French colonialism. He blamed President Roosevelt for planting the seeds of the anticolonial tempest that followed in North Africa and the Far East. He noted that in fact the Americans were the real colonialists, as they had eliminated the local race—"the red skins," as he called them—and were now practicing discriminatory policy against blacks. The French, so the general wrote, rejected the accusation of being colonialists. France had the right to be proud of what it had created in its overseas territories.

Borgnis-Debordres then presented the French colonizers as the saviors of the Africans, rescuing them from their own barbarity and their bloodthirsty rulers, such as Haj Umar and Samory Touré.[5] He rejected Valluy's suggestion that the word "colonial" should be removed from the army's name and clarified that the French were proud to be colonial but were not colonialist. In fact, so he noted, the invention of the word "colonialist" proved that there was nothing wrong with the term "colonial." Otherwise, he asked, why would there be a need for a different word? Borgnis-Debordres also referred to the practical issues Valluy's proposal was supposed to solve. He declared that the existence of the colonial army in no way damaged the unity of the French army and that in fact it solved the problem of having to send metropolitan soldiers overseas for long periods.

Though Borgnis-Debordres's response to Valluy's proposal was firm and critical, General Nyo's report was even stronger in its tone. Nyo did not mince words when attacking Valluy and his team. He did not hesitate to use terms such as "holocaust" and "dangerous" to describe the results if the proposal was adopted and words such as "criminal," "unqualified," and "irresponsible" to portray its initiators.

Nyo interpreted Valluy's proposal as referring not only to the future of the colonial army but also to the future of the entire French Union. He maintained that Valluy actually suggested turning the French Union into a sort of commonwealth. This, however, would be a commonwealth without the power of a crown, the sterling bloc, or confidence in the power and the majesty of Great Britain. This idea was actually a policy of renouncement that would turn the French military system into a series of local militias and accelerate French military decadence.

Nyo repeated Borgnis-Debordres's assertions regarding the true colonialist nature of the Americans and added that they did not understand the French idea of the equal vocation of two different human groups that live side by side but do not wish to fuse into one another through *métissage*, two different societies with different aptitudes that justify their coexistence. According to Nyo, the colonial army, which Valluy suggested eliminating, was a space in which the coexistence of and true comradeship between these two groups was manifested in the best possible manner.

With regard to the conclusions Valluy had drawn from the Indochina war, Nyo agreed with Borgnis-Debordres that the colonial troops performed perfectly in Indochina and mentioned that the correct lesson to be drawn from this war was the need to encourage the professionalization and maintenance of these units rather than dissolving them.[6]

The two generals' harsh and critical response to the idea of dissolving the colonial army reflects, to a large extent, the position of these forces' high-ranking officers toward the future of French colonialism. The interesting linguistic analysis Borgnis-Debordres offers regarding the invention of the term "colonialist" highlights this position: colonialism in the form it took after World War II was nothing to be ashamed of. Through the implementation of vast political reforms, it had lost all its negative characteristics and now described the coexistence of two human societies with unique dispositions but a common mission. This description, of course, does not include real equality between the two groups, as it speaks only of an "equal vocation" and not of equal rights. Nevertheless, as Nyo noted, this coexistence was manifested within the colonial army in equal pensions and service conditions. Therefore, the suggestion to dissolve the colonial army was in fact a suggestion to negate the existence of a benevolent colonialism in which the general had firmly believed.

While Valluy's proposal was eventually rejected and the colonial army survived until after the independence of the territories of AOF, the term "colonial" was in fact removed from the name of the army in April 1958. It is interesting that the "new" name that was chosen in its stead was in fact the old name of these forces, Troupes de Marines (Naval Troops), a name they had held until 1900. Therefore, even when the term "colonial" was eventually removed, the return to the old appellation indicated that colonial pride was still very much part of the military perception.

The endemic lack of resources, the political and strategic threats, especially after 1956, and the vote of no confidence raised by a general who was once part of the colonial army's command all contributed to the precarious position of the colonial army in AOF. Apart from the attempts to fight the military threats from the north using the meager manpower at its disposal, the military command in AOF was also occupied by fighting against the so-called radical forces threatening to destabilize the only part of the empire in which no war was taking place. The armed forces in the federation did not underestimate this parallel war of ideas and took a major part in it, mostly because the military command believed that the civilian administration was not handling the situation very well. This attitude toward the perceived weakness of the civilian colonial administration reflects the general suspicion and hostility of French military commanders during the Fourth Republic toward the political authorities, especially regarding the latter's colonial policy. In order to negate the influence of anticolonial ideas on the population of AOF, the army resorted to the use of propaganda and to surveillance of African soldiers and of those civilians considered dangerously influential.

Military Propaganda in AOF

The concept of psychological operations was examined in chapter 5, as this mode of operation first gained the attention of French military commanders during the Indochina war, but it was developed into a clear military policy with the escalation of the conflict in Algeria. The situation in AOF was of course completely different and much calmer. Nevertheless, during the 1950s, especially between 1956 and 1958, the growing African political activity caused the army to resort to this form of persuasion in AOF as well. We have already seen in chapter 3 how the army used its ties with the veterans to distribute promilitary and pro-French propaganda. Here I would like to focus on two examples of this kind of psychological activity and examine some of the African reactions to it. The first example is the use of films to win African support, and the second is the celebrations of the centennial of the African soldiers units known as the Tirailleurs Sénégalais in 1957. These two examples clearly demonstrate the role of the army in diffusing propaganda to both civilians and soldiers, the aims of this propaganda, the problems with its implementation, and the difficulty of disseminating an image of a glorified army at a time when it was losing so many battles.

Before we examine these activities in AOF it is necessary to discuss another concept closely related to that of the psychological operations, one that has existed in the military lexicon since the nineteenth century and is often cited in documents discussing the psychological operation in AOF: the concept of army-nation relations. These two linked ideas are vital to our understanding of the army's attitude toward the political changes in the French empire during the late 1950s. The concept of army-nation relations served as the basis for the army's politicization during the twentieth century. According to it, the French army represented the nation and was the nation's army more than it was the official state's army. Thus, the army's loyalty was first and foremost to the nation. It was this conviction that allowed some of the army's leaders to resist the government's policy during the two main conflicts of the 1950s in Indochina and in Algeria.[7] The rather frequent use of this concept in the context of AOF and the fact that the African population of the federation was included in the "nation" are quite remarkable and point to the military's attempts to present the army as the colonial organ that best represented the aspirations of Africans and supposedly treated them as equals.

Films as a Tool of Psychological Operations

While the army used various means of propaganda such as newspaper articles and radio broadcasts, which we have discussed in previous chapters, films certainly held a special allure for the military authorities, as films were both highly attractive to Africans and did not require the ability to read in French. The French army had begun using films as a means of propaganda as early as World War I. This practice intensified during the 1930s and later in World War II. The army under both the Vichy regime and the Free French forces used films to present these regimes' ideals. After the war, the military hierarchy recognized the effectiveness of cinema as a means of propaganda and established the Service Cinématographique des Armées (Army's Cinematographic Service), which was responsible for the production of all propaganda films.[8] The link between the psychological operations and films was formalized in 1952 when the Ministry of Defense combined the Army's Cinematographic Service with the newly established Service d'Action Psychologique et d'Information de la Défense Nationale (Service of Psychological Operations and Information of National Defense).[9] During the 1950s the French used films extensively as part of their psychological operations in Indochina and Algeria. In 1957, for example, the army screened eighty-eight films in the federation.[10] Not all of those films targeted audiences in the colonies, though. Some were shown only to French audiences, and occasionally these films were also screened outside France and its empire. Their aim was to convince their viewers to support the continuation of the French presence in Indochina and later in Algeria. Films about Indochina presented the purpose of the war as pacification and attempted to convince their viewers of its necessity. The films on Algeria presented soldiers as maintaining order and bringing education, health care, and aid to the Algerians. In other words, the films ignored the fact that a war was actually going on.[11] What is important for our discussion is that apparently for lack of funds or interest none of the films shown in West Africa were produced specifically for West African audiences. The military and colonial authorities had to rely on the supply of films from France, films that were intended for completely different purposes and audiences. This, as we shall see, proved to be quite problematic.

The films that were sent from France to assist the psychological operations were screened in the major territories once every two months in all districts and subdivisions capitals and occasionally in various villages. The audience mostly included veterans and schoolchildren, the two groups that were most accessible to the colonial authorities but also very significant in military eyes.[12] Although the administrators who reported on the screening of these films attempted to present many of these events as a great success, a careful reading of the documents points to the contrary. In fact, the only time in which the film screenings could be regarded as a success was when veterans watched documentaries describing familiar battlefields. Most of the other films were actually extremely boring to their viewers or, worse, detrimental to colonial and military interests.

As mentioned before, the main problem of most films was that they were not originally designed for audiences in AOF. In 1954 the high commissioner complained to the minister of the colonies that the films sent to AOF did not fulfill their aim. As an example he gave the film *Nos soldats en Afrique noire* (Our soldiers in black Africa), which was aimed at attracting young French people to the army but was of no interest to the African public.[13] When the film *Le grand cirque* (The great circus), which tells the story of three men who fought with the Free French in World War II, was shown in Bamako, only women and young children attended, and, according to the report, they did not find the film interesting at all.[14] Other films were reported as being too technical or tediously long.[15]

Films that failed to attract the attention of their African audience for more than a few minutes were not useful as tools of propaganda, but at least they were not harmful. On the other hand, showing the public in AOF documentaries filmed in Indochina before the French defeat in Dien Bien Phu in 1954 was in fact contrary to propaganda purposes. In 1956 the governor of Upper Volta remarked in his report regarding the psychological operations in his colony that it was not worthwhile to screen documentaries filmed in Indochina at a time when it still seemed that the problem would be solved in a favorable manner. He added that the film *Les armées de la paix* (The armies of peace), for example, was considered a military propaganda film at the time but achieved the opposite results when the outcome of that war was taken into consideration. In general, the governor recommended not screening any film that related to a military operation whose outcome was not politically favorable for France.[16] This, unfortunately, did not leave many options.

At first glance, the extensive use of films that were not adapted to African audiences and that occasionally presented an unflattering image of the French army might seem surprising. However, in spite of their obvious disadvantages, these military films had a vital role in the so-called psychological operations. They symbolized a shared past glory and a common aim for French and African soldiers. The military authorities saw African veterans—who apparently were the only ones who appreciated these films—as a key element in reaching the hearts of the African population. The military documentaries sought to emphasize this shared destiny and thus to present the entire colonial project in a different light. After all, even shared defeats can evoke the brotherhood in arms, and it was this brotherhood that ensured the loyalty of both soldiers and veterans in AOF. It was also this notion of the brotherhood in arms that stood in the center of the celebrations of the centennial of the African colonial units that we shall examine next.

The Celebrations of the African Troops' Centennial

In February 1957 Gaston Deffere, the minister of overseas France, sent a letter to the minister of defense to remind him that 1957 marked the centennial of the Tirailleurs Sénégalais—a fact that he believed should be used to emphasize the French gratitude to the soldiers and, by extension, the French attachment to its overseas territories. He suggested that the minister declare 1957 as the *année de centenaire des troupes africaines* (centennial year of the African soldiers).[17] About a month later, such a law proposal was in fact submitted to the National Assembly.[18]

In general, 1957 was not an easy year for the French army. It was sinking deeper and deeper in the Algerian swamp, and it faced, as we have seen so far, increasing criticism in the colonial, national, and international arenas. The centennial was perceived as an excellent opportunity to assert the military vision of France's relations with its overseas territories. An examination of the correspondence about the preparations for the event, the speeches written for the celebrations, and the way in which they were organized and performed is an excellent prism to the military perception of French colonialism in the late 1950s and, even more, to the link created by the army between its African soldiers and this perception.

In the introduction to the proposed program of the celebrations in Paris, the state secretary of the armed forces described the African soldiers whose centennial was being celebrated. These soldiers, according to the text, had liberated their people from slavery and from the rule of bloodthirsty chiefs.

(This was of course a reference to the soldiers' participation in the colonial wars that enabled France to conquer its empire.) They fought gloriously in the two world wars and in the "ungrateful" Indochina war (the writer ignored the Algerian war), and finally, they represented the best example in all military history of brotherhood in arms.[19]

The importance the army, as well as the Ministry of Overseas France, assigned to the centennial of the African troops is evident through the decision to organize the main celebrations in AOF and in the metropole during the week beginning July 14, Bastille Day, absorbing the colonial calendar of the celebration into that of the French metropolitan one. In this manner, a clear and unequivocal link was created between France's national celebration and the celebration of its colonial troops and empire. No one could be clearer regarding this link and the embodiment of the merits of French colonialism in France's African soldiers than Gen. François Ingold, who declared in a speech in Paris, "Let us be proud facing the world. One hundred years of friendship, of glory and of sacrifices. . . . Yes, our black troops are 'our' pride. Facing the world, facing our adversaries, facing the exaggerations of these times . . . let us remain proud. We have the right to be proud, and if anyone would like to deny this today, the presence of veterans on our side will brilliantly prove them wrong." Ingold then told the story of a young French lieutenant who died while saving one of his African soldiers and added, "Never, anywhere in the world, in any military history, have I met a more beautiful example of love and fraternity. I am still waiting to be offered one!"[20]

Ingold's speech summarizes the French military view of its relations with its African soldiers, idealized of course, as a mirror of the ties between France and its empire. At a time in which the world went mad, pointing a blaming finger at France despite its efforts to reform its colonial rule, the loyalty of the African soldiers and the moral support of the veterans served as the best proof that the whole world was wrong and France was right. The willingness of African soldiers to sacrifice their lives for France proved that the ties between France and its colonial subjects—now citizens of the French Union—were based on friendship, shared glory and sacrifices, and brotherhood in arms. The celebrations in France included not only soldiers and veterans but also African pupils from the EMPAs of the federation. While the veterans represented the past and the soldiers the present, these children represented the future—a future in which the army had confidence. In fact, by the time these children reached the end of their studies, the African units would no longer exist. In 1957, though, Ingold and his comrades were determined to let nothing destroy the celebrations. In spite of the difficulties the Algerian war created; in spite of the political reforms in AOF, which changed the rules of the game; and in spite of the growing international criticism, which even led, as we have seen, to a proposal to eliminate the colonial army, the celebrations were conducted in full glamor, ignoring the changing reality and clinging to the old paternalist narrative of loyal African soldiers grateful to the French for using them to save their people from themselves.

Although it seems as if the celebrations represented an old and unchanged colonial discourse, in fact this is not entirely accurate. While the recruitment of African soldiers to fight in Europe during World War I was justified by the debt they ostensibly owed the French for liberating them from their tyrants, in 1957 the debt became mutual. France was also indebted to its African soldiers, who had helped liberate it from the Nazis. On the last day of the celebrations in Paris, the veterans and soldiers met with several ministers, including the minister of overseas France and the minister of defense. The report's writer noted that they should have met with one more, nonexistent, minister—the minister of public debt. This public affair was meaningful, as it demonstrated that the debt was no longer only perceived as that of the soldiers toward France but also vice versa.[21]

The efforts invested in the organization of the celebrations in the metropole exemplify the importance the army allocated to these events as the manner in which they could relay to the French public and to the world the true meaning of French colonialism and the future of this project. The proposed program for these celebrations included an opening ceremony planned for June 23, three weeks before the peak of the celebrations on July 14, at the Tata Sénégalais, the graveyard in the village of Chasselay near Lyons, where African soldiers were massacred by the Germans in 1940. This date was probably chosen because it marked the liberation of the city of Toulon in 1944, in which a great number of African soldiers took part.[22] On July 14, an official ceremony was to be conducted in Paris in which African music would be played. It was suggested that a mixed paratrooper

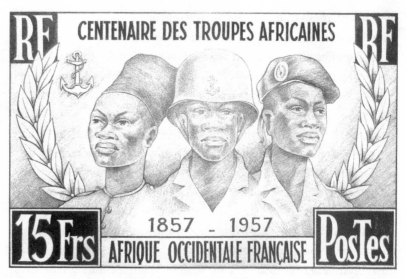

FIG. 5. The stamp issued for the celebration of the centenary of the Tirailleurs Sénégalais. Courtesy Centre d'Histoire et d'Études des Troupes d'Outre-Mer, Fréjus, 15H 17.

company be invited to march in this ceremony. Other ceremonies were to take place in Marseille, Toulon, and Fréjus.

A week later, on July 21, the monument for Gen. Charles Mangin, the initiator of the idea to recruit African soldiers to defend the motherland even before World War I, was to be inaugurated in the Invalides, next to the military museum. This monument was to replace the one that the Germans had destroyed during the occupation. In addition to the ceremonies, several propaganda measures (and this was indeed the term used in the military documents) were taken: the initiation of a special stamp and a medal marking the centennial, lectures, radio broadcasts, special articles in the journal *Tropiques*, and the distribution of brochures.[23]

This proposed program was sent to several generals and people connected to the French Union authorities, and a number of replies were received. One of the replies was from a person named de Jonquières whose exact identity is unclear, though he seemed to be connected to high-level officials in the French Union. He was pleased with the program but had two suggestions. One was to take advantage of the opera season in Paris and organize a gala of black dances. De Jonquières emphasized that this should be a performance in good taste, attended by the president, ministers, the diplomatic corps, and an audience of five thousand guests. The performance should include the big masks of the Dogon dances similar to those photographed in *Tropiques* and be choreographed by the opera.[24] For some reason, de Jonquières was worried that the black male dancers might give "the beautiful French ladies" in the audience nightmares. One might assume that in fact de Jonquières meant that such a performance before French ladies would give French men nightmares. The concerned de Jonquières thus suggested that only half of the performance should include black dances; the rest of the performance should include a ballet—*Giselle*, for example—a much safer option as far as the ladies were concerned. He also proposed that after the performance the president should deliver a speech and the flag of the Premier Régiment des Tirailleurs Sénégalais should be raised.[25] This, so he believed, would attract the attention of the important newspapers. De Jonquières's second suggestion was to approach the French academy and ask that great authors publish articles about the centennial in the Parisian press.[26]

While it is unclear whether any or all of these proposals were implemented, and, if so, to what extent, their common aim was obvious: exposing the French public to the centennial celebrations and turning this event into a major national festival involving French political and cultural elites. The military command also felt that the participation of representatives from the Ministry of Overseas France would be important. It was also vital to include African political leaders in the celebrations, and Gen. Roger Blaizot, the president of the centennial committee, was proud to announce that he had already secured the participation of Félix Houphouët-Boigny.[27]

Despite this grandiose proposal, the celebrations of the African troops were not appreciated by all African politicians. For example, the party of Léopold Sédar Senghor (1906–2001, Senegalese poet and politician and the nation's first president), the Bloc Populaire Sénégalais, a merger of several Senegalese parties created that year, published an announcement against the decision to celebrate this centennial on the day that symbolized the struggle against tyranny. They noted that the party was ready to celebrate the destruction of the Bastille and any other regime of oppression and exploitation and was also willing to celebrate any type of human advancement. The party protested the celebration of black Africa within the so-called centennial of the African troops, which was supposedly invented for the needs of the French Union and was combined with the anniversary of the takeover of the Bastille. It also deplored the fact that, contrary to the legitimate sentiments of any African conscience, so the announcement said, the high commissioner of AOF had decided to celebrate the creation of an instrument of conquest specifically in the first year of the autonomy created by the Loi-Cadre.[28] In August 1957 demonstrations were organized in Saint Louis, the capital of Senegal, against the celebrations of the centennial that were planned for that month due to the participation of African soldiers in the brutal repression of several incidents that had taken place a short time before. An organization by the name of the Comité de Défense des Intérêts du Sénégal (Committee for the Defense of the Interests of Senegal) called the population not to participate in these celebrations.[29]

The military authorities were highly upset by the attempts to attack the celebrations of the centennial. They were quite horrified by the allegation that the forces they saw as the embodiment of everything that was just and right in the French colonial project were in fact a vicious tool of conquest and colonial violence. However, they still had one important consolation: veterans did not take part in the demonstrations against the centennial, and many of them took an active part in the celebrations. The support the military authorities in AOF received from veterans was also manifested in their participation in ceremonies, sports events, and, as we saw in this chapter, film screenings. The continued support of the veterans was priceless, as they served as living proof of the theory regarding the merits of French colonialism and the legitimacy of the French Union. It is no wonder that in the intelligence report of 1957–58 an important place was dedicated to a decision of the general assembly of the veterans' association, brought to a vote on January 18, 1957. The decision was presented as a glorification of France, to which the veterans owed everything—from liberation from slavery through receiving a means of communication between them to becoming civilized and even being elected to the French parliament. The text assured the minister of the veterans in France of the loyalty of African soldiers who fought in Algeria against *anarchistes meurtriers* (murderous anarchists).[30]

Even this public reassurance did not put the military mind at ease. While propaganda was an important measure to control the African mind, other measures had to be taken against those who apparently were not persuaded by the presentation of this information and were determined to disseminate dangerous ideas among supposedly naive and nonpolitical African soldiers and loyal African veterans.

Monitoring "Dangerous" Civilians

Until 1958 the military authorities in AOF were not greatly concerned about their soldiers' loyalty, as the authorities were positive that most soldiers were not interested in politics but only in their material conditions. As we have just seen, the authorities were even less worried about the veterans' support, which was reinforced after the reforms of 1950. Nevertheless, they certainly realized that soldiers and veterans did not live in a vacuum and could potentially be lured by politically motivated civilians.

In order to monitor such a political influence, the army closely followed any African political activity that was related to soldiers or veterans. It was of course much easier to prevent soldiers from becoming politically active, as this was prohibited for all soldiers—metropolitan French or Africans. When asked about political discussions during their military service, one veteran explained that of course soldiers held political opinions (contrary to the military perception), but politics were not allowed in the army, so the soldiers did not discuss their views openly.[31] It was impossible, though, to prevent veterans from getting involved in politics, and this was indeed a source of concern for the military authorities. They were especially worried about the danger of the veterans' potential rapprochement with the RDA. Both the IOM, which was tolerated by the French, and the RDA, which was considered to be the enemy, attempted to win over veterans during that period. The RDA had even falsely attempted to take the credit for the equation of the pensions (see chapter 3).

In an interview with Aissatou Diagne, Mbaye Seck, a veteran from the Indochina war, told her how he was courted by various political militants upon his return home: "A few days after my arrival, Mbaye Diagne Degaye came to see me. . . . He told me: 'Here we have two parties, the party of the Goors [men in Wolof] which is the BDS and the party of the traitors— Lamine Guèye's party.' He wanted me to join Senghor's party [the BDS]. I answered that I am a military man. I know nothing about politics."[32] In order to convince him, his interlocutor promised Seck that Senghor would solve all Seck's problems regarding his pensions and papers that he had left in Indochina. To further persuade Seck, Degaye also brought him two sheep. At that point, Seck felt that he had to be honest with the man and explained to him that he had met Senghor and did not like him because he was not nice to him and had obviously preferred the company of intellectuals from Réunion and Martinique. Senghor's Christianity also bothered Seck, who eventually decided to join Lamine Guèye's party.[33]

The military authorities were aware of these attempts to court veterans and closely monitored any attempts made by political parties, and especially of the RDA, to win veterans' support. Although the RDA cut itself off from the Communists in 1950, it was still highly antimilitarist, and it is therefore not surprising that the military authorities aspired to keep veterans out of this party's reach. In fact, while the RDA considered veterans as an important group politically, its antimilitarist position did little to attract them to its ranks.

African veterans won not only the attention of the political militants but also that of the African representatives in the French parliament. The positions of some of these parliamentarians regarding the deployment of Africans in France's imperial wars, which the army also followed attentively, were often quite complex. The actions of Ouezzin Coulibaly, RDA's representative from Upper Volta in the National Assembly, demonstrate well the complexity of the party's position toward the service of Africans in the French army.

In June 1949 Coulibaly confronted the minister of the colonies in parliament, asking him why France was breaching the agreement it signed in Indochina, according to which no African soldiers would be sent to fight there. The minister responded that the soldiers were volunteers, but Coulibaly asserted that it was known that the way in which volunteers were recruited was dubious and that in fact these soldiers had not really volunteered. Moreover, so Coulibaly maintained, no one had ever explained to these so-called volunteers that they would have to serve under such difficult conditions. Coulibaly then concluded that France was in fact involving Africans in a fraternal war.[34] Needless to say, most African soldiers who served in Indochina would have hardly agreed with this definition. Yet from the army's point of view this was certainly a challenge emanating from an African member of parliament.

On another occasion, Coulibaly drew loud objections in the National Assembly when he compared the deployment of African soldiers in Indochina to cancer. Coulibaly vehemently protested against the use of one people in the French Union against another and claimed that this was contradictory to the spirit of the union's constitution. In fact, he said, French Africa was being sent to reconquer French Asia. Coulibaly went on to say that while the use of African soldiers was common during the colonial conquest, he had believed that French methods had evolved and had become more humane. He was disappointed to discover that in fact Africans were again being used as mercenaries of the republic. He also mentioned that the French sent ex-Nazis (probably referring to some of the German soldiers recruited to the Foreign Legion after World War II) to fight in Indochina side by side with African soldiers, though the Nazis had tortured these soldiers in their camps during World War II just because of the color of their skin. The African soldiers, who had fought against fascism and racism, were now in Asia under the command of their former enemies, fighting against democracy and the liberty of the Vietnamese people.[35] These allegations shed light on the complexity of Coulibaly's view regarding the service of Africans in the French Army. While he fiercely objected to the use of African soldiers against the Vietnamese, whose fight for liberty he considered legitimate, he did not object to the principle of the Africans' service in the French army and even took pride in the Africans' contribution to the war against Nazism. The response of the minister of the armed forces to Coulibaly's accusations clarifies this perspective quite coherently.

The minister first claimed that the deployment of African soldiers in Indochina was not against the constitution, quoting the relevant article. He then objected to the term "mercenaries," which Coulibaly had used, saying that the Africans in fact volunteered in great numbers to fight in Indochina. When Coulibaly was allowed to respond, he immediately adjusted his main argument in light of the minister's explanation. Coulibaly asked the minister: If Africans were not mercenaries but were just like French metropolitan soldiers, why did they not receive exactly the same benefits as French soldiers?[36] This was obviously an interesting shift from a more nationalist discourse to the one that prevailed among African politicians and trade union leaders in AOF: the discourse of equality.[37] In fact, this type of argument was not unexpected. Coulibaly not only fought against the use of African soldiers in Indochina but also struggled for soldiers' and veterans' rights, especially in the immediate aftermath of World War II. Between 1947 and 1949 Coulibaly gave six speeches in the National Assembly in which he called upon the French government to award equal service conditions to African soldiers. He referred to various kinds of discrimination, from the different uniforms and food supplied to the African soldiers to the refusal of the army to teach them proper French. He also spoke against the discrimination between the African subjects and citizens in the army, for which he saw no basis, and between French and African soldiers of the same rank.[38]

It is interesting that while fighting for the soldiers' rights Coulibaly had adopted the same discourse of "brotherhood in arms" that was promoted by the African veterans and the French military authorities, but this brotherhood was limited to World War II, which he had perceived as a just war, and did not include the ongoing wars of decolonization. It is not surprising that on May 20, 1949, Coulibaly reinforced his claims during a ceremony in which Félix Eboué, the black governor of Chad who allied with de Gaulle, was buried in the Pantheon side by side with the great abolitionist Victor Schoelcher. In an article written on this occasion, Coulibaly reminded his readers that Eboué opposed the Vichy regime, which was a blemish in the history of France, and together with him many African soldiers refused to surrender and preferred to die for France, while many Frenchmen chose otherwise. Coulibaly pointed to the symbolism of the burial of two great people, one black and one white, side by side and called for the same kind of equality between black and white living soldiers.[39]

African politicians such as Coulibaly, who obviously did not support the French deployment of African soldiers, adopted the veterans' discourse regarding comradeship in arms based on shared sacrifices during the two world wars. Coulibaly, who was especially critical regarding France and its deployment of African troops in Indochina, did not question France's right to recruit Africans to World War II and their service for France in general after the war. In fact, in August 1958, nine years after his vehement speech in the National Assembly, Coulibaly called the youth in Upper Volta to register for a new school that had been established in the colony and that prepared its students for the prestigious military academy of Saint-Cyr. Coulibaly urged African youth to follow the preceding generations who had brought honor to their country (not clarifying if he meant France or their native land) by their military service. He emphasized his appreciation of this military academy and declared that any officer who graduated from it was a "temple of honor." Africa, so he said, should become part of this: it has to have its own Saint-Cyr graduates.[40] This call to African youth to become officers in the French army at a time when Africans were fighting against the Algerian independence movement is rather surprising if we take into account the vehement opposition of the RDA to the use of African soldiers in Algeria. It demonstrates, however, that the ambiguity regarding the service of Africans in the French army was not only a tactic to attract veterans to the RDA. It was also an acceptance of a discourse of equality that was best represented in glorious (and even the less glorious) battlefields.

Speeches and law proposals of African representatives in the French National Assembly drew the attention of the military command, which became worried about their potential influence over French politicians. Nevertheless, it was the political activity on the ground in AOF that was threatening to infiltrate the ranks of African soldiers. While soldiers usually did not follow the debates of African parliamentarians in Paris, they had many occasions to meet these militants in the streets, in places of entertainment, and even at home, among their families.

The deep involvement of the army in the political life in AOF is evident in the military reports, which did not settle for describing military activities or threats to public order in the federation but also elaborated on political events and processes. Periodic intelligence bulletins issued by the armed forces in AOF reported on every political gathering, convention, or major publication of political parties (especially those regarded by the colonial administration and the army as radical), trade unions, and student movements. The army also monitored the local press's reports of any criticism voiced against the Algerian war or any expression of supporting independence. As described in the intelligence report of 1957–58, that period was full of significant political activities displaying a rise in the African political consciousness. The two organizations that the report referred to as the most dangerous that were mentioned in chapter 5 were the West African students' union (UGEAO) and the West African trade union (UGTAN). For example, the conference of the youth council of Senegal in January 1957 culminated with a moment of silence in memory of the victims of French colonialism in Algeria and Cameroon, an act that evoked some concern. Especially alarming was the participation of a number of African NCOs in this meeting and in others similar to it. One NCO was mentioned as participating regularly in meetings of the youth wing of the RDA during his vacations.[41]

As we have seen, most morale reports concluded that the morale of African soldiers in general did not seem to be affected by this political activity, since they believed that Africans were preoccupied mainly by their material situation. Yet some concern was raised that this situation might change in the future. A list of incidents appeared at the end of the report, all involving soldiers who, contrary to the supposed general trend, were involved in political activity. One of these soldiers, serving in Kaolack, Senegal, and portrayed as a person who spent time among the milieu of "progressive young *évolués*" wrote in a letter: "I am under the flag wearing the uniforms of a criminal." Another soldier from AOF wrote in a letter he sent to a comrade serving in Morocco: "The black suffers too much in the army. The French take us for animals, for their captives, and this is why their subjects revolt one after the other to be released from their heavy yoke.... One day, if God wishes so, we will find ourselves free as well."[42] The army's sensitivity to any mood change among the African soldiers, especially regarding service in Algeria, is also evident from these reports, as every change of attitude or refusal to serve in Algeria generated a thorough investigation. The army thus attempted to "protect" its African soldiers from what it saw as the negative and dangerous influence of African political organizations, especially those of workers and students.

The military command perceived the young students of the EMPA as even more vulnerable and susceptible to this kind of propaganda, especially when it emanated from students their own age studying in civilian schools. The most problematic were Africans who were sent to study in military schools in France, as the level of politicization of African students in the metropole was high. On September 4, 1958, a few weeks before the referendum on the Franco-African Community, the superior commander of the forces in AOF, Gen. Pierre Garbay, complained to the minister of overseas France about the negative influence of African students studying in Aix-en-Provence, whom he accused of organizing demonstrations during their vacation in Dakar. The general asserted that the source of their behavior lay in their detachment from their surroundings and the subversive propaganda they were exposed to during their studies. He offered two possible solutions to the problem. One was to make sure the students were kept in their own cultural surroundings while in France. The other, which he preferred, was to turn the EMPA of Saint Louis into a college and thus avoid sending African students to France altogether.[43]

The assumption that the main problem was the presence of the African students in France was far from accurate, as by January 1957 the students of the EMPA in Bingerville, Ivory Coast, went on strike and refused to participate in classes. The students declared that they did not wish to become soldiers, that they had been sent to that school without their consent, and that they aspired to receive diplomas equivalent to those accorded to students of the best schools of the federation. Although the formal reason for the strike was a punishment inflicted on one of their classmates, the students' actual motives are perhaps best illustrated in a telegram one of them sent to the president of the Enfants de Troupes Africaines in Dakar: "We have started a strike due to bad food, bad command, and racism." While these motives sound valid, General Bourgund did not accept them and maintained, as usual, that the strike was motivated by the negative influence of the students studying in the nearby civilian technical college. After a thorough investigation it was concluded that the recent school strikes in civilian establishments had inspired this strike. A note of criticism is heard in this conclusion, blaming the civilian administration for failing to deal in a determined manner with these student strikes and disorders. Bourgund emphasized that the lack of any sanctions against the striking civilian students encouraged their military comrades to follow suit. He warned that if the violent incidents in Lycée Faidherbe in Saint Louis were not dealt with on a disciplinary level, it would become clear that the students were the ones who set the rules.[44]

This criticism of the manner in which the colonial administration dealt with political threats exposes an interesting facet of the relations between the civilian and the military administrations at a time of high tension in the federation. As I intend to show in the following pages, the attitude of the colonial administration to this kind of criticism was rather ambivalent. On the one hand, the colonial officials were aware that the army possessed better tools to deal with political threats. On the other hand, they were wary of the military attempt to take over areas of control from the colonial administration. In order to demonstrate this ambivalence, I will examine two opposite examples of the civilian attitude toward offers of military assistance in controlling the federation. The first one is the civilian initiative to assign a military officer to each District commander, who would become part of the civilian administration. The opposite example is the fierce resistance of the colonial administration to the military attempts to transfer a branch of the police, the district guards (*gardes de cercle*), from administrative to military control.

The idea of designating officers who would be affiliated with the civilian administration organization known as Officers for African Affairs was suggested by the high commissioner of AOF in 1955, and it was implemented in April 1956.[45] The colonial administration's motive for this idea was to receive assistance from the military in the everyday management of the districts. This help was especially needed in the organization of the "bush tours," which were discussed in chapter 3. Since the beginning of this practice in the early colonial period, it had been extremely difficult to convince the district commanders to carry out the tours on a regular basis. The idea that this duty could be passed on to military officers was probably very attractive to the reluctant administrators and to their superiors. The officer assigned to the colonial administration was to become an outsider and an insider at the same time. Officially, this officer was introduced as part of the administration so that the population would not view him as a spy. Nevertheless, when it was convenient, the officer presented himself as being "outside of politics" and as a soldier who was not really affected by the political considerations of colonial administrators. Each of the thirty officers assigned to this mission had to learn the local dialect (or at least one of them if there were several) and read a monograph about the region he was assigned to. Assuming that this policy was actually carried out, the officers' knowledge of the local society was probably better than that of the district commanders, who were not required to learn the local languages. The officers were especially useful in two domains in which their military training and prestige were important: maintaining order and establishing contacts with veterans. It was the second role that made this initiative worthwhile for the military command in AOF. The officers also served as the representatives of the Office des Vétérans, the administrative organ responsible for the veterans in the federation. They had to ensure that the veterans' centers were lively and active, they organized events for local veterans, and they had to open a file for every one of them, making sure that they knew each veteran personally. The officers' duties included monitoring Koranic school pupils and pilgrims returning from Mecca. They were also assigned with gathering information about any potential threats from political dissidents. In a letter from August 1957, five months after the independence of the Gold Coast (which became Ghana), one of these officers, posted in central Savalou subdivision in Dahomey, sent a letter to his supervisors describing his tours along the border of the newly independent country to collect information. Another officer, posted in the Pada N'Gourma district in Upper Volta, referred to his job as a game that one must play the best one could. He noted that he had managed to gain the trust of Africans elected for administrative posts and to avoid all political solicitations by presenting himself as an impartial soldier who was not involved in politics.

Although the system of the Officers of African Affairs was presented in official documents as a success, even the enthusiastic report admitted that it had some disadvantages as well, as the officers were not administrators and were not trained as such. Therefore, they were also liable to cause damage.[46] In addition, while the colonial administration had initiated the cooperation with the army, this took place at around the same time that a heated debate had begun between the military and civilian authorities in AOF regarding the status of the district guards. Colonial officials, it seems, did not always welcome military intervention in the colonial administrative system.

In November 1955 the district guards, first in the Ivory Coast and then in Senegal, claimed that they were being discriminated against. They demanded that their compensation be compared to that of employees of other administrative services and gendarmes with similar duties who were part of the army and therefore enjoyed the benefits offered to soldiers as of 1950. The district guards decided to take advantage of their civilian status and profit from the right accorded to civil servants in AOF to establish a syndicate and, if necessary, go on strike.

The response of the military authorities to this demand was swift.

According to the military cabinet of AOF, the only solution to the problem was the immediate incorporation of the district guards into the army. As soldiers were not allowed to organize, this measure was supposed to put an end to the growing unrest among the guards. The director of political affairs in the federation, Léon Pignon, fiercely rejected this proposed solution and saw it as an attempt by the army to annex all civil forces to its authority. He noted that as the problem was the guards' work conditions, the solution was to improve these conditions rather than transfer the force to the army. Pignon acknowledged the fact that the guards' material situation was indeed inferior in comparison to other services, such as the gendarmes. He emphasized that their demands were not related only to their salaries but also to more symbolic features, such as their uniforms.[47]

But Pignon's argument was not altogether convincing in the colonial reality of the mid-1950s. First, the clear boundaries he had depicted between military and civil forces were in fact quite blurred, as we have seen in the case of the Officers of African Affairs. Second, most of the district guards were actually veterans who were employed in this service after they had completed their military service. In fact, their military experience was one of the factors that initiated their protest, as they were able to compare their conditions in the civil forces to those of their military service. Third, while Pignon's suspicion of the army's intentions to take over the civil forces is quite understandable, he neglected to mention that there was no contradiction between the idea of transferring the civil guards to the army's authority and his suggestion to improve their conditions, as such a transfer would have automatically equated their conditions to those of the gendarmes, whom they had envied.

The district guards' protests reached the highest level of the colonial administration when in November 1955 the leaders of this movement sent a letter to the minister of overseas France complaining about the treatment they had received since they began lobbying for their right to organize. It is interesting to note that their principal complaint was against a military agent rather than an administrative official. The leaders of the district guards asserted that a certain commander by the name of El Hadji Soumana told them that he had received orders to physically subdue them if they continued with their campaign. They doubted if such orders were actually given.

It must be noted that it is not clear what the official position of this military commander was, as the system of the Officers of African Affairs formally began to function only a few months later. We can assume, though, that this commander fulfilled a similar role to that of the future African Affairs officers. The movement leaders complained that Soumana's aim was not to help veterans, as he claimed, but rather to fight against veterans and against the district guards. According to them, he came to their treasurer's office with a captain by the name of Desbases and took at gunpoint all the money the movement had raised for its campaign. He also recruited six gendarmes in order to gather information about their activities. The leaders had explained to the commander that they were not soldiers but civilians, and they therefore held the right to organize and would do so even at the cost of their lives. They then complained in the letter about the daily harassment by both the commander and the captain, who came to search their huts regularly, gave their new uniforms to European gendarmes, and arrested thirty-seven guards for no reason at all. They claimed that the high commissioner of AOF, Pierre Messmer, gave the two men permission "to break the movement leaders to pieces." They asked the minister to save them from the two, emphasizing that they were all veterans who only wished to get a bit of rest after fighting in the wars. They could not understand why the conditions of employees in the police, water, forests, and customs commissions were so much better than theirs. These employees were well dressed, they said, and lived in nice houses, while they, the district guards, were being treated like disgusting prisoners.[48]

When it was clear that the district guards' protest would not be crushed by arrests and repression, and the movement began to spread into Senegal, the high commissioner acknowledged that swift action was needed. The first administrative move to prevent the consolidation of this force was to declare that the nature of the guards' job contradicted their right to organize. The high commissioner realized, though, that this would not be enough. As he noted, contending with this solution would raise three problems: discontent among the guards would harm the security of the colonies; it would be impossible to deny the guards the same conditions the auxiliaries of the gendarmerie received; and finally, it was legally problematic to deny a person who did not hold military status the right to organize. As he rejected the military idea to transfer the entire force to military control, he suggested a compromise: incorporating the more educated guards into the gendarmerie and transferring the others to the rural police, which was under the control of the civilian administration. He admitted that this idea was far from perfect, as the transfer of guards into the rural police might be detrimental to their training and quality. He then suggested a second option that was almost identical to the army's original solution: incorporating the entire force into the gendarmerie, leaving some guards as detached personnel in the districts' brigades and under civilian control.[49]

The establishment of the system of the Officers of African Affairs and the struggle over the control of the district guards both reflect the complex relations between the military and administrative authorities in AOF at a time when political tension was on the rise. Both examples seem to show that the dangerous political situation and the common fear of the civilian and military authorities of losing control led to a certain dependence of the civilian administration on military assistance. The fact that the administration was willing to incorporate into its ranks military officers who did not undergo any administrative training exemplifies the extent of this dependence. Even when the civilian administration endeavored to reject what it saw as military attempts to take over civilian forces, it was eventually obliged to succumb to military demands, as it was not able to reconcile the political rights it owed its civil servants with the necessity to protect the federation against threats to its political stability.

As we have seen in this chapter, while the French army did not have to contend with an enemy threat in AOF, it was involved in its own local struggle. This was not the same kind of military struggle as in Indochina and in Algeria, but it had some similarities to one aspect of these two wars: it involved a war of ideas that pushed the army to act beyond its military duties and invade areas that were supposed to be under civilian responsibility. Although the army invested energy, as well as much of its meagre budget and manpower, in this struggle, it was gradually losing due to political reforms that kept changing the rules of the colonial game. The next chapter will examine the ways in which the army saw the political transformations of the late 1950s, which eventually led to the independence of all the territories of AOF, and how it adjusted to the new reality imposed on it, even managing to save some of its control over the newly independent African states.

7

Adjusting to a New Reality

The Army and the Imminent Independence

When Gen. Roger Gardet, the superior commander of the French forces in AOF in the crucial years between 1958 and 1960, summarized his term, he used the following words: "We could not insist more, in fact, on the fundamental change that had occurred in less than two years in the conditions of the French presence and consequently in the missions of our military apparatus."[1] This was hardly an overstatement. The political reality in AOF changed rapidly within this short period of time, and from the army's point of view, not in a positive manner.

In the previous chapter we examined the distinct political vision the army had for AOF and the ways in which it attempted to keep the federation French despite the difficulties in Algeria, the political reforms that accorded more and more autonomy to African governments, and the international hostility toward French colonial rule. We saw the army make use of propaganda materials and closely monitor veterans' and soldiers' contact with political movements in the federation, often encroaching on civilian authority in order to advance its own political agenda. In this chapter, we will examine the army's response to a series of political reforms that were not intended to secure independence but eventually resulted in it. My main argument is that the army saw these reforms as dangerous and tried to minimize their damage in order to keep control of the federation. Once it became clear that there was no way to prevent these political processes, the army played an active part in establishing national armies in the various territories of AOF and tried to ensure continued control through a series of military agreements with the newly independent countries. I will discuss the effects of independence on African soldiers and veterans and will show that many of them, just like the military authorities, did not consider decolonization as a process that necessarily leads to independence. This final chapter sheds light on the various meanings of the concept of decolonization and on the impact of the military bond, discussed in the introduction, on the postcolonial period in AOF. This impact was reflected not only in a series of military coups d'état, led by ex–African soldiers and officers in some of the federation's ex-territories, but also in a continued French military involvement in the entire region.

In this chapter I will first examine the ways in which the army perceived the various political events in the federation, namely, the May 1958 crisis and the establishment of the Franco-African Community, the independence of Guinea, the formation of the Mali federation and its collapse, and finally the independence of all the other territories in AOF. Next, I will examine the French involvement in establishing the national armies of the newly independent countries and the military agreements signed with most of these states as a way to ensure continued military control in the region. The third part of the chapter will be dedicated to the ramifications of independence and the dismantling of the African units in the French army on the African soldiers and veterans. Finally, I will briefly examine the involvement of African veterans in military coups d'état after independence as a means of demonstrating the impact of the military bond on the postcolonial political process in some of the former colonies of AOF.

The May 1958 Crisis and Its Impact on the Military Command in AOF

The political reforms in AOF were directly influenced by France's problems in Algeria and by the concern of facing another colonial war in this region. It is clear that the aim of the Loi-Cadre of 1956 was not to grant independence to the African territories of AOF but rather to prevent this occurrence. In retrospect, this law triggered a chain of reforms that eventually resulted in independence.

The Loi-Cadre is widely recognized as a turning point in the history of French Africa. While it was later condemned by African intellectuals as the law that put an end to the federal structure of the French colonies, or, as Léopold Sédar Senghor defined it, the "balkanization" of Africa, at the time many African politicians considered it a victory. Most of their political demands were accepted, including universal suffrage, a single electoral college, and territorial assemblies with real power. The French, on the other hand, freed themselves from having to confront the growing demands of African workers for a salary equal to that of their metropolitan colleagues, as the law established that each African territory would be responsible for its own local budget.[2] As for the military, the Loi-Cadre encouraged the Africanization of the middle ranks of African colonial troops and removed the racial barriers that had hindered their promotion within the military hierarchy.[3]

Even though the Loi-Cadre preserved French control over the area of defense, a fact that had upset some African RDA leaders, as we have seen in the previous chapter, the military command in AOF was not happy with this law, as military policy was not adjusted to the new law accordingly. While no outright criticism was raised against these reforms, at least not directly, military commanders in the federation complained that the policy outlining the military budget and conditions remained unchanged and had not been adjusted to the new political reality shaped by these reforms. However, these were minor concerns in comparison to what was to follow. Ironically, it was the return of the man who was supposed to save the French empire—Charles de Gaulle—that brought about another political reform far more dangerous in the eyes of the military command in AOF than the Loi-Cadre: the new Franco-African Community.

In May 1958 France experienced a serious political crisis that was a direct result of the Algerian war. While the collapse of the Fourth Republic and the return of de Gaulle as the man who would save France for the second time took place in a seemingly democratic procedure, the events that preceded it were much more similar to a coup d'état. The army was the principal actor in this drama. The military command became exasperated by the governments of the Fourth Republic and what it perceived as their weakness in facing the FLN. That, and the army's growing involvement in areas normally under civilian authority in Algeria, caused the command to act in order to keep Algeria French by calling for the comeback of General de Gaulle, whom the army's commanders trusted. The eventual return of de Gaulle to power and the establishment of the Fifth Republic brought hope to the army, which could not bear to see its military achievements annulled by "feeble" politicians. Quite soon, though, its commanders realized that the man whom they brought to power to keep Algeria French was determined to dismantle the French empire in Africa; first, de Gaulle offered full autonomy to the territories of AOF, a decision that led to the independence of Guinea in October 1958. Next, he negotiated with the FLN and put an end to the 132-year control of Algeria. The army was thus faced with a whole new reality within which it had to find ways to keep control of AOF. This was a reality that changed rapidly within a very short period of time. Certain terms, such as "colonialism," were suddenly conceived as pejorative and were replaced by more egalitarian, even if far from accurate, terms such as "cooperation." The army lost control over entire territories now ruled by African governments, some of which saw the French military presence as obstructing their sovereignty and demanded the withdrawal of French army units. Even when French units were allowed to stay, the officers found themselves training and advising the same units they had once used to command.

In February 1958 the military command in Algeria decided to bombard the Tunisian village of Sakiet without official permission from the French government. This action, which cost the lives of a large number of inno-cent civilians, was performed to prevent Tunisian aid to the FLN. The French government was too weak to rebuke the army, but it succumbed to international pressure and allowed British and American mediators to investigate the area that had been bombarded. This move enraged the senior military commanders. On May 13, 1958, during a memorial for three French soldiers who were captured and executed by the FLN, the French *colons* (settlers) who attended the ceremony began to riot and attacked the office of the governor-general in Algiers. The army did not try to stop them and instead called for the return of de Gaulle to power so that order in Algeria could be restored. The military commanders refused to see Pierre Pflimlin, the intended prime minister, in power because of his willingness to negotiate with the FLN. The Committee of Public Safety was established in Algeria and quickly took over the authority of the civilian administration. On May 22 the army staged a coup d'état in Corsica, and the French government was in a state of panic. The generals in Algeria also planned a similar coup in France. In the meantime, de Gaulle declared his willingness to take power, ensuring worried parliament members that he did not intend to begin a career as a dictator at the age of sixty-seven and refusing to condemn the army's actions, stating that such an approach would harm his status as an arbiter. On May 27 Foreign Minister René Pleven summed up the situation as follows: "We are the legal government, but what do we govern? The minister for Algeria cannot enter Algeria. The minister for the Sahara cannot go to the Sahara. The minister of information has no control over the police. The minister of defense is not obeyed by the army."[4] The assembly had to decide whether to give in to the military pressure and bring de Gaulle back to power without elections, or resist and risk a coup d'état in France. A left-wing Gaullist member explained to the hesitant assembly: "You are not abandoning power—it has abandoned you."[5] In June 1958, after eliminating all technical and parliamentarian obstacles, the politically unstable Fourth Republic gave way to the Fifth Republic, with de Gaulle as its leader. A new age in French political history had begun.

The events of May 1958 left a deep impression on other parts of the French empire. The military command in AOF, as well as the colonial administration, followed them attentively. On May 16, 1958, Gen. Gabriel Bourgund, the superior commander of the French forces in AOF, threw a cocktail party with his wife celebrating their imminent departure at the end of Bourgund's two-year term. Up until the last moment there were rumors circulating that Gaston Cusin, the high commissioner of the federation, would not attend the party due to the tension between him and the military command. Cusin did arrive finally, but as the British consul in Dakar reported to his superiors, most guests, who belonged to the military, treated him coldly, and he felt quite isolated.[6]

The background for this tension, which apparently ruined the party for the high commissioner, was the ongoing crisis in Algeria. Cusin, who according to the British consul had joined the French resistance during World War II and therefore was an ardent admirer of de Gaulle, was nonetheless rather upset by the course the events in Algeria were taking and was worried that the rebellio.⟍ ⟍blems in his otherwise rather calm territory. Immediat⟍ ⟍vents, Cusin spoke on Radio Dakar and delivered a clear warning to the armed forces in the federation who, again according to the British consul, overwhelmingly supported the generals in Algeria. Cusin declared that he would not tolerate defiance on the part of civilian and military personnel. He specifically forbade any marches in support of the generals in Algeria, as he was worried that these would spark an African response, specifically from the UGTAN workers' organization, and might result in clashes and disorder. This speech deeply insulted Bourgund, who responded by declaring that the army needed no reminder of its duties.[7]

This report of a British outsider reflects the deep tensions between the civilian and military authorities in AOF, each with their different sets of concerns and worries. The high commissioner, who had apprehensively followed the events in Algeria and saw how enraged settlers could bring about a military take-over of what was left of the civilian authority there, was certainly worried that similar riots might erupt in his own territory. Gaullist or not, he could not afford to lose control over the federation by allowing the army to implement measures similar to those taken in Algeria.

Although the May 1958 crisis was relatively short and ended in a calm transfer of power to de Gaulle, it had left a mark on the army and on its African soldiers. The military contempt toward the civilian administration in Algeria and the official governments of the Fourth Republic had certainly impressed some of the African officers serving at the time. As we shall see at the end of this chapter, after independence these African officers would show the same contempt toward their own governments and would be convinced that weak and quarrelling politicians should be replaced by the army, which was supposedly apolitical and represented the "true interests" of the nation. These ideas were certainly not born in postcolonial Africa. African officers who performed military coups in the 1960s and 1970s found a convenient example in the French army of the late 1950s.

The Army and the Political Developments in AOF:
From the Community to Independence

On December 1, 1958, the units of the former Tirailleurs Sénégalais were scheduled to officially lose their pejorative misnomer and be integrated into the infantry regiments of the marines (RIM). African infantrymen considered this a major achievement, as this transfer meant that their prestige would now be equal to that of the *originaires* and metropolitan troops. The results of the 1958 referendum, which de Gaulle initiated upon his return to power, undermined this important triumph.[8]

De Gaulle's return to power in June and the establishment of the Fifth Republic put an end to the May 1958 crisis, and both events were greeted with enthusiasm by the military authorities in AOF.[9] Soon after, however, de Gaulle began speaking of a new federal or confederal structure for the French Union based on a freely negotiated contract with the overseas territories. The result was a referendum that would allow all the territories to vote on whether they would like to stay within the framework of a Franco-African Community with full autonomy or opt for immediate independence.[10] This new colonial policy introduced unprecedented challenges to the military command in AOF.

African political leaders presented de Gaulle with a list of demands pertaining to this new structure. They wanted recognition of the right to self-determination, full autonomy for all territories, economic support from France, and the right of the various territories to decide whether to join the community separately or as a federation with other territories. Their main demand for the right to self-determination was immediately denied. During a tour to AEF, de Gaulle promised that territories that would vote for the community and later decide to opt for independence would be allowed to do so while maintaining links with France.[11] De Gaulle made sure to warn African leaders that territories that would opt for immediate independence would suffer serious consequences. This warning helped persuade most African leaders to encourage a favorable vote. Sekou Touré, Guinea's leader, was not deterred by this threat, and his territory was the only one to reject de Gaulle's community. The decision to count the September 1958 referendum votes based upon individual territories rather than on a federal basis enabled Guinea to gain immediate independence after 94 percent of its voters rejected the community. All the other territories voted with a decisive majority for joining the community. After the vote, de Gaulle became president of the republic and the community, and the Ministry for Overseas France was replaced with the Ministry of Cooperation.[12]

The referendum and its results changed the political reality in AOF, and although the military authorities expressed no formal objection to the idea, this new reality caused them several difficulties, about which they complained in official reports. One of the major complaints mentioned the difficulty the new situation had created for maintaining order in the various territories of the community. The Franco-African Community replaced the French Union. As the French Union ceased to exist, the army—which was supposed to serve it—became the army of the community. The African territorial governments were supposed to be responsible for fulfilling the needs of the strategic bases and of the military infrastructure. These governments were also supposed to guarantee public order, assisted by the local police forces, which were at their disposal. They had control over part of the gendarmerie, but the gendarmes maintained their military status and could be employed only according to the rules of their units. In case of serious trouble, the head of the territorial government could invite the army to intervene, but under no circumstances could he control these forces, which remained under the military authority.

Inevitably, the army lost part of the control it had before the establishment of the community. In principle, it was able to maintain order in the various territories only at the request of the African head of government. Its official role was reduced to protecting the borders of the federation against external enemies, a mission the army had to implement mainly at the northern border of Mauritania. In order to allow itself some measure of control over the internal security in the states of the community, the army made sure that it would be allowed to intervene in case of subversion within a territory, if led by an external factor.[13] As we have seen previously, the military authorities saw all African anticolonial activities as influenced by an external factor. So, in fact, this addition to the terms of the community accorded the army much more freedom of action.

As much as the newly established community created difficulties for the army, it was Guinea's decision to opt for independence that the military authorities in AOF considered as the real danger. This decision, and even more so the French reaction to Guinea's position, separated this country from the rest of the community members both legally and politically. Mairi MacDonald maintains that Guinea's leader, Touré, began creating an ideology of independence only a few months before the vote, and even after he rejected the community he still hoped for some sort of cooperation in the areas of defense, diplomatic relations, currency, and higher education. It was, in fact, de Gaulle's reaction, which was directed by vengeance and by a desire to prove that Guinea was not ready for independence, that increased Touré's ideological fervor.[14] Elizabeth Schmidt shows that the French were so adamant in their attempts to dissuade Guinea from voting against the community that even before the vote they took several steps toward total desertion of the territory. French teachers who were supposed to return to Guinea after the summer break were detained until the results of the referendum were known, which made it difficult to open the school year in Guinea. Civil servants vacationing in France received similar orders, and discussion about the new credit available for Guinea was suspended. France began to treat Guinea as a hostile territory even before the referendum and its results. After the referendum, these preliminary warning actions turned into a radical vengeance campaign during which the French severed all of its economic ties with Guinea, suspending all bank credits, development assistance, and most cooperative projects. Technical services were sabotaged. Telephone wires were cut, even in the main government building. Military camps were stripped of their equipment and hospitals of their medicines. Although independence was supposed to be a legitimate option in the referendum, France refused to recognize the independence of Guinea even after the United States urged France to do so. France's vindictive reaction and its insistence on isolating Guinea internationally eventually left the new nation little choice but to become closer to the Soviet Union and the Eastern Bloc.[15]

The army's horror at this political development can be inferred from a military report written after Guinea's independence in which the ex-AOF federation was described as "amputated."[16] Guinea was the traditional place of recruitment for the French forces in the federation, and a great number of Guinean soldiers were serving in Algeria. The army had to evacuate Guinea within two months and to demobilize five thousand soldiers. It also had to improvise the recruitment of four thousand soldiers from other territories to make up for this loss.[17]

The Guinean decision caused the African governments of the states remaining in the community much concern about the opposition parties in their territories, and they continuously called upon the army to ensure their authority in the face of this opposition. The army was also worried by Guinea's relations with the Eastern Bloc and specifically by the purchase of weapons from Czechoslovakia in April 1959. This concern turned the borders with Guinea, which had until recently been within French territory, into a dangerous area that demanded special attention. The establishment of the Ghana-Guinea Union in November 1958 also alarmed the French authorities. Ghana, formerly the British colony of the Gold Coast, had been a source of deep concern ever since it was clear that it too was marching toward independence. The close ties between this ex-British colony and Guinea were therefore seen as especially dangerous. The only consolation to the military command was the difficult economic and social problems the young country faced, which reduced its ability to stir trouble in the diplomatic arena. The military report covering this period noted with joy the rupture between the Senegalese and Guinean worker unions.[18]

One of the negative consequences of Guinean independence, as far as the military was concerned, was its influence on the other countries in the community. The military authorities were deeply concerned that Guinea's independence would influence other countries to follow the same path. Shortly after the establishment of the community, on April 4, 1959, Senegal and French Sudan formed the Mali federation. Although this new entity stayed officially within the framework of the community, it was one of the early signs of the community's demise. As far as the army was concerned, French Sudan was the problematic partner in this federation, which was initially supposed to include also Dahomey and Upper Volta. Soon after the founding of the federation, the Sudanese leaders pushed for the establishment of a national army, contrary to the principles of the community. This demand upset General Gardet, who pointed to the harm such a move would cause to the army's morale and dignity. He lamented the fact that soldiers who had once "pacified" a certain territory would now have to evacuate it for the benefit of a national army.[19] Although in October 1958 General Gardet expressed his relief in the face of the obvious tension between Guinea and Mali following the Sudanese government's refusal to accept the Guinean ambassador, concerns were still raised regarding Mali's so-called independent views in the UN and its orientation toward neutrality and even collaboration with the Eastern Bloc, especially with China. Mali's intentions of joining the Afro-Asiatic delegation in the UN were viewed with hostility, as well as its protest against the ongoing French nuclear experiments in Algeria.[20]

The military authorities also followed closely and with great concern the political developments in the other countries belonging to the community. The reports they produced did not focus only on military issues but also dealt with matters that had nothing to do with the army, at least not directly. For instance, one report described the draconian measures that the leader of Niger, Hamani Diori, took against the opposition party in his country, Sawaba, which had objected to the creation of the community and called for independence. These actions, according to the report, left the government the ability to do as it wished. The writer of the report seemed to have been relieved by Diori's undemocratic conduct, but he also sadly noted that the situation was still less than ideal, as some politicians had received financial help from Ghana.[21] The appreciation for Diori's decisive actions against the opposition was later reflected in the French military support of his regime. Yet, as we shall see later in this chapter, when Diori was toppled by a military coup in 1974, the French army did not bother to save him, as he had become a nuisance in their eyes.

The military authorities in the former AOF looked upon the formation of the Mali federation unfavorably, especially because of the independent views manifested by the former French Sudan. It is not surprising, then, that when the federation collapsed on August 19, 1960, the Sudanese leader, Mobido Keita, accused the French authorities of plotting this split. There are various hypotheses regarding the measure of truth in this accusation. As we have seen, the Mali federation caused concern among both military officials and colonial administrators. Obviously, there were internal reasons for the federation's failure, such as the different political cultures of the ruling elites in both countries and the different views regarding the mode of relations with the former colonizer. Using recently opened documentation, Alexander Keese closely examined the events that led to the breakup of the Mali federation. He demonstrates that shortly before the decisive night of August 19, the French were certain that the federation's crisis was temporary. The course of events on that night was influenced by the lack of proper army forces in the federation, who may have opted to support the Sudanese leader. The only significant armed unit available was the gendarmerie of Senegal, which was planned to become the gendarmerie of the federation of Mali. The commander of this unit was a French officer by the name of Lt. Col. François Pierre. He was supposed to take orders from the prime minister of Senegal, although according to the planned changes he could also be called upon by the president of the federation, a position in which the Sudanese leader, Keita, was serving at the time. But as these changes had not yet gone into effect, when Lieutenant Colonel Pierre received a phone call on the night of August 19 from Keita, ordering him to meet him regarding an urgent matter, he chose to follow the rules and report this call to his direct superior, the Senegalese prime minister, Mamadou Dia. This decision led to the arrest of Keita and other Sudanese officials, their expulsion from Senegal, and the final breakup of the federation. Keese maintains that this episode in the history of the decolonization of AOF demonstrates that even if the French wished to influence the course of events, it was difficult for them to conspire and scheme in such a rapidly changing political reality.[22] What is also relevant to our discussion in this story is how radically the situation of French military commanders had changed since 1958. A French officer who had previously commanded an African unit within the French colonial army was now obligated to obey African authorities.

The disbanding of the Mali federation did not improve the situation the army had to deal with in the region. In some ways it even made it worse. After the split, Senegal agreed to sign military cooperation agreements with France, but Sudan, which now became the Republic of Mali, refused to do so. To add insult to injury, on January 20, 1961, while speaking before the official diplomatic corps in Bamako, Keita demanded the immediate evacuation of the French troops from his territory. Keita expressed his willingness to cooperate with France but explained that his country's wish for sovereignty and nonalliance necessitated the withdrawal of the former colonizer's troops. As we shall see, unlike Mali, other territories chose to keep their military ties with France. Mali's refusal to do so was an especially bitter pill to swallow, as, like French Guinea, French Sudan was also an important source of African soldiers throughout the entire colonial period.[23] As requested, the army had withdrawn its troops by July 1961. The disbanding of the Mali federation also encouraged other members of the community to opt for independence. While Côte d'Ivoire, Dahomey, and Niger signed defense agreements with France, Upper Volta agreed only to sign a cooperation agreement and, like Mali, demanded the withdrawal of French troops, which it termed "foreign troops." In the military report, this term appears in quotation marks, emphasizing the improper and even insulting choice of adjective.[24]

In the military reports for the period of 1958-60 there is no doubt about the emotional reaction to the fact that the French army, which had once conquered, or "pacified," according to military jargon, the territories of AOF was now considered by some of their leaders as an unwanted foreign army. Even the term "cooperation" was somewhat resented, as it implied the existence of two separate parties.[25] The military commanders of the forces in AOF were reluctant to see their units as external to the territory of former AOF. Nevertheless, the reality around them was changing rapidly, and it was necessary to act swiftly in order to retain at least part of their control over this territory. Therefore, despite their initial hostility toward the idea of establishing national armies in the newly independent countries, the military authorities found it essential to be involved in the formation of these armies and to formulate different kinds of military agreements to replace the former colonial bonds with these territories.

Military Agreements and the Establishment of the National Armies

As we have seen so far, the military command in AOF was far from pleased with the political reforms that resulted in independence and the dismantling of the colonial units to create national armies. Still, this was the new reality that had to be dealt with. At the time of independence the colonial army had to be disbanded, and its troops had to be reassigned, unit by unit or sometimes on an individual basis, to their country of origin. The dissolution of these troops, which were comprised of approximately 61,000 African soldiers, would produce some fourteen national armies in AOF and AEF.[26]

Formal independence, however, did not mark the moment in which everything had changed. Sovereignty was gained gradually and had begun four years earlier with the formulation of the Loi-Cadre. Independence was just another step in this process, and it certainly did not dissolve overnight the colonial ties in the cultural, political, economic, and military spheres. The colonial dependency of the newly independent countries on their former colonizer was too deep to vanish so quickly. The military sphere was crucial in this respect, as military control ensured all other forms of domination.

In spite of the necessity to dissolve the colonial units, France could ensure its military control after independence in three ways: military assistance agreements; defense agreements; and direct military interventions, usually in support of the recognized local authorities.[27]

Surprisingly enough, there was not much correlation between French military interventions in postcolonial Africa and the African states with which it signed the two types of agreements. During the first thirty years of independence, France had intervened in sub-Saharan Africa thirty-five times, but in most cases these interventions did not involve states with which it held either assistance or defense agreements.[28] In any case, as these interventions are beyond the chronological scope of this book, I will focus here on the first two tools France had used to ensure the continuation of French military control over its ex-colonies: military assistance agreements focused mainly on establishing, training, and maintaining the African national armies; and defense agreements, which aimed at gaining control over wider spheres and therefore further infringed on African sovereignty.

The military assistance agreements were initially a vehicle to assist the formation of new African armies, but later they evolved into an ongoing cooperation network, with African officers educated either in France or in French-sponsored military schools in Africa. The Ministry of Cooperation, which replaced the Ministry of Overseas France, was in charge of the military cooperation. This domain remained the army's responsibility under the charge of a two-star general and a team of thirty officers. The agreements that were signed with the ex-colonies concerned three main areas: dispatching French military cadres to advise and train African military personnel; hosting African military trainees at French military schools or sponsoring African training centers; and assisting African armies by directly supplying equipment.[29]

During the first three years of independence, separate national armies were established in all ex-AOF states. According to the French military report of 1962, the African governments tried to give their national armies a character of their own, different from that of the colonial army. They also wished to reduce expenses and use their armies as much as possible for immediate missions of maintaining public order. The first national army to be created was that of Mali. Even while the short-lived Mali federation still existed, the armies of Sudan and of Senegal were formed separately, a fact that casts doubt over the willingness of both countries to preserve their federation in the long run and demonstrates the deep mistrust that existed between its two members even before the its final collapse.[30]

As we have seen, after the collapse of the federation, Sudan, which now became Mali, severed all military relations with France. In response to its demand to withdraw all French troops, France ceased all funding for the upkeep of the Malian army starting January 1, 1961. Malian soldiers serving in Algeria and in Cameroon were quickly repatriated. The French army rapidly pulled out of Mali, leaving by December 1960 only thirty officers, all belonging to the medical corps and working alongside local army forces. These remaining officers were recalled to France following the demand of the Malian government. Although this demand was expected, the French daily *Le Monde* still described it as an unfriendly gesture. Military relations between Mali and France finally came to an end on September 5, 1961.[31]

All other ex-AOF colonies, excluding Guinea, signed military assistance agreements with France, accepting support in equipment and training. Gen. Michel de Brebisson, whose official title was changed after independence to "the delegate for the defense of Overseas Zone number 1" (the new name for the ex-AOF territory), was not particularly impressed by most national armies of the ex-AOF states. The only two that had some potential, according to him, were the armies of Senegal and Ivory Coast. The Senegalese army was undoubtedly the most valued in his report. It initially included 2,500 men but in February 1961 had adopted an ambitious plan of reaching 3,500 and even 7,000 soldiers at a later stage. Brebisson estimated that the Senegalese army was a relatively cohesive force, solid and significant, that included specialists trained in the French army. The general also noted that thanks to a strict selection process and a more lively national sentiment than in other African countries, the quality of recruitment for 1960 was excellent. He appreciated the high level of morale among Senegalese military men who were proud of their previous service in the French army and kept excellent relations with their former French comrades.

The general was also pleased with the Ivoirian army, which was expanding quickly and was already the same size as the Senegalese. Although it lacked specialist personnel and resources, was less cohesive, and depended greatly on French technical aid, Brebisson predicted a bright future for it, similar to that of the Senegalese army.

Another army that the general seemed to appreciate, at least potentially, was that of Upper Volta, established in November 1961. It consisted only of 750 men but had 24 officers, good recruitment, and professional reservists and therefore had the potential of becoming one of the best armies in Africa, according to Brebisson. The general feared that the main hindrance to that army's success was the country's extreme poverty, and he suspected that its government might not lead a wise and stable military policy. Therefore, he concluded, the Voltaic army would never be brilliant. The armies of the other ex-AOF states—Mauritania, Niger, Dahomey, and the ex-mandate of Togo—did not impress the general at all. He saw them as no more than local militias, small and lacking in professional personnel and a sense of military duty. These insignificant forces remained entirely dependent on French military assistance.

The general's conclusion from his survey of the new African armies was that although the political evolution in AOF made it necessary to form national armies, this step diminished the potential of the military forces in the federation without re-creating a force equivalent to that of the dismantled units. Therefore, the military ability of the forces stationed in AOF could not be compared to that of the forces stationed there three years earlier. There was no longer a united command in the federation, and the value of the forces greatly decreased. The armies at the disposal of the new states were a symbol of their sovereignty, and they could perhaps help them maintain public order. In case of serious difficulties, the general warned, most of these forces, except the Senegalese and the Ivoirian armies, would be useless.[32]

One way to overcome this weakness was to persuade the new African governments to sign defense agreements with France in addition to the military assistance agreements. The idea behind this type of agreement was to ensure French control over the major military decisions in the African countries, thus turning the ex-colonies into consensual zones of influence. In the framework of defense agreements, internal security remained in the hands of local authorities, although France could provide some additional assistance upon request. France had the mission of guaranteeing overall defense, providing technical cooperation, and supporting local forces in case of aggression or subversion. The specific conditions regarding military interventions usually remained confidential, but they were based on two elements: a widespread network of French bases, and light and mobile French forces in the host country. The presence of French troops was one of the clauses in these agreements that infringed the most on African sovereignty. The countries that decided not to sign such agreements usually resented this presence. Some of these agreements also gave France privileged access to strategic materials and minerals, including uranium. France also gained a monopoly over the supply of military equipment to the new armies.

During the first three years of independence, all ex-AOF states except Guinea, Mali, and Upper Volta signed a defense agreement with France in addition to the military assistance agreement. These agreements enabled France to dismantle the least essential part of its costly colonial network of bases in these areas without compromising its influence and its ability to send forces to protect desired African regimes from external and, even more so, internal threats. The weaker partners in these agreements, the African governments, could ensure French support and in this manner consolidate their bases of power. Nevertheless, France had the liberty of choosing to refrain from action, and its support was not automatic. These agreements allowed it to control African leaders who knew that they would receive French support only as long as they cooperated with its political demands.[33] In 1974, for example, the president of Niger, Hamani Diori, attempted to renegotiate the price of uranium with France due to his country's dire economic situation. This endeavor to change the rules of the game did not please the French, and when a short while later a coup d'état against Diori's regime was led by Lt. Col. Seyni Kountche, a former sergeant in the French colonial army, the French forces stationed near the president's palace watched the events from the sidelines and did not intervene. It was obvious that the French government was in fact happy to get rid of an ally who was beginning to show signs of independence.[34]

The military assistance and defense agreements France had signed with its ex-colonies in AOF filled the vacuum created by the dismantling of the colonial units. Although, as we have seen, the army found it difficult to get used to the idea of renouncing its colonial vision to give way to African independence, it eventually accepted this changed reality and made the best of it.

While the focus of this book is on the French military perspective, the story will not be complete without considering the ways in which African soldiers and veterans perceived the political transformations that had eventually led their countries to independence and changed the course of their professional career, as well as their lives in general.

The Transfer to Independence and the African Troops

Malic Guèye served in Indochina and witnessed the defeat in Dien Bien Phu. He was later sent to Morocco and, when this country gained its independence in 1956, was transferred to Algeria, where he won a decoration for his service. He served three tours of duty in Algeria and during the last one was repatriated to Senegal at the demand of its government in order to serve in its new national army. Like almost all other African soldiers, he did not have a say in the matter. When asked in what respects his service in the army of independent Senegal was different from that in the French colonial army, he said: "In the French army I saw the world. I had served in different and varied places. In the Senegalese army it was always Dakar-Casamance-Dakar. It was boring."[35] This short paragraph summarizes the African soldiers' career course transformation following the political developments in AOF. What Guèye describes here is actually the closing of a door to a much wider world. Instead of serving in an imperial army, he was now transferred to the small army of an independent African country in which all he could hope to see was the problematic area of Casamance on the southern border with the Gambia or the border area with the northern neighbor, Mauritania, which had been in conflict with bordering Senegal after independence. Being prevented from seeing the world was only one facet of this transformation. Saliou Badji was instructed to leave the French army only in 1962, since the demobilization of Africans was gradual and finally ended in 1964. While he then joined the Senegalese army, he felt betrayed by the French. He had joined the French army because he wanted a secure job and a salary that would help him support his parents, as he was their only child. He resented the fact that no one had asked him whether he would like to stay in the French army. After two years of service he decided to leave the Senegalese army and found it extremely difficult to find a job. After a while, he managed to find employment as a gardener.[36]

Some African soldiers, though, found it easier to adjust to the new political reality. Marc Guèye, who served in Indochina until 1955 and then in AOF, was released from the French army at the rank of chief sergeant in 1963 and found it easy to integrate into the Senegalese civil service.[37] Papa Figaro Diagne also did not seem to mind this transfer so much. He transferred to the Senegalese army in 1962 and served there until the end of his contract. He was pleased by the educational opportunities he had received in the French army and used them to his advantage in his civilian life. He also appreciated the fact that he had received pensions from both armies after his final demobilization.[38]

In his memoirs, Mamadou Niang recounts the festive welcome he received in his hometown, Thiès, when he was demobilized in 1961. He was greeted with songs and dances, and his mother was proud that "her baby" fought in the French army for France. One of his young nieces did not recognize him at first, as he had been away for over two years, but later she was happy to sit on his lap and listen to his stories. Other people who gathered to welcome him were also eager to hear all about France. The women sang traditional songs praising his ancestors, and Niang, who seems to have been deeply satisfied by his service in the French army, felt that his long stay away from home had alienated him from his traditions. After a short stay at home, he decided to join the Senegalese army. What is clear from this description is that Niang did not see a contradiction between his patriotism for France and his pride in serving in its army, and the same patriotism and pride he felt toward the newly independent Senegal and its army.[39]

Even if some African soldiers managed to adapt to the political upheavals that caused abrupt changes to their plans and their lives in general, the fact that such a major decision—whether to stay in the French army or join the army of their country of origin—was not in their hands was at least potentially a source of distress. This was probably even more annoying due to the fact that only a short while earlier, Guinean soldiers had indeed had the right to choose between these two options. While Touré demanded the immediate repatriation of all Guinean soldiers serving in Algeria after the results of the referendum were known, the French military decided to leave the choice up to the soldiers. Voting on this matter took place in October 1958. While it seems that the choice given to Guinean soldiers, a privilege that other African soldiers did not receive at a later stage, afforded them some control over their destiny, this control was rather precarious. In fact, both options—repatriation or continued service until the end of contract—proved problematic for the soldiers. Guinean soldiers who opted for repatriation lost their salary from the French army and some of their pension rights due to the suspension of their contracts. They had returned to a country in which they had no political ties and little economic security. To make matters worse, they soon found out that their leader, Touré, was highly suspicious of them and had put many of them under constant surveillance, as he often suspected them of spying for the French. On the other hand, Touré was even more hostile toward those soldiers who chose to complete their service in the French army. Some were not able to return home until the end of his rule in 1984 and had to find refuge in other African countries. These soldiers also found themselves in an impossible situation regarding their citizenship. They had lost their French status following the departure of their country from the community but were refused Guinean citizenship because of their decision to stay in the French army. They were able to apply for French citizenship, but this was a long, tedious, and not always successful process. Both groups of soldiers lost their access to their pensions in Guinea after demobilization due to a disagreement between the French and Touré. The French insisted on transferring the pensions directly to the veterans, while Touré wanted control over the money in order to gain control over the veterans.[40]

We can see, then, that even the option to choose was often no more than an illusion, and the former AOF territories' independence would change the destiny of African soldiers. It is, of course, possible to claim that soldiers never have much control over their destinies. African soldiers rarely engaged in politics or even discussed it. They were not involved in the political debates that had eventually shaped the path the French African colonies had taken. African veterans, on the other hand, played an active role in these debates, and although they claimed to be "above politics," they were highly engaged in political activity during these crucial years.

African Veterans and the Political Debates of the 1950s

In his book *Native Sons*, Gregory Mann refers to the debate regarding the veterans' role in the national struggle and asks what made this idea so necessary in the first place. He argues that, "collectively, veterans did not seek independence *for* a nation so much as they sought independence *from* an emerging idea of a nation, specifically one in which their claims to privilege might carry little weight."[41]

As we have seen, as soon as World War II was over, the African veterans' main aim was their struggle for equality and protection of gained privileges. In this respect they were no different from any other sector within African society at the time, and yet there was a major difference between them and others. Unlike workers or teachers, African veterans could use the valuable discourse of brotherhood in arms and shared sacrifices to demand their equality, which they had won with their blood. Interestingly enough, it is the same discourse used during the recent decade by African veterans, as well as by African migrants in France who had nothing to do with military service, in their attempt to gain equality within French society. In using their military service during the two world wars as the basis for their demands for equality, veterans positioned themselves above politics. They demanded political rights in a seemingly apolitical way. As we have seen in chapter 3, this strategy proved to be extremely efficient.

It is important to bear in mind that African veterans did not speak in one voice. There were differences in the political views of veterans from different territories and between those who were close to the urban centers and took part in veterans' politics and those who lived in rural areas and were physically far from any political activity. I will examine here the official discourse of the main veterans' organization in Dakar, Fédération des Anciens Combattants, as it was reflected in the organization's journal, *La Voix de Combattants et des Victimes de Guerre*. This organization's general secretary and the force behind it until his retirement in 1957 was Papa Seck Douta, who was mentioned in chapter 3. Seck was a teacher at Malic Sy School in Dakar. He was born in Saint Louis in 1887 and therefore was considered an *originaire* and held French citizenship. In 1946 he began a political career within the framework of the RDA, but his political opinions became more moderate, and he began to support the West African branch of the French Socialist Party (the SFIO) and its leader, Lamine Guèye. While serving as the association's general secretary he tried to maintain political neutrality in order to represent all veterans. As noted, his organization's so-called apolitical stance was not supported by all veterans and territorial organizations, such as the organization in French Sudan, which often diverged from this line and backed the RDA's political line.

Despite these divisions, it can be argued that most veterans adopted a so-called apolitical approach during the 1950s and attempted to further improve their conditions within the existent colonial framework. Although they had achieved their main aim of equating the pensions in 1950, they did not consider the battle over. In theory, veterans were entitled to many advantages, such as chief positions, interest-free loans, subsidized housing, and so on, but in reality these advantages were not always easily realized. Veterans were often frustrated by the manner in which African society perceived them—as people who had served France and not their own society and who had largely benefited personally from this service. Veterans felt that people around them envied and therefore resented them and that this animosity had no basis.[42] Nevertheless, they continued to struggle for their rights and generally believed that their relations with the French military authorities should be carefully maintained. Cooperation was seen as the best strategy. This did not prevent the veterans from seeking alliances among African politicians in order to advance their interests. African veterans actually conducted what was basically a trade union struggle, maneuvering between the military authorities and African politicians while clinging to what they defined as an apolitical position. An examination of the veterans' main journal in this period allows us a clear example of this strategy. Although our aim is to examine the veterans' attitude to the main political transformations of the late 1950s, it is essential to go back farther, to the late 1940s and early 1950s, in order to better understand this attitude.

The journal's first issue was published on April 1, 1948, and its last one on January 2, 1959. It was first published from Malic Sy School, where Seck had worked as a teacher, and later moved to better accommodations in Dakar. The journal was financed by the main veterans' organization mentioned above, while the organization's budget consisted only of membership fees, which covered just above half of its expenses and administrative support.[43]

From its very first issues the journal's articles used a discourse of brotherhood in arms that demanded equal rights for the veterans based on the soldiers' sacrifices during the two world wars. It was also combined with another discourse that evolved mainly after the Vichy episode in AOF: the concept of "true France." This concept meant that all cases of discrimination and racist behavior toward African soldiers and veterans stemmed from people who acted against the principles of an ostensibly "true France," which was represented during World War II by de Gaulle and the Resistance.[44] To these two discourses one can add the journal's tendency to use military terms derived from the battlefield. The journal's editors saw themselves as leaders in a new kind of veterans' battle: the battle for their rights. This is best illustrated by an ad published in March 1949 aimed at encouraging readers to persuade their friends to subscribe to the journal: "We are in full battle. To fight one needs weapons. Our journal is a weapon. Make it stronger every day! Find new subscribers for the journal!"[45]

Armed with these two main discourses and a hefty dose of military vocabulary, the journal had set out to battle. However, reading the journal's issues since its inception onward, it is possible to detect a certain change of tone and emphasis after 1950, the year in which the African soldiers' pensions were equated to those of the French soldiers. Until 1950 the most recurring complaints were those that referred to cases of discrimination and racist conduct toward soldiers and veterans. The journal distinguished between those individuals who were responsible for the discrimination and what it perceived as the general French approach. Colonial administrators who opposed the rights accorded to veterans were labeled by the journal as non-French, making it clear that a "true Frenchman" cannot be a racist.[46]

When the demand for equal pensions was finally met in 1950, the journal's tone softened considerably, and accusations against military and administrative authorities regarding racism and discriminations diminished significantly. The journal still complained about bureaucratic obstacles that the veterans living in remote areas had to tackle in order to receive their pensions, but it no longer accused the authorities of deliberate discrimination.

The journal not only changed its tone after 1950, it also changed its strategy. Instead of petitioning the colonial authorities complaining about specific incidents, it was now directing all its energy at the African deputies in the French National Assembly. In any case, the veterans' general discourse, of brotherhood gained with blood, did not change. Again, the African soldiers' participation in the two world wars was the basis for the demands made before the African deputies.

From 1951 onward, a permanent section titled "The Activities of Our Deputies" was published on page 2 of the journal. This section described all the African deputies' actions on behalf of the African veterans.[47] African deputies were also reminded of their duty to the veterans every time a new session of the French parliament was opened.[48]

As expected, African deputies who advanced veterans' rights in the French parliament won the journal's recognition and gratitude. The journal published their actions in detail, along with letters of praise from various organizations and occasionally even from the military authorities. Such was the case of Mamba Sano, the Guinean deputy who gave an endless speech in the National Assembly in August 1955 in support of his amendment proposing to augment the budget of the colonial gendarmerie and thus raise the gendarmes' salaries. Sano's efforts to exhaust the members of parliament until they approved his amendment were such that he began his speech with a review of the gendarmerie in the times of the Roman Empire. This long-winded speech, which finally achieved its goal, was quoted in full in the journal along with a letter of praise from the National Gendarmerie.[49]

Not all the articles in the journal were of a positive nature. When the veterans thought it necessary, they did not hesitate to admonish African parliamentarians who hindered or opposed their cause. In September 1953, after seventeen African deputies voted in parliament against an amendment of a law that purported to improve the veterans' benefits, the journal published a blacklist of their names under the title "Our Adversaries." This list included well-known and influential African politicians such as Félix Houphouët-Boigny from Côte d'Ivoire, Mamadou Konaté from French Sudan, and Joseph Apithy from Dahomey.[50]

The veterans' journal saw African deputies not only as a weapon that must be used but also as a group that should be emulated. When the editor explained the importance of joining the veterans' organization, he described a hypothetical encounter with a veteran who raged at the fact that African deputies had managed to get their salaries raised while the veterans remained with the same pensions. The editor explained to the frustrated veteran that this was because African deputies were united and knew how to fight for their rights as a group. Therefore, instead of being angry with the deputies, the veterans should learn from them.[51]

This call for the unification of veterans in order to act in unison, similarly to a trade union, reflects to a large extent the manner in which the Federation of the Veterans of AOF saw its role in the years after World War II. The similarities between the organization and various trade unions that acted in the region at the time are easily detected. There were two basic differences, though, between the veterans and other African workers. First, the veterans' organization at least professed to represent vaster interests than those of its members. One example of this attempt to present the organization as contributing to the general community is a rather defensive article published in October 1951, according to which veterans were seen by the general public as *revendicateurs* (demanding people). The article stated that the veterans' demands were raised because the governments in France did not recognize even their basic rights. It also emphasized that the veterans' organization did not act solely to promote its own interests but contributed to the social life in the country. To demonstrate this claim the author quoted the establishment of social and medical services, summer camps, and homes for the elderly.[52]

The second and more significant difference between the veterans' organization and African trade unions is the former's claim to be above politics. This supposedly apolitical stance is reflected in the refusal of the journal to recommend to its readers whom to vote for in the local elections, although the blacklist that was mentioned earlier may have certainly helped readers decide whom not to vote for.

The organization's attempt to stay out of politics was also reflected in the small number of reports that appeared in the journal on political and military events and the few articles dealing with the political future of the federation. The rare exceptions, such as an article dealing with the future of the French Union written by the journal's editor, Babacar Camara, in 1953, only prove the rule.[53] It is especially surprising that the veterans' journal almost totally ignored the ongoing wars in Indochina and Algeria, though the African soldiers participated in them. Neither the November or December 1954 issue, for instance, mentioned the beginning of hostilities in Algeria. One of the few exceptions is, once again, an article written by the editor, Camara, in which he expressed his anger at the French refusal to respond to what he termed "the modest and legitimate demands of the veterans." Camara noted that this was especially infuriating in light of the fact that African soldiers were concurrently risking their lives in Indochina to save humanity from slavery.[54]

Despite the veterans' pretense of being above politics, it is not possible to conclude that their true position, as reflected in their main journal, was indeed as apolitical as claimed, as it is difficult to separate the veterans' interests from their involvement in politics. The mere defending of their interests was, in fact, a political action. Nevertheless, it is clear that at least until the referendum of 1958, the veterans separated themselves from internal and international politics. This was not simple to do during a time in which the French army and its African soldiers were deeply involved in the wars in Indochina and in Algeria. As discussed above, this military involvement was practically ignored by the veterans' journal. The only wars that were discussed at length were the heroic ones of the past, the two world wars, which served as the moral basis for the veterans' claim for equality.

Independence and Its Repercussions for Veterans

A major diversion from this abstention from a direct discussion of politics and from political recommendations to veterans occurred just before the 1958 referendum for the Franco-African Community. The journal recommended an affirmative vote, claiming that this could not be considered a political stand because de Gaulle was such an important military figure that it was only natural for African veterans to support him.[55] A more plausible explanation for this shift from the so-called apolitical stand is the deep concern of the veterans' organization caused by the prospects of independence. In fact, from 1956 onward it became increasingly difficult for veterans to abstain from a clear stance regarding the political future of AOF. The principle which the Loi-Cadre evoked was the transfer of budget responsibility to African governments, effectively renouncing the practical implications of assimilation and rejecting the right to colonial claims based on a metropolitan standard. This was certainly a warning bell for the veterans, whose entire discourse was based on such claims. At the time it seemed that they had nothing to worry about, as it was difficult to reject the idea of brotherhood in arms, which distinguished the veterans' discourse from other struggles for equality in the federation. But the referendum of 1958 was another step in a direction that threatened veterans' interests. Most veterans voted for the community, since this ensured their relations with France. As Mann shows, even veterans who later advocated independence demanded that some form of association with France be retained.[56]

Just like the military command of AOF, the African veterans had to adjust to a dizzying rate of political transformations that had changed their reality unrecognizably within a few years. They had to cope with the hostility and suspicion of the political elites toward them and redefine their relations with France. The greatest blow to their interests, however, came in the form of article 71 in the French Finance Law of 1960. This article redefined French obligations toward veterans living in countries that had left the French community, freezing their base pension rates in such a way that the pensions of the veterans living in the newly independent states would decline steadily in years to come. According to Mann, this article became the center of the veterans' politics and an important element of French-African relations only when its impact began to be felt, years after it was passed in the French National Assembly. This article saved the French coffers millions, if not billions, of francs. Although this was certainly an unjust measure, it was not vindictive but rather part of a move that began the year before to reduce payments to veterans in general, including French metropolitan ones. This decision affected half a million veterans, one-third of all French veterans.[57]

Even so, it is clear that in the postcolonial period veterans' politics have evolved around this unjust article and the struggle to equate their pensions to those of French veterans. They also focused on the demand that France remember the sacrifices of African veterans and their contribution to its victory in both world wars. Just like the veterans' journal in the 1950s, veterans today continue to ignore the wars of decolonization. This is quite understandable, as the controversial nature of these wars does not suit the veterans' discourse of equal sacrifices for a noble cause. This return to the world wars tends to create a hole in the history of the veterans' relations with France and its army. The period in which veterans felt deep attachment to France and managed to win the battle of equality seems to disappear from the public debate regarding their current struggles. Some academic studies also tend to skip this important period, thus emphasizing the freezing of the pensions as a sign of French ingratitude toward its African soldiers, without even referring to the equation of the pensions ten years before—an achievement that was indeed unique in the political struggles in post–World War II AOF.

Most African veterans concentrated on the struggle to be remembered by France and to be treated with equality and respect. Yet some Africans who had previously served in the French colonial army and had developed a military career in the new national army of their country of origin took active part in military coups in the postcolonial period. These soldiers and officers were the minority, but it is important to consider their role and the influence of their military service for France on their postcolonial actions.

Veterans' Involvement in Military Coups in Ex-AOF Territories

On the morning of December 17, 1967, Gen. Christophe Soglo, who was one of the young African officers in charge of the BAA of Indochina mentioned in chapter 4 during the Indochina war, found his house surrounded by a unit of paratroopers. Their aim was to force Soglo to resign from his post as the leader of the seven-year-old republic of Benin (formerly Dahomey), a post he had acquired following a second coup d'état he had performed two years earlier, the first being in 1963, only three years after independence. Quite understandably, Soglo chose not to argue with the paratroopers and decided to withdraw from involvement in politics altogether. Interestingly enough, the motive for his overthrow was his supposed weakness in the face of strikers who were upset by his decision to cut salaries by 25 percent and to cancel family allocations from the sixth child onward. When Soglo took over power for the first time in 1963, an accusation of weakness would have sounded quite surprising. The motive for the two coups Soglo had led was the inability of the three leading politicians in Benin—Hubert Maga, Sourou Nigan Apithy, and Justin Tomentin Ahomadegbé–to come to terms and run the country efficiently. Soglo saw these politicians as people who did not represent the nation's interests and were not able to rise above their insignificant quarrels. We can see here a reflection of the French military idea of the army-nation relations discussed in chapter 6, which presented the army as the only true guard of the nation's interests. Protests from trade unions further destabilized the regime, and in October 1963 the army, led by Soglo, took over. The French local army commander based in Dahomey assured the French that the protests were not anti-French, and as a result, the French army did not stand behind the threatened regime.[58] The fact that Soglo was once a trusted officer in the French army probably contributed to this decision.

After his first intervention, Soglo prepared the ground for new elections and promulgated a new constitution. He then withdrew from power, returning authority to civilian rule. As the conflicts between the different political groups in Benin continued to paralyze the regime, Soglo intervened again in November 1965, demanding the creation of one party. This time he tried to cling to power longer, but, as we have seen, he was overthrown by another coup d'état, which was certainly not the last one in Benin's turbulent postcolonial history.[59]

Soglo was not the only French-trained African officer to perform a coup d'état in his country. In Upper Volta, when manifestations threatened to topple the RDA, the army was the only institution that was able to fill the political vacuum that was created, as the party oppressed all opposition groups. Lt. Col. Sangoulé Lamizana took power and imprisoned President Maurice Yaméogo. In Mali Lt. Moussa Traoré overthrew Mobido Keita's regime in November 1968 and brought the country back to the franc zone. As we have seen, the French army supported a similar coup d'état in Niger against Hamani Diori by abstaining from protecting the president. On the whole, during the first two decades of independence, twelve Africans who had served in the French colonial army before independence executed coups d'état in ex-AOF territories.[60]

Table 2. Military coups d'état in the former territories of French West Africa

DATE	COUNTRY	OVERTHROWN PRESIDENT	NEW PRESIDENT
January 13 1963	Togo	Sylvanus Olympio	Nicholas Grunitzky
October 20 1963	Benin (Dahomey)	Hubert Maga	Christophe Soglo
December 22 1965	Benin (Dahomey)	Sourou N. Apithy	Christophe Soglo
January 4 1966	Upper Volta (today Burkina Faso)	Maurice Yameogo	Sangoule Lamizana
January 13 1967	Togo	Nicholas Grunitzky	Etienne Eyadema
December 17 1967	Benin (Dahomey)	Christophe Soglo	Maurice Kouandété

November 18 1968	Mali (ex-French Sudan)	Mobido Keita	Moussa Traoré
December 10 1969	Benin (Dahomey)	Emile Zinsou	Maurice Kouandété
October 26 1972	Benin (Dahomey)	Justin Ahomadegbe	Mathieu Kerekou
February 8 1974	Upper Volta (today Burkina Faso)	Gérard Ouedraogo	Sangoule Lamizana
April 15 1974	Niger	Hamani Diori	Seyni Kountche
October 25 1980	Upper Volta (today Burkina Faso)	Sangoule Lamizana	Saye Zerbo

Source: Jean-Pierre Pabanel, *Les coups d'état militaires en Afrique noire* (Paris: L'Harmattan, 1984), 177–78.

Military coups in sub-Saharan Africa stemmed from a variety of reasons and were linked primarily to the weakness of the states in question and that of the civil societies within these states, as well as a severe lack of cohesion and unifying identity. I propose that the ability of relatively young officers, serving in small and underequipped armies, to overthrow civilian regimes with comparative ease stems primarily from the experiences of these officers in the French army. One experience that no doubt influenced them most was witnessing the May 1958 crisis and the return of de Gaulle, always regarded as a military figure more than a politician, to power with the help of the army. It is also related to the way in which the French army ensured its control over the territories of ex-AOF with the help of cooperation and defense agreements. In addition to reflecting the weakness of the African independent states, these military coups also mirrored the continuity in the French army influence over the territory of ex-AOF and its ability to allow coups against leaders who no longer served French interests. In this respect it is quite clear that after the initial shock of the military command in AOF at the political reforms that undermined French colonial control over the federation, the French army managed to secure its privileged position there long after independence.

The Price of Independence

As we have seen in this chapter and the previous one, the French army deeply resented the political reforms that allowed a growing autonomy in the territories of AOF and eventually led to their full independence. The military command in AOF firmly endorsed the myth of a benevolent colonialism, which had supposedly enabled two societies—French and African—to cohabit peacefully and share one vocation. Unlike in Indochina and Algeria, opposition to colonial rule in AOF was usually nonviolent, and the main goal of most African political leaders was equality within a French framework rather than independence. The reason this struggle led eventually to independence was the high price the French government had to pay for this kind of equality. The army, however, had already paid this price when it equated the pensions and service conditions of Africans to those of their metropolitan comrades, and its commanders thought the price was worthwhile. Thanks to the extensive military reforms of 1950, the army managed to ensure the continued loyal service of Africans in the complex and morally dubious wars of decolonization. There was no reason, then, for the military authorities to doubt the success of their colonial vision in AOF, if only the French politicians would guard the "true interests" of the French nation—a term that also included the African citizens of the French Union and later the Franco-African Community.

But as in Algeria, the politicians chose to succumb, as the military command saw it, to international pressure and the winds of decolonization. Their reforms finally resulted in the demise of the entire French empire, including the relatively peaceful AOF. When the military authorities realized this, they decided to support the establishment of African national armies to which they had previously objected and attempted to safeguard their control over AOF with the help of military agreements. While some of the ex-territories of the federation tried to limit French military involvement, others were more willing to allow the army to keep a large part of its previous control. This was done mainly out of weakness and fear of losing power to opposition forces without French protection after independence.

Even though the French army managed to maintain some control over large parts of ex-AOF territories, its colonial units were dismantled within a few years after independence. This meant an end to the careers of many African soldiers for whom the French colonial army was a source of income, pride, and social security. Some managed to find alternative careers either in the military of their independent country or in its civil service. Others did not. For veterans, independence often meant a loss of a patron, as well as that of their major achievement after World War II: the equation of their pensions to those of their French comrades. Although it took some time for the veterans to feel the effects of the freezing of the pensions, when this happened they began organizing again, just like they had after World War II. Along with the decorations they had won for their honorable service, they took out their old and most trusted weapon—the notion of shared glories and sacrifices between French and Africans—and set out to their last battle for equality and recognition, a battle they finally won in 2011, although most of them were no longer around to enjoy the victory.

Conclusion

Just before the fiftieth anniversary of Senegal's independence in April 2010, its president, Abdoulaye Wade, managed to persuade the French government to evacuate its main military base in central Dakar, situated on a valuable piece of land along the beach, and rescind the defense agreement between his country and France. Wade presented the French military withdrawal from Senegal as another step in the direction of supposedly "true independence." A news item produced by the English-speaking French channel France 24 discussing this decision revealed that not all the inhabitants of Dakar were especially enthusiastic about this move. The French army employed 3,000 workers in this city and procured from local suppliers all the external services the French soldiers needed, from laundry to food and entertainment. The departure of the French military from Dakar saved the French taxpayer some money and did not bother the French government very much due to the political stability of Senegal and the traditional friendly relations with this ex-colony. However, it posed a difficult problem for a large segment of the people of Dakar, not only those working directly for the military but also the service providers who indirectly benefited from the army's presence and whose livelihood depended on the army.[1]

This was not the first time a Senegalese president used the military relations with France to present his professed objection to French neocolonialism. President Abdou Diouf made a similar statement in 1983 when he ordered the removal of a World War I French monument depicting two soldiers, one French, the other African, raising their rifles. The words "Vers la victoire" (Toward victory) were inscribed at their feet. The statue, popularly known as "the Demba and Dupont monument" (using two ostensibly typical Senegalese and French names), was moved from the central Tascher square facing the National Assembly to a marginal and obscure location— the Catholic cemetery at the fringes of Dakar. The square, named after Charles Tascher, a French nineteenth-century politician, was renamed on the same occasion as Place Soweto, emphasizing the anticolonial nature of this act. By removing the monument, which Diouf deemed "colonial," from the center of the capital and changing the name of the square, he could express his professed objection to French neocolonialism while avoiding any substantial move that might truly upset the French.[2] As we shall soon see, this was not the end of Demba and Dupont's interesting itinerary.

There is, of course, a great difference between the two presidential actions. While the removal of the monument was purely symbolic, the evacuation of the French military base was far more significant. More than any assertion of "true" Senegalese independence, though, the French consent to withdraw its soldiers from Dakar demonstrated its government's inclination to abandon its Franceafrique policy, which had come under increasing international and internal criticism. What is interesting in these two examples, separated by almost thirty years, is the connection that Senegalese leaders established between the concept of independence and the severing of former military alliances—symbolically and practically. The emblematic monument reflects both the brotherhood in arms between French and Africans and the former's paternalism, as illustrated by the French soldier putting a reassuring and guiding arm over the shoulders of his African comrade. The military base in Dakar mirrors both Senegalese military dependence on France and the economic benefits of these relations. In both cases, the military sphere represents the complexity of Senegal's postcolonial relations with France.

The complaints about the loss of livelihood due to the evacuation of the French soldiers from Dakar remind us that the colonial past continues to have a real and tangible effect on France's ex-colonies. In fact, even the Demba and Dupont monument affected the livelihood of Africans when in 2004 President Wade decided to relocate it again. His decision stemmed from a new awareness regarding the participation of African soldiers in the two world wars and the debate around the freezing of their pensions. Wade decided to adopt and pursue the veterans' political aims and as part of a wider set of commemoration activities moved the Demba and Dupont monument to Place de la Gare, now Place du Tirailleur, a central square facing the railway station, one of the main landmarks of colonial Dakar. This "comeback" of the two World War I heroes caused major distress to a large number of Malian traders who used this space to sell their goods and were evacuated in order to make room for the monument. Within less than a decade it became obvious that the removal of living soldiers and the return of two virtual ones had unequivocally harmed African economic interests to varying degrees.

It seems, then, that in both the African and French minds there is a tight connection between the concepts of colonialism and what is generally considered its opposite, independence, and the military relations between France and its African territories during and after the colonial period. This confirms Tony Chafer and Alexander Keese's assertion that the narrative of the military bond has the best potential of explaining the decolonization of AOF; the French army's destiny was entwined with that of the French empire. This was the force that occupied its territory and established French rule there, relying heavily on African soldiers. After the conquest of the empire, in spite of the transfer to civilian rule in most of the federation of AOF, the army continued to be deeply involved in shaping colonial policy. This was also the institution that tried to protect the empire to the last moment. In the post–World War II era, the empire seemed to justify much of the army's existence. Therefore, the military aspect of French colonial rule in AOF can largely explain France's colonial presence in this region. What prevents this narrative from best portraying the process of decolonization in AOF is that often there is an important piece of the puzzle missing. It is this missing piece that is depicted in the military relations described in this book.

As I have shown in this book, the fact that Africans served in great numbers in the French army both in the empire and in Europe along the entire colonial period resulted in an important military bond. The nature of this bond was changed and reshaped by the post–World War II years and the extensive military reforms of that time. After an initial period of contention and protest that even led to extreme colonial violence, Africans who served in the army gained what other sectors in African society could not: a recognition of the principle of equal pay for equal work. While the arena was certainly still the discriminatory and nonegalitarian colonial sphere, the military service offered Africans benefits and a feeling of belonging as never before. In this sense, it is quite surprising that so much literary attention had been given lately to the freezing of the pensions in 1959 and so little to their comparison to those of metropolitan veterans a decade before. As we have seen in chapter 3, the decision to equate the pensions, which at present can be viewed as natural and even obvious, was in those years no less than revolutionary. It was the first time that a regulation regarding the metropole was applied to Africans *talis qualis* with no adaptation.

The "new army," which we examined in chapter 3, was indeed new from this point of view. While many of the paternalistic modes of thought regarding African soldiers remained constant during the 1950s, the army still managed to professionalize its African units, improve the level of their education, and offer them a venue to ameliorate their social and economic status. More than any of the propaganda and monitoring measures examined in chapters 4 and 5, this was the main reason for the military command's success in maintaining African loyalty. Most Africans who served in Indochina and Algeria saw their service as their job—no more and no less. This was the career they chose, and these wars were just part of their duties. Contrary to their commanders' view, they were indeed interested in politics, especially as these politics were about to change the course of their professional lives, but they did not think politics had anything to do with the performance of their duties in the army in which they served.

As we have seen in chapter 6, the military authorities played a very significant role in the political developments in AOF during the 1950s. The army tried to encroach on the civilian authorities in the federation whenever its commanders thought these authorities might be liable to lose control. In light of the international atmosphere and what it considered as the weakness of French politicians, the army was determined not to lose the empire. Despite the defeat in Indochina and the growing difficulties in Algeria, especially in the political and diplomatic spheres, its commanders still believed that AOF could remain under French control until almost the last moment. They were also keen to prove the significance of AOF and to diffuse its continuous contribution to France. As we have seen in the centennial celebrations of the Tirailleurs Sénégalais and in the generals' reports objecting to the idea of dismantling the colonial army, the army had its own vision for the future of the French empire. Its commanders firmly believed that the military reforms had set a model for continued colonial rule that would be able to resist the growing international criticism against the French empire, as it would be stripped of all the negative aspects formerly inherent in this form of control. The loyalty of African soldiers and veterans, even in the turbulent times of the wars in Indochina and Algeria, was in the commanders' eyes solid proof of the validity of this colonial vision.

What is interesting in this military colonial vision is that in some ways it is quite similar to that of many of the African politicians and trade union leaders during the years of decolonization. They, too, did not see independence as the desired goal of their anticolonial struggle. What they fought for was equality within a French framework. The military model did not embody, of course, the equality strived for by the African politicians and trade union leaders. The army was a highly hierarchical and nondemocratic institution in which concepts such as freedom of speech and unionization were irrelevant. Unlike the civilian sector, the military authorities did not have to worry that their reforms might be met with strikes and further demands; it was much easier to initiate such reforms in the highly controlled military sphere than in the civilian one. In fact, as we have seen in chapter 6, when the district guards expressed their wish to organize, the military authorities' solution to this new problem was to transfer them from civilian to military control.

Eventually, French politicians opted for the simpler solution in AOF: independence. The French army had to accept that the territories that it once conquered (or "pacified," according to the colonial military jargon) now had the power to evacuate its soldiers and refer to them as "foreign," a deeply insulting term as far as the military command was concerned.

The army did its best to retain its control over the French former colonies through different means. It helped build their national armies, signed military cooperation and defense agreements with African states that were willing to do so, and kept military bases wherever allowed. The continued military presence in the former French colonies was doubtless one of the major symbols of the French controversial policy of Franceafrique.

In interviews Aissatou Diagne conducted with Senegalese veterans who fought in the Indochina War, many of them told her that Senegal had gained independence without bloodshed thanks to the African veterans.[3] This is a very interesting statement considering the fact that, as we have seen, veterans in general did not support independence and had a great deal to lose with the departure of the French. In fact, the African political leaders who had pushed for independence, such as Séckou Touré and Mobido Keita, treated the veterans with deep suspicion after independence.[4] The veterans' seemingly contradictory statement may be resolved, though, if viewed from their own perspective. The veterans felt that as they had shed their blood in the battlefields of Europe, their sacrifices entitled them to demand equality and improved conditions. Therefore, the veterans believed that they had enabled Africans in general to demand full rights—a demand that eventually led to independence.

There is still a basic problem with this assertion. The veterans' struggle was for the main alternative to independence: equality within a French framework. It is true that their participation in World War II enabled veterans to achieve this goal within the limits of a military hierarchical sphere. However, it did not allow the rest of the African population to do so. When demands for equality intensified in other sectors of colonial society, the French opted for the easier way out and granted autonomy and then full independence to their sub-Saharan African territories.

The recent struggle of African veterans for equality and the commemorative attention given to African veterans in West Africa and in France seventy years after the end of World War II only prove that the military bond between France and its sub-Saharan African colonies cannot be easily unraveled. The complex relations between the French army and its African soldiers involved various and often contradictory aspects, moving between comradeship and hostility, obligation and discrimination, respect and oblivion, paternalism and brotherhood. As I have shown in this book, it is through these complex relations that we can fully understand the nature of the unique decolonization process in AOF. However, we should not be tempted to skip over the years in which the military experimented with an alternative model to independence and in which Africans who served in its ranks opted for this model, which offered them some measure of equality. Despite the violence that erupted in other parts of the French empire, after the initial years of protest in AOF the military relations were the best they had ever been. Comradeship, obligation, and respect, admittedly often expressed in a paternalistic manner, were certainly more dominant in this period than hostility, discrimination, and oblivion, which were gradually resumed only when independence became the only political option available to the territories of AOF. The continued French military control over some of the ex-territories of AOF reflected a clear extension of the colonial relations into the postcolonial era without the previous obligation toward France's African veterans. This demonstrates that independence, when not accompanied with a real change in the nature of the colonial relations, could not improve the lot of the former colonial subjects and was certainly not enough to bring about a decisive end to the colonial era.

NOTES

INTRODUCTION

1. All military ranks appear in an English translation of their French form. For equivalents in the U.S. Army, see Fogarty, *Race and War in France*, 295-96.
2. Chafer, "Chirac and 'La Franceafrique,'" 7-12. One of the more recent military interventions was operation Serval in Mali, although, unlike other cases, it definitely played in favor of the vast majority of the Malian population. See Galy, "Pourquoi la France," 76-77.
3. Foccart (1913-97) was the chief advisor for the French government on African affairs for most of his career and served in various positions related to France's activities in the continent.
4. Chafer, "Chirac and 'La Franceafrique,'" 7-12.
5. Rouvez, *Disconsolate Empires*, 102-3.
6. The main recent publication on colonial soldiers, including Africans, in World War I is Fogarty, *Race and War in France*. Recent studies on World War II include Scheck, *Hitler's African Victims*; Scheck, *French Colonial Soldiers*; Mabon, *Prisonniers de guerre "indigènes."*
7. Shipway, *Decolonization and Its Impact*, 5.
8. Cooper, *Africa since 1940*, 38.
9. Clayton, *France, Soldiers and Africa*; Evrard, "Transfer of Military Power," 90-96; Joly, "The French Army," 75-89.
10. Two other studies deal with the participation of Africans in two colonial conflicts: Bodin, *Les Africains*; and Ba, *Les "Sénégalais" à Madagascar*.
11. See, for example, these publications in English: Evans, *Algeria*; Shepard, *The Invention of Decolonization*.

1. HISTORICAL BACKGROUND

1. On the *métis*, the *originaires*, and the early French presence in the four communes, see Johnson, "The Ascendancy," 235-53; Lambert, "From Citizenship to Negritude," 241-47; Jones, "Rethinking Politics," 325-44; Jones, *The Métis of Senegal*.
2. On the *indigénat*, see Mann, "What Was the *Indigénat*?," 331-53.
3. On the French colonial practice of forced labor, see Fall, *Le travail forcé*.

4. On the difference between the military service of *originaires* and colonial subjects, see Woodfork, "'It Is a Crime,'" 115-39.
5. On the French conquest of the territory that was to become French West Africa and the deployment of Africans for this purpose, see Echenberg, *Colonial Conscripts*, 7-24; Vandervort, *Wars of Imperial Conquest*, 27-32, 40-44, 70-84, 122-36.
6. Clayton, *France, Soldiers and Africa*, 6-8.
7. Le Naour, *La honte noire*, 16-18.
8. Mangin, *La force noire*, 350.
9. Lunn, "'Les races guerrières,'" 521.
10. Ingold, *Avec les troupes noires*, 3.
11. Michel, *Les Africains*, 192-93. The official number of African soldiers who were sent to Europe during the war presented in military reports is 134,000. This number is also cited by other scholars. However, according to Michel, the number he quotes corresponds with census data in AOF.
12. Echenberg, *Colonial Conscripts*, 42-46.
13. Koller, "The Recruitment," 115-18.
14. Ginio, *French Colonialism Unmasked*, 129. This decree was temporarily abolished under the Vichy regime in 1942 but was renewed after the war.
15. In the early 1920s several governors refused to contribute funds toward a monument for African soldiers who perished in the war, planned to be built in Bamako, the capital of French Sudan (contemporary Mali). See Archives Nationales du Sénégal, Dakar (hereafter ANS), 17G 282 (126), July 1, 1921, letter from Raphaël Antonetti, governor of Côte d'Ivoire, to Gen. Louis Archinard; December 5, 1922, correspondence between the governor of Dahomey and General Archinard.
16. Conklin, *A Mission to Civilize*, 33-42; Clayton, *France, Soldiers and Africa*, 19.
17. ANS, 17G 199 (104), March 25, 1925, Paris, Philippe Pétain, the army's situation in French West Africa.
18. On the Brazzaville Conference, see Chafer, *The End of Empire*, 56-61.
19. For a detailed account and analysis of the latter strike, see Cooper, "'Our Strike,'" 81-118.
20. Chafer, *The End of Empire*, 61-70.
21. Chafer, *The End of Empire*, 104-10.
22. Chafer, *The End of Empire*, 163-72. For a detailed analysis of the process of the formulating of the Loi-Cadre and the French and African debates around it, see Cooper, *Citizenship*, 215-78.
23. Chafer, *The End of Empire*, 172-85.

2. THE AFTERMATH OF WORLD WAR II

1. See, for example, the various chapters of Byfield et al., *Africa and World War II*.
2. Echenberg, *Colonial Conscripts*, 88. For a more recent and detailed overview of the *tirailleurs*' service during World War II, see Fargettas, *Les Tirailleurs Sénégalais*.

3. On the deployment of African troops in the Rhineland and the international protest campaign that followed, see Nelson, "The 'Black Horror,'" 606-27; Roos, "Women's Rights," 473-508. On the massacre of African soldiers in Chasselay, see Echenberg, "'Morts pour la France,'" 370.

4. Sheck, "French Colonial Soldiers," 427-37.

5. Sheck, "French Colonial Soldiers," 437-41.

6. Officially, Vichy rule in the federation had already ended in November 1942, following the Allied landing in North Africa, but the real change of power took place only when Boisson left the federation and was replaced by the Free French governor Pierre Cournarie. See Ginio, *French Colonialism Unmasked*, 26.

7. On the establishment of the Vichy regime in French West Africa, see Ginio, *French Colonialism Unmasked*, 3-9. On the Free French rule in French Equatorial Africa, see Jennings, *La France libre*.

8. Zimmerman, "Living beyond Boundaries," 82-91.

9. On the whitening of the army, see Le Naour, *La honte noire*, 247-48.

10. Jennings, *La France libre*, 166-70.

11. On relations between African soldiers and French women in World War II and the women's quest after their lost lovers in AOF, see Ginio, "African Soldiers," 324-38.

12. Fargettas, *Les Tirailleurs*, 267-82.

13. ANS, 4D 60, Dakar, October 15, 1943.

14. On the tragic events at camp Thiaroye, see Echenberg, "Tragedy at Thiaroye," 109-27; Fragettas, *Les Tirailleurs*, 288-92; Mabon, *Prisonniers de guerre "indigènes,"* 193-211.

15. ANS, 4D 60, October 31, 1944, letter from the minister of the colonies to the high commissioner of AOF.

16. ANS, 4D 60, November 15, 1944, an extract from the *Journal Officiel* of French Guinea.

17. ANS, 4D 60, November 28, 1944, renseignement.

18. ANS, 4D 60, November [sic] 1944. The handwritten date that appears on this document cannot be accurate, as the document refers to the echoes of the Thiaroye incidents among the local population. Therefore, it is obvious that this document was formulated after December 1, 1944.

19. ANS, 4D 60, December 7, 1944, letter from the high commissioner of AOF to the minister of the colonies regarding the events in Thiaroye.

20. ANS, 4D 60, December 2, 1944, letter from the governor of Dakar to the high commissioner.

21. ANS, 4D 60, December 12, 1944, letter from the high commissioner of AOF to the minister of the colonies.

22. ANS, 4D 60, November [sic] 1944, report from Ziguinichor, Senegal, Conakry, December 18, 1944.

23. ANS, 4D 60, August 23, 1945, letter from the high commissioner of AOF to the minister of the colonies.

24. "Senator Jane Vialle," *Crisis* 57, no. 4 (April 1950): 208.

25. ANS, 4D 60, November 13, 1946.

26. ANS, 4D 60, March 1946.

27. ANS, 4D 60, March 1946.

28. ANS, 4D 60, April 3, 1946.

29. ANS, 4D 60, Conakry, December 18, 1944.

30. ANS, 4D 60, Dakar, January 4, 1945.

31. ANS, 4D 60, January 28, 1948, information report.

32. ANS, 4D 60, June 26, 1946, report of the military cabinet.

33. ANS, December 6, 1945.

34. ANS, Dahomey, February 1946.

35. ANS, 4D 60, July 27, 1945, letter from the governor of Dakar to the high commissioner.

36. ANS, 4D 60, April 29, 1947, letter from the minister of the colonies to the high commissioner.

37. ANS, 4D 60, July 3, 1945, letter from the high commissioner to the commander of the French Forces in AOF.

38. On data regarding recruitment of Africans to the Free French Forces, see Jennings, *La France libre*, 11.

39. ANS, 4D 60, June 5, 1947.

40. ANS, 4D 60, April 29, 1947, letter from the minister of the colonies to the high commissioner of AOF.

41. ANS, 4D 60, Bathurst, July 20, 1946.

42. ANS, 4D 60, October 20, 1946.

43. ANS, 4D 60, March 7, 1947.

44. ANS, 11D1 380, September 7, 1944, circular from the high commissioner of AOF to the governors of the colonies.

45. ANS, 11D1 380, September 6, 1944, letter from the high commissioner of AOF to the British consul general.

46. ANS, 11D1 380, February 15, 1945, letter from the high commissioner to the governor of Senegal. Both the British and the French administrators were confused regarding the choice of this date and even argued about it. Apparently it is related to the departure of the Vichy governor-general, Pierre Boisson, on July 23, 1943.

47. ANS, 11D1 380, January 5, 1945, letter from the head of the subdivision of Ossouye to the commandant of the Ziguinchor district.

3. THE MILITARY REFORMS

1. Mann, *Native Sons*, 122.

2. Mann, *Native Sons*, 122.

3. Mann, *Native Sons*, 126–32.

4. On the French formal status of pupils of the nation, see Office National des Anciens Combattants et Victimes de Guerre, "Le status de pupille de la nation," http://www.onac-vg.fr/fr/missions/pupille-de-la-nation/, accessed November 25, 2014.

5. Archives Nationales, Section d'Outre-Mer, Aix-en-Provence (hereafter ANSOM), DSM/275, Veterans' Office of AOF and Togo, annual report, 1952.

6. ANS, 4D 59, note from the minister of the colonies, December 1, 1952.

7. See Ginio, "La politique antijuive," 109–18.

8. On this debate, see Mann, "Immigrants and Arguments," 362–85.

9. ANS, 11D1 256, September 21, 1950, circular from the governor-general of AOF to the governors of the colonies.

10. *Journal Officiel de la République Française*, Débats Parlementaires, Assemblée Nationale, July 27, 1950, 6023–24. On the RDA's short-lived alliance with the PCF, see Chafer, *The End of Empire*, 104–6.

11. These numbers varied, of course, according to the need in various periods. Echenberg, *Colonial Conscripts*, 105–8.

12. Echenberg, *Colonial Conscripts*, 108–9.

13. Echenberg, *Colonial Conscripts*, 108.

14. Zimmerman, "Living beyond Boundaries," 102.

15. The Office du Niger was an irrigation project that was based on the model of the British project of El-Jazeera in Sudan. Its aim was to enable cotton cultivation, which requires much water. The agency responsible for the project was established in 1932, and work was based on forced labor. Soon after World War II the French government acknowledged the failure of this project. See Van Beusekon, "Disjunctures," 79–99.

16. Bogosian Ash, "Free to Coerce," 109–10.

17. Bogosian Ash, "Free to Coerce," 118–19. It is interesting that Louveau, who served as the lieutenant-governor of Ivory Coast at the beginning of World War II, was a fierce resister of the Vichy regime and was even sent to a concentration camp in France. His support of the practice of forced labor even after it was officially abolished proved that the link French and African politicians tried to create between repressive methods of colonial rule and the so-called Vichy spirit was rather dubious. On Louveau, see Ginio, *French Colonialism Unmasked*, 27.

18. Echenberg and Filipovich, "African Military Labor," 541–42, 550.

19. Bogosian Ash, "Free to Coerce," 109, 117–25.

20. ANS, 11D1 256, October 26, 1950, superior command of the terrestrial forces of AOF, instructions for African recruitment, class 1950.

21. ANS, 11D 195, August 2, 1951, letter from the governor of Senegal to the commandant of Thiès district.

22. ANS, 11D1 256, December 6, 1950.

23. Until the establishment of Dakar University (today Cheick Anta Diop University) in 1957, the pinnacle of the education system in AOF was a number of schools that trained Africans as teachers and administrators. These were called *grandes écoles*. The most prestigious was the William Ponty School.

24. After 1945 francs in AOF were officially called CFA, but often the term *francs* was also used. Here and in other cases in which the sums mentioned are related to AOF the currency is actually CFA. The exchange rate of CFA was 1 CFA = 1.70 French francs. Between 1948 and 1959 the rate was 1 CFA = 2 French francs. The exchange rate was changed again several times after independence.

25. Echenberg, *Colonial Conscripts*, 110.

26. ANS, 11D1/256, head of subdivision of Velingara to the district commandant of Ziguinchor, March 9, 1955.

27. An ethnic group in Senegal to which the first president of Senegal, Léopold Sédar Senghor, belonged. This group resisted any kind of hierarchy, fought against Wolof domination in the precolonial period, and opposed French colonial rule. They were finally subdued by the French with the help of the Wolof, but the Serer continued to perform acts of defiance toward various colonial policies.

28. ANS, 11D1/130, March 26, 1953, report on the recruitment operations of "ex-subject" Africans of the class of 1952 in the district of Diourbel.

29. Echenberg, *Colonial Conscripts*, 111–12.

30. Echenberg, *Colonial Conscripts*, 112.

31. ANS, 11D1 256, October 26, 1950, Superior Command of the Terrestrial Forces of AOF, instructions on the African recruitment of the class of 1950.

32. ANSOM, DSM/281, Paris, October 1, 1945, War Ministry, direction of colonial troops, note of organization concerning the regional propaganda centers. The original sentence in French: "Rien n'épate plus le badaud français qui est encore à la conception du tirailleur type 'y'a bon' que d'être en présence d'un tirailleur s'exprimant comme lui." On the Banania commercial and the image of African colonial soldiers in France, see Hale, "French Images," 138–45.

33. ANS, 4D 77, June 4, 1950, letter from the governor of Ivory Coast to the high commissioner of AOF.

34. One example is a declaration of a father from Ziguinchor in Senegal whose son refused to enlist, requiring the father to pay for half the cost of his son's studies in the EET of Saint Louis. Such cases seem to be very rare. ANS, 11D1 376, June 16, 1949.

35. ANS, 4D 78 (10), March 13, 1954, superior command of AOF-Togo, directions for the military instruction given in the EMPA.

36. ANS, 4D 78 (100), March 13, 1954, directions for the military instruction given in the EMPA. On the military involvement in sports in the federation after World War II and its competition with the civilian authorities in this area, see Deville-Danthu, *Le sport*, 236.

37. Centre d'Histoire et d'Études des Troupes d'Outre-Mer, Fréjus (hereafter

CHETOM), 16H 423, September 1, 1957, military command of Upper Volta, EMPA of Upper Volta, operations and activities log.

38. ANS, 4D 78 (100), March 13, 1954, directions for military instruction, EMPA.

39. ANS, 4D 78 (100), March 9, 1954, academy inspector to the general commander of the First Brigade of AOF.

40. ANS, 4D 78 (100), February 28, 1954, studies director of the EMPA of Saint Louis to the general superior commander of the defense zone AOF-Togo.

41. ANS, 4D 78 (100), February 9, 1954, academy inspector, opinion of Capitaine Mazeline, commander of the EMPA of Saint Louis.

42. ANS, 4D 76 (100), September 10, 1949, général de corps d'armée Magnan, instructions about the functioning of the EMPAs; ANS, 4D 78 (100), October 23, 1952, service note, EET, Saint Louis.

43. CHETOM, 16H 423, *Tropiques*, no. 356 (November 1953): 30.

44. ANS, 4D 76 (100), May 9, 1953, governor of Upper Volta to the high commissioner.

45. ANS, 4D 76 (100), August 19, 1952, war orphans; October 4, 1951, EET; November 10, 1951, EET.

46. ANS, 4D 59, July 21, 1954, letter from Papa Seck Douta to the high commissioner of AOF; August 4, 1954, Lieutenant Colonel Villard, chief of the military cabinet, to Papa Seck Douta.

47. ANS, 4D 59, August 10, 1954, admission to the EMPA in 1954 of young Coulibali Lougozie.

48. Echenberg, *Colonial Conscripts*, 112, 120.

49. Echenberg, *Colonial Conscripts*, 111.

50. ANS, 4D 59, September 20, 1945, letter from Léopold Sédar Senghor to the high commissioner of AOF; September 28, 1945, letter from Général Magnan to the high commissioner of AOF.

51. ANS, 4D 77, instructions concerning the young students of the *grandes écoles* of AOF.

52. ANS, 4D 77, September 6, 1954, minister of overseas France to the high commissioner of AOF.

53. Echenberg, *Colonial Conscripts*, 120.

54. Echenberg, *Colonial Conscripts*, 117.

55. Echenberg, *Colonial Conscripts*, 120-21.

56. Echenberg, *Colonial Conscripts*, 121.

57. In 1959, under pressure from Africans who resented the implied inferiority of the term *transitional regime*, the same acronym came to stand for École de Formation des Officiers Ressortissants des Territoires d'Outre-Mer. Echenberg, *Colonial Conscripts*, 122.

58. Echenberg, *Colonial Conscripts*, 123.

59. Echenberg, *Colonial Conscripts*, 123, 125.

60. Echenberg, *Colonial Conscripts*, 125.

61. ANS, 11D1 405, Dakar, recruitment for 1957.

62. ANS, 11D1 405, February 21, 1956, letter from the superior command of AOF to the Health Department of the terrestrial forces.

63. Niang, *Mémoires synchrones*, 47–48.

64. ANSOM, DSM/275, July 25, 1958.

65. ANS, 17G 638 (152), July 10, 1957, letter of complaint on behalf of 180 soldiers from Ivory Coast posted in Bouaké to the general commandant of the Second Brigade.

66. Service Historique de l'Armée de Terre, Vincennes, France (hereafter SHAT), 5H 24, annual report, 1950, armed forces of AOF.

67. Echenberg, *Colonial Conscripts*, 128.

68. ANSOM, DSM/275, Veterans' Office of AOF and Togo, annual report, 1952.

69. ANS, 11D1 1265, August 12, 1948, letter from the general inspector of the colonies, general secretary of the high commissioner of AOF, president of the Office for War Victims in AOF, to the governors and presidents of the Offices of the Veterans and War Victims.

70. ANS, 11D1 1265, Tivaoune, January 19, 1951, letter from the head of the subdivision of Tivaoune to the district commandant of Thiès.

71. ANS, 11D1 1265, September 1, 1949, letter from the governor of Senegal to the mayor of Saint Louis and the district commandants; 11D1 1265, Saint Louis, September 10, 1949, letter from the president of the local committee of veterans of Senegal to the mayor of Saint Louis and the district commandants.

72. ANS, 11D1 1265, Saint Louis, October 6, 1951, letter from the local president of the veterans of Senegal to the governor of Senegal, the mayor of Saint Louis, the district commandants, and the heads of subdivisions.

73. ANSOM, DSM/275, Veterans' Office of AOF and Togo, annual report, 1955.

74. ANSOM, DSM/275, Veterans' Office of AOF and Togo, annual report, 1952.

75. ANS, 4D 59, September 11, 1948, letter from François Saiba to the high commissioner of AOF.

76. ANS, 4D 59, April 20, 1950, letter from the general director of the Department of Finance to the head of research service, Dakar.

77. ANS, 4D 59, September 28, 1948, letter from the Veterans' Office of AOF to the general director of the Department of Finance in Dakar.

78. SHAT, GR 5H 24, February 18, 1952, report on the functioning of the social service of the land forces of AOF, 1951.

79. Here are a few examples: ANS, 11D1 118, Mbacké, June 17, 1957, letter from Samba Gaye, ex–district guard; Conakry, May 18, 1957, letter from Camara Hassana, guard fourth class; Diourbel, April 6, 1957, letter from M'Baye N'Diaye, veteran, class of 1939, ex-POW.

80. ANS, 11D1 119, Diourbel, November 9, 1957, excerpt from a report by Chief-Sergeant Gaudry, itinerant NCO for the veterans of Senegal, to the governor of Senegal and the president of the local veterans' committee.

81. ANS, 11D1 405, December 1, 1953, letter from the army commander in AOF to the high commissioner of AOF.

82. Echenberg, "Slaves into Soldiers," 322–24.

83. ANS, 5D 213, January 26, 1954, superior commander of the armed forces of defense zone AOF-Togo to Cornut-Gentille, propaganda activity in favor of recruitment; ANS, 17G 520, Upper Volta, report on the psychological operations in September and October 1955.

84. ANS, 11D1 903, August 30, 1957, Lami, governor of Senegal, to the district commandants.

85. ANS, 11D1 903, August 30, 1957, Lami to district commandants.

86. ANS, 11D1 195, May 9, 1955, Note de service—Tournées de brousse.

87. General Garbay played an active role in the rallying of Chad to the Free French Forces in 1940. After the liberation of France, in which he also played a decisive role, Garbay continued his military career in Madagascar, where he commanded the brutal repression of the 1947 revolt, in Indochina, in Tunisia, and finally in Senegal. The reservation request is in ANS, 5D 213, February 22, 1955, Garbay, superior commander of the army in AOF, to Cornut-Gentille.

88. ANS, 5D 213 (143), February 22, 1955, Garbay to Cornut-Gentille.

89. ANS, 5D 213 (143), April 13, 1955, Bonifay, mayor of Dakar, to Jourdain, governor of Senegal.

90. Echenberg, *Colonial Conscripts*, 115.

91. ANS, 5D 214, February 7, 1955, high commissioner to the governors of the colonies, photographic documents.

92. ANS, 5D 213 (143), May 3, 1954, radio interview with Colonel Saquet.

93. ANS, 11D1 1412, May 15, 1948, Thiès.

94. ANS, 5D 213 (143), March 24, 1954, General Nyo to the minister of the colonies, Dakar.

95. ANS, 5D 213 (143), March 30, 1954, high commissioner to the minister of the colonies, Dakar.

96. ANS, 5D 213 (143), March 17, 1954, cabinet militaire.

97. ANS, 5D 213 (143), April 5, 1954, high commissioner to the director of civil aviation.

98. ANS, 5D 213 (143), May 3, 1954, radio interview with Colonel Saquet.

99. ANS, 5D 213 (143), October 16, 1953, note for the director of information.

100. Niang, *Mémoires synchrones*, 46–47.

101. On the establishment of the French Union and the 1946 constitution and its limitations, see Cooper, *Citizenship*, 67–123.

102. Cooper, "'Our Strike,'" 115.

103. Mann and Fogarty both provide many examples of the policy of separating African soldiers and European soldiers and civilians during their service in France during World War I: Mann, *Native Sons*, 166–68; Fogarty, *Race and War*, 98–119, 205–19.

104. Echenberg, *Colonial Conscripts*, 116.

1. I have chosen to use the term *war*, which best characterized the nature of this conflict, even though the French government recognized the hostilities in Algeria as a war only in 1999.

2. I have chosen not to examine this conflict at length, as Amadou Ba has already discussed the participation of African troops in it. Nevertheless, the Malagasy Uprising and the major role of African troops in its repression are vital to our understanding of the later participation of Africans in the wars of decolonization. Although chronologically the beginning of the Indochina war preceded the Malagasy Uprising, the latter was over before 1949, a year in which most African soldiers were recruited to fight in Indochina. Therefore, the discussion of the rebellion precedes that of the Indochina war.

3. Ba, *Les "Sénégalais,"* 197.

4. Tronchon, *L'insurrection malgache*, 22–67; Benot, *Massacres coloniaux*, 116–20.

5. This was a reference to the massacre of hundreds of villagers, including children, of Oradour-sur-Glane in Nazi-occupied France, committed by German Waffen-SS soldiers on June 10, 1944.

6. Ba, *Les "Sénégalais,"* 200–208.

7. Echenberg, *Colonial Conscripts*, 140–44.

8. Bodin, "Les 'Sénégalais,'" 110.

9. Echenberg, *Colonial Conscripts*, 112–13.

10. According to army regulations, Africans who wanted to volunteer to serve in Algeria needed their parents' consent.

11. Interview with Mamadou Niang (born in 1936 in Tambacounda), performed by Cheick Anta Mbaye, March 2011.

12. Interview with Papa Figaro Diagne (born in 1932), performed by Cheick Anta Mbaye, March 2011.

13. Interview with Sadibou Badji (born in 1937), performed by Cheick Anta Mbaye, March 2011.

14. Interview with Marc Guèye (born in 1934), performed by Cheick Anta Mbaye, March 2011.

15. Zimmerman, "Living beyond Boundaries," 103.

16. Bradley, *Vietnam at War*, 42–45; Marsot, "The Crucial Year," 337–54.

17. Bradley, *Vietnam at War*, 49–67; Cooper, "Dien Bien Phu," 445–57.

18. Zimmerman, "Living beyond Boundaries," 106–7; Goscha, *Historical Dictionary*, 31.

19. Bodin, *Les Africains*, 54–55; Bodin, "Les 'Sénégalais,'" 105–6, 134.

20. Clayton, *The Wars of French Decolonization*, 53–56.

21. Bodin, "Les 'Sénégalais,'" 109–10.

22. Bodin, "Les 'Sénégalais,'" 113–14.

23. SHAT, 10H 420, July 28, 1951, report on the morale of the African units.

24. SHAT, 5H 24, May 26, 1952, annual report 1951, instructions and activities of

the terrestrial forces of AOF-Togo, superior command of the armed forces in defense zone AOF-Togo, Third Bureau.

25. See interviews conducted by Zimmerman, "Living beyond Boundaries," 107.

26. Diagne, "Le Sénégal," 52.

27. Diagne, "Le Sénégal," 60.

28. Diagne, "Le Sénégal," 109.

29. Interview with Marc Guèye.

30. SHAT, 5H 24, May 31, 1951, annual report 1950, chap. 4.

31. See, for example, a case of a complaint dated August 24, 1948, sent by the governor of Senegal to the high commissioner of AOF regarding the way a French lieutenant and some French soldiers in Indochina treated an African sergeant from Saint Louis who was an *originaire*, ANS, 4D 76 (100). This case is also quoted by Diagne, "Le Sénégal," 73.

32. Bodin, *Les Africains*, 190.

33. SHAT, 10H 420, May 19, 1953, January 20, 1954, and March 28, 1954, African affairs.

34. For a detailed description of these investigations, see Ginio, "French Officers," 69–73.

35. Diagne, "Le Sénégal," 135–36.

36. SHAT, 5H 24, annual report of the terrestrial forces in AOF, 1951; 5H 26, annual report, 1953.

37. Zimmerman, "Living beyond Boundaries," 110–11; on the nature of the investigations that these African officers had to carry out, see Ginio, "French Officers," 69–73.

38. SHAT, 10H 420, January 6, 1953, Saigon, Captain Guedou to the director responsible for Caravelle.

39. SHAT, 10H 420, January 6, 1953, Saigon, Guedou to the director.

40. See, for example, ANS, 11D1 380, February 25, 1949, letter to the governor of Senegal about an African farmer living in the subdivision of Kolda who had not heard from his brother serving in Indochina. This file contains many more such complaints.

41. ANS, 11D1 380, October 20, 1948, circular from the governor of Senegal to the district commanders.

42. ANS, 4D 76 (100), December 17, 1948, Porto Novo, governor of Dahomey to the high commissioner of AOF; April 7, 1949, circular regarding soldiers' morale.

43. ANS, 11D1 394, October 8, 1952, North Vietnam, Social Service.

44. ANS, 11D1 1265, September 16, 1948, letter from the minister of the colonies to the high commissioner of AOF.

45. Mann, *Native Sons*, 177–78.

46. Diagne, "Le Sénégal," 75–76.

47. Zimmerman, "Living beyond Boundaries," 115.

48. Mann, *Native Sons*, 158–59.

49. Mann, *Native Sons*, 158–59.

50. ANS, 4D 76 (100), October 2, 1952, report from the chief of the military cabinet in AOF.

51. ANS, 4D 76 (100), January 29, 1953, letter from General Salan to the high commissioner of AOF.

52. ANS, 4D 76 (100), September 10, 1953, letter from General Navarre to the high commissioner of AOF.

53. ANS, 4D 76 (100), September 25, 1953, letter from General Navarre to the high commissioner of AOF.

54. On the construction of the mosque in Fréjus, see Mann, "Locating Colonial Histories," 426–27.

55. Mann, *Native Sons*, 160–61; Diagne, "Le Sénégal," 75–85.

56. Goscha, *Vietnam*, 127.

57. Guèye, *Un Tirailleur Sénégalais*, 16–19.

58. Bodin, "Les 'Sénégalais,'" 118. *Congaïe* is a French term derived from the Vietnamese word *con gai*, which means "young woman" or "girl." During the colonial period it went through a semantic transformation that also implied the meaning "mistress" or "whore." See Proschan, "'Syphilis, Opiomania, and Pederasty,'" 614. I would like to thank Sarah Zimmerman for providing me with this reference.

59. Vo Nguyen Giap (1911–2013) was Ho Chi Minh's chief commander in both the Indochina and the Vietnam wars. The phrase "Giap's women" meant that these women were sent to seduce African soldiers as one of Giap's strategic schemes.

60. Diagne, "Le Sénégal," 110.

61. Stoler, "Sexual Affronts," 198–237.

62. ANS, 11D1 903, December 22, 1955, letter from the minister of defense to the commander of the French forces in the Far East.

63. SHAT, 10H 420, March 22, 25, 1952, African affairs, morale reports, 1952–53.

64. Diagne, "Le Sénégal," 110–11.

65. SHAT, 10H 420, March 22, 25, 1952, African affairs, morale reports, 1952–53.

66. SHAT, 10H 420, March 22, 1952, report of Lt. Ketty Amara.

67. While never considering their African soldiers as savages, French commanders often tried to present them as such to their enemies (notably the Germans). For more on the manipulation of the Africans' violent image within the French army, see Ginio, "French Officers."

68. Interview with Papa Figaro Diagne.

69. Pahlavi, "Political Warfare," 54.

70. Diagne, "Le Sénégal," 72.

71. Bodin, *Les Africains*, 196.

72. Zimmerman, "Living beyond Boundaries," 109.

73. Bodin, *Les Africains*, 194–95. This is a very low figure, as estimates regarding desertion in the entire French forces, including the North Africans and the

French Legion, refer to 16,550 desertions during this same period. See *The Indochina War, Historical Dictionary*, "Desertion, French Union Forces," http://indochine.uqam.ca/en/historical-dictionary/388-desertion-french-union-forces.html, accessed April 26, 2015.

74. Zimmerman, "Living beyond Boundaries," 109.

75. Zimmerman, "Living beyond Boundaries," 109.

76. Diagne, "Le Sénégal," 95–98.

77. Guèye, *Un Tirailleur Sénégalais*, 83. On the practice of lecturing POWs in Indochina about Communism and anti-imperialism, see Edwards, "Traître au colonialism?," 193–210.

78. ANS, 4D 76 (100), September 12, 1953, letter from the federal secretary of the Red Cross to the high commissioner of AOF.

79. SHAT, 10H 424. These files contain 680 forms.

80. ANS, 11D1 195, September 30, 1954, letter from the governor of Senegal to the district commanders.

81. Bodin, "Les 'Sénégalais,'" 125–26.

82. ANS, 11D1 405, May 8, 1954, telegram from the high commissioner to the governor of Senegal regarding the defeat in Dien Bien Phu.

5. ALGERIA, 1954–1962

1. Quoted in Thomas, *Fight or Flight*, 288.

2. Mann, *Native Sons*, 22.

3. SHAT, 1H 2454 d. 1, May 7, 1956, information file concerning African personnel arriving in AOF as reinforcements.

4. Zimmerman, "Living beyond Boundaries," 122–23.

5. Niang, *Mémoires synchrones*, 65–82.

6. Niang, *Mémoires synchrones*, 78.

7. Pahlavi, *Guerre révolutionnaire*, 28.

8. Villatoux, *Guerre et action*, 5–11.

9. Villatoux, *Guerre et action*, 26–29.

10. Ouellet and Pahlavi, "Institutional Analysis," 804–5.

11. Pahlavi, *Guerre révolutionnaire*, 23–25.

12. Villatoux, *Guerre et action*, 37.

13. Ouellet and Pahlavi, "Institutional Analysis," 804.

14. Ouellet and Pahlavi, "Institutional Analysis," 810–19.

15. Ouellet and Pahlavi, "Institutional Analysis," 820.

16. ANS, 19G 16 (17), April 27, 1957, tract; March 23, 1957, radio text; May 13, 1957, tract.

17. ANS, 19G 16 (17), May 13, 1957.

18. ANS, 19G 16 (17), March 23, May 13, 1957.

19. Chafer, *The End of Empire*, 118.

20. See, for example, Frederick Cooper's analysis of the long railway workers' strikes in AOF in 1947–48: Cooper, "'Our Strike,'" 81–118.

21. Chafer, *The End of Empire*, 124.

22. Chafer, *The End of Empire*, 126–27.

23. Chafer, *The End of Empire*, 129–30.

24. ANS, 19G 16 (17), June 25, 1957, Radio-Tanger.

25. On these events, see Whitfield, "Algeria in France," 412–32.

26. ANS, 19G 16 (17), July 21, 1956, intelligence report.

27. This was the annual conference of African and Asian independent countries. The most famous of these conferences was the one in Bandung in 1954, which was a significant step toward the nonaligned movement.

28. ANS, 19G 16 (17), January 11, 1958, Paris.

29. ANS, 19G 16 (17), April 26, 1957, letter from a priest in Niamy to an African soldier in Algeria written on March 3, 1957, and seized by the military censor. The original text of the last paragraph is: "Il faut espérer que la guerre d'Algérie sera bientôt finie. Dieu ne veut pas la guerre, ça apporte que le mal. *Dieu veut que les peuples soient libres*, qu'ils soient de n'importe quelle race, et il nous demande de nous aimer et de nous aider vraiment comme des frères les uns les autres. Je prie pour que Dieu t'accorde la santé et la paix dans ton corps et dans ton âme, Bonjour à tous les Nigériens."

30. SHAT, July 9, 1956, annual report, superior command of the armed forces in zone AOF-Togo.

31. SHAT, July 9, 1956, annual report, AOF.

32. ANSOM, DSM/275, April 24, 1956, letter from Mademoiselle Ploix, social assistant for the terrestrial forces for overseas France, to Mademoiselle Ruellan, social assistant, French North Africa, allocations for families of soldiers serving in Algeria.

33. ANSOM, DSM/275, October 24, 1957, letter from General Missonier, director of military affairs, to lieutenant colonel, commander of the general staff company of colonial troops, barracks of Clignancourt, Paris.

34. See, for example, SHAT 1H 2454 d. 1, May 5, 1956, report of Colonel Loisy concerning the morale of African soldiers.

35. SHAT, 1H 2454 d. 1, May 24, 1956, Constantine.

36. SHAT, 1H 2454 d. 1, June 5, 1956, military report on African Muslims.

37. SHAT, 1H 2454 d. 1, September 18, 1956, file concerning the morale of African soldiers.

38. SHAT, 1H 2454 d. 1, May 7, 1956, a census of African Muslim soldiers to be conducted in units of colonial troops stationed in Algeria.

39. SHAT, 1H 2454 d. 1, June 5, 1956, report, African Muslim soldiers.

40. Robinson, *Paths of Accommodation*, 75, 85.

41. Grandhomme, "La politique musulmane," 243–44.

42. Mann and Lecocq, "Between Empire," 377–78.

43. Orwin, "Of Couscous and Control," 272–76.

44. Mann and Lecocq, "Between Empire," 368.

45. Mann and Lecocq, "Between Empire," 375.

46. Mann and Lecocq, "Between Empire," 372–73.

47. Quoted in Mann and Lecocq, "Between Empire," 381.

48. Quoted in Mann and Lecocq, "Between Empire," 381.

49. Fall refers here to Gaston Monnerville, the grandson of a slave from French Guiana who studied law in Toulouse and served as the president of the Senate between 1947 and 1959.

50. On the French attack on Coca-Cola as a symbol of Americanization during the 1950s, see Kuisel, "Coca-Cola and the Cold War," 96–116.

51. SHAT, 1H 2454 d. 1, September 7, 1956, Lt. Tiemoko Konaté, report on the pilgrimage, Paris.

52. Mann and Lecocq, "Between Empire," 374.

53. Mann and Lecocq, "Between Empire," 381, 374.

54. Cheick Bamba Dioum, "Pèlerinage à la Mecque: Pourquoi la privatisation est la solution," http://bambadioum.seneweb.com/pelerinage-a-la-mecque-pourquoi -la-privatisation-est-la-solution_b_30.html, accessed April 9, 2014.

55. Niasse (1900–1975) was the son of Abdoulaye Niasse, the founder of one of the branches of the Tijaniyya order. On Niasse and his father, see Piga, *Les voies du soufisme*, 264–75.

56. ANS, 17G 602 (152), September 26, 1956, text regarding Arab and Muslim propaganda in black Africa.

57. Bloom, *French Colonial Documentary*, 60–63.

58. Interview with Sadiq Sall, Dakar, January 24, 2014.

59. Guèye, *Un Tirailleur Sénégalais*, 27.

60. Interview with Mamadou Niang (born in 1936), April 16, 2010, African Oral History Workshop, funded by the British Academy through the UK-Africa Academic Partnerships Scheme. I am grateful to Ibrahima Thioub for allowing me to use this interview for my research.

6. ALTERNATIVES TO INDEPENDENCE

1. On the UPC struggle against French colonial rule, see Sharp, "The Changing Boundaries," 189–203.

2. Evrard, "Transfer of Military Power," 91–92.

3. Evrard, "Transfer of Military Power," 93.

4. SHAT, 5H 28, Dakar, May 16, 1958, report of the end of command of General Bourgund, superior commander of the armed forces of AOF-Togo, September 12, 1956–May 16, 1958.

5. Two African precolonial leaders who established empires in West Africa and confronted the French when they later attempted to colonize the area. Haj Umar Tal was born in Futa Toro, now Guinea, in approximately 1794 and died fighting against the French in 1864. Samori Touré was born in around 1830 also in today's Guinea. He founded the Tukolor empire and fiercely resisted the French. He was

finally captured in 1898 and died in exile in 1900. On Haj Umar Tal, see Robinson, *The Holy War*. On Samori Toure, see Killingray and Hadley, *Samori Touré*.

6. CHETOM, 15H 06, February 25, 1955.

7. Bankwitz, "Maxime Weygand," 157-59.

8. Launey, "Les services," 27, 35.

9. Challéat, "Le cinéma," 10-11.

10. SHAT, GR 5H 24, March 28, 1958, annual report, 1957.

11. Pinoteau, "Propagande cinématographique," 55-58, 64.

12. ANS, 17G 520, February 27, 1955, Bonfils, letter from the governor of Dahomey to Cornut-Gentille, high commissioner of AOF.

13. ANS, 17G 520, February 1954, letter from Cornut-Gentille to Jacquinot, minister of overseas France, psychological activity through films.

14. ANS, 17G 520, May 29, 1954, letter from Geay, governor of Soudan, to Cornut-Gentille.

15. ANS, 17G 520, July 22, 1954, Cluset, commander of the second brigade of AOF.

16. ANS, 17G 520, Upper Volta, report on the psychological operations in September–October 1955, 1956.

17. CHETOM, 15H 17, February 7, 1957, letter from the minister of overseas France to the minister of defense.

18. CHETOM, 15H 17, March 12, 1957.

19. CHETOM, 15H 17, February 1957, secretary of state of the armed forces.

20. CHETOM, 15H 17, February 1957.

21. CHETOM, 15H 17, the centenary of the African troops in Paris.

22. This has been the official Memorial Day for African colonial soldiers in Senegal since 2004.

23. CHETOM, 15H 17, February 1957, secretary of state of the armed forces.

24. The Dogon, an ethnic group located in the central plateau in Mali (colonial French Sudan), is known for its rich religious culture and ability to agriculturally develop an especially challenging land.

25. The first regiment of African colonial soldiers established in 1884, when two companies of these soldiers were combined.

26. CHETOM, 15H 17, February 5, 1957, letter from A. de Jonqières.

27. CHETOM, 15H 17, February 7, 1957.

28. ANS, 17G 638 (152), August 24, 1957, Dakar, information bulletin, AOF-Togo, May 15–August 20, 1957.

29. ANS, 17G 638 (152), August 24, 1957, Dakar, information bulletin, AOF, Annex II.

30. ANS, 17G 638 (152), information bulletin, superior command of the armed forces of AOF, 1957-58.

31. Interview with Malic Gueye (born in 1930), Dakar, January 2011.

32. Diagne, "Le Sénégal," 142-43.

33. Diagne, "Le Sénégal," 142-44.

34. Coulibaly, *Combat pour l'Afrique*, 259-65.

35. *Journal Officiel de la République Française*, Débats Parlementaires, 2e séance du 31 mai 1949, 2950-51.

36. *Journal Officiel*, 2951-52.

37. Mann, *Native Sons*, 123.

38. Mann, *Native Sons*, 225-58.

39. Mann, *Native Sons*, 267-68. This same discourse was also adopted by other African deputies, such as RDA member Hamani Diori from Niger, who spoke in parliament against the ongoing discrimination against African soldiers. See *Journal Officiel de la République Française*, Débats Parlementaires, 1ere séance du 30 décembre 1947, 6533.

40. "Le président Coulibaly lance un appel à la jeunesse voltaïque," *Troupes d'*AOF: *Mensuel militaire d'information des armées de terre-air-mer*, no. 11 (August 1958): 6.

41. ANS, 17G 638 (152), information bulletin, AOF, 1957-58.

42. *Évolués* is a colonial term designating Western-educated Africans who did not possess French citizenship and were therefore not *originaires*. The letters are in ANS, 17G 638 (152), May 25, 1957, Dakar, trimestral bulletin AOF-Togo, February 15-May 15, 1957.

43. ANSOM, DSM/275, September 4, 1958, Paris, note for the attention of the minister of overseas France, incidents in Dakar caused by pupils of the EMPA of Aix-en-Provence.

44. ANS, 17G 638 (152), information bulletin, AOF, 1957-58.

45. ANSOM, DSM/275, Ministry of Overseas France, Paris, April 20, 1956.

46. ANSOM, DSM/275, October 17, 1957, Paris, General Larroque, director of the military center of information and specialization of overseas France, in search of officers of African affairs.

47. ANSOM, DSM/275, June 5, 1956, note from the department of political affairs to the director of the cabinet; June 16, 1956, note of the director of political affairs to the director of military affairs.

48. ANSOM, DSM/275, November 15, 1955, syndicate of the district guards of the Ivory Coast, Abidjan, to the minister of overseas France.

49. SHAT, 5H 38, June 29, 1956, Dakar.

7. ADJUSTING TO A NEW REALITY

1. SHAT, GR 5H 28, report on the end of command, General Gardet, May 25, 1958-February 15, 1960.

2. Cooper, *Citizenship*, 214.

3. Zimmerman, "Living beyond Boundaries," 125.

4. Philips, "How the Fourth Republic Died," 31.

5. Philips, "How the Fourth Republic Died," 31.

6. Public Record Office, London, FO 371, May 17, 1958, British Consulate of Dakar.

7. Public Record Office, London, FO 371, May 17, 1958, British Consulate of Dakar.

8. Zimmerman, "Living beyond Boundaries," 126.

9. SHAT, GR 5H 24, annual report, 1959.

10. Chafer, *The End of Empire*, 174.

11. Chafer, *The End of Empire*, 174.

12. Chafer, *The End of Empire*, 175-79.

13. SHAT, GR 5H 28, situation in overseas zone no. 1 in mid-January 1960.

14. MacDonald, "A Vocation for Independence," 34, 40-41.

15. Schmidt, *Cold War*, 167-74.

16. SHAT, GR 5H 28, situation in overseas zone no. 1 in mid-January 1960.

17. SHAT, GR 5H 27, Dakar, annual report, 1962. See also Joly, "The French Army," 79.

18. SHAT, GR 5H 27, Dakar, annual report, 1962. See also Joly, "The French Army," 79.

19. SHAT, GR 5H 28, report on the end of command, General Gardet, May 25, 1958-February 15, 1960.

20. Joly, "The French Army," 79.

21. SHAT, GR 5H 28, situation in overseas zone no. 1 in mid-January 1960.

22. Keese, "French Officials," 44-55.

23. Joly, "The French Army," 75.

24. SHAT, GR 5H 28, June 30, 1962, report on end of command of General de Brebisson, delegate for the defense of overseas zone no. 1.

25. SHAT, GR 5H 28, June 30, 1962, report on end of command.

26. Rouvez, *Disconsolate Empires*, 21.

27. Rouvez, *Disconsolate Empires*, 14-15.

28. Rouvez, *Disconsolate Empires*, 31.

29. Rouvez, *Disconsolate Empires*, 105-6.

30. SHAT, GR 5H 28, June 30, 1962, report on end of command.

31. Joly, "The French Army," 85-86.

32. SHAT, GR 5H 28, June 30, 1962, report on end of command.

33. Rouvez, *Disconsolate Empires*, 102-3.

34. Pabanel, *Les coups d'état militaires*, 142-44.

35. Interview with Malic Gueye.

36. Interview with Sadibou Badji.

37. Interview with Marc Guèye.

38. Interview with Papa Figaro Diagne.

39. Niang, *Mémoires synchrones*, 100-104.

40. Zimmerman, "Living beyond Boundaries," 127-32.

41. Zimmerman, "Living beyond Boundaries," 109.

42. Echenberg, *Colonial Conscripts*, 138-39.

43. Echenberg, *Colonial Conscripts*, 132.

44. On the idea of "two Frances" in AOF, see Ginio, "Vichy Rule," 205-26.

45. *La Voix des Combattants et des Victimes de Guerres: Organe de la Fédération des Anciens Combattants de l'*AOF *et du Togo*, no. 25, March 30, 1949, 1.

46. "Ils ont des droits sur nous!," *La Voix des Combattants*, no. 3, May 13, 1948, 1; *La Voix des Combattants*, no. 5, May 29, 1948, 1-2.

47. See, for example, *La Voix des Combattants*, no. 54, April 5, 1951, 2.

48. See, for example, *La Voix des Combattants*, no. 110, January 19, 1956, 1.

49. "Brillant intervention de M. Mamba Sano, député de la Guinée," *La Voix des Combattants*, no. 105, August 25, 1955, 3.

50. "Nos adversaires," *La Voix des Combattants*, no. 83, September 14, 1953, 2.

51. *La Voix des Combattants,* no. 67, May 7, 1952, 3.

52. *La Voix des Combattants*, no. 60, October 11, 1951, 4.

53. *La Voix des Combattants*, no. 82, August 18, 1953.

54. "Le sort de l'Union français," *La Voix des Combattants*, no. 90, April 15, 1954, 1.

55. *La Voix des Combattants*, no. 139, September 2, 1958.

56. Mann, *Native Sons*, 137-38.

57. Mann, *Native Sons*, 141-44.

58. Keese, "First Lessons," 602.

59. Pabanel, *Les coups d'état militaires*, 91-99.

60. Pabanel, *Les coups d'état militaires*, 131-32, 140-45.

CONCLUSION

1. France 24, "French Army to Close Senegal Base after 50 Years," https://www.youtube.com/watch?v=_ub548mj6rg, accessed June 9, 2010.

2. Ginio, "African Colonial Soldiers," 144-45.

3. Diagne, "Le Sénégal," 138. Seck was born in 1912 in Rufique, Senegal.

4. Mann, *Native Sons*, 212-13.

BIBLIOGRAPHY

MANUSCRIPTS AND ARCHIVES

Archives Militaires, Paris, Service Historique de l'Armée de Terre (SHAT)

Archives Nationales du Sénégal, Dakar (ANS)

Archives Nationales, Section d'Outre-Mer, Aix-en-Provence (ANSOM)

Centre d'Histoire et d'Études des Troupes d'Outre-Mer, Fréjus (CHETOM)

Public Records Office, London (PRO)

PUBLISHED WORKS

Ageron, Charles-Robert, and Marc Michel, eds. *L'heure des indépandances*. Paris: CNRS, 2010.

Ba, Amadou. *Les "Sénégalais" à Madagascar: Militaires ouest-africains dans la conquête et la colonisation de la Grand île, 1895–1960*. Paris: L'Harmattan, 2012.

Bankwitz, Philip C. F. "Maxime Weygand and the Army-Nation Concept in the Modern French Army." *French Historical Studies* 2, no. 2 (1961): 157–88.

Benot, Yves. *Massacres coloniaux, 1944–1950: La IVe République et la mise au pas des colonies françaises*. Paris: La Découverte, 2001.

Bloom, Peter J. *French Colonial Documentary: Mythologies of Humanitarianism*. Minneapolis: University of Minnesota Press, 2008.

Bodin, Michel. *Les Africains dans la guerre d'Indochine, 1947–1954*. Paris: L'Harmattan, 2000.

——. "Les 'Sénégalais' de la guerre d'Indochine." In *Défendre l'Empire: Des conflits oubliés à l'oubli des combattants, 1945–2010*, edited by Frédéric Garan, 103–35. Paris: Vendémiaire, 2013.

Bogosian Ash, Catherine. "Free to Coerce: Forced Labor during and after the Vichy Years in French West Africa." In *Africa and World War II*, edited by Judith A. Byfield, Carolyn A. Brown, Timothy Parsons, and Ahmad Alawad Sikainga, 109–26. Cambridge: Cambridge University Press, 2015.

Bradley, Mark Philip. *Vietnam at War*. New York: Oxford University Press, 2009.

Byfield, Judith A., Carolyn A. Brown, Timothy Parsons, and Ahmad Alawad Sikainga, eds. *Africa and World War II*. Cambridge: Cambridge University Press, 2015.

Chafer, Tony. "Chirac and 'La Franceafrique': No Longer a Family Affair." *Modern and Contemporary France* 13, no. 1 (2005): 7–23.

———. *The End of Empire in French West Africa: France's Successful Decolonization?* Oxford: Berg, 2002.

Chafer, Tony, and Alexander Keese, eds. *Francophone Africa at Fifty*. Manchester: Manchester University Press, 2013.

Challéat, Violaine. "Le cinéma au service de la défense, 1915–2008." *Revue Historique des Armées* 252 (2008): 3–15.

Clayton, Anthony. *France, Soldiers and Africa*. London: Brassey's Defence Publishers, 1988.

———. *The Wars of French Decolonization*. London: Longman, 1994.

Conklin, Alice. *A Mission to Civilize: The Republican Idea of Empire in France and West Africa, 1895–1930*. Stanford CA: Stanford University Press, 1997.

Connelly, Matthew. *A Diplomatic Revolution: Algeria's Fight for Independence and the Origins of the Post–Cold War Era*. Oxford: Oxford University Press, 2002.

Cooper, Frederick. *Africa since 1940*. Cambridge: Cambridge University Press, 2002.

———. *Citizenship between Empire and Nation: Remaking France and French Africa, 1945–1960*. Princeton NJ: Princeton University Press, 2014.

———. "'Our Strike': Equality, Anti-colonial Politics, and the 1947–48 Railway Strike in French West Africa." *Journal of African History* 37, no. 1 (1996): 81–118.

Cooper, Nikki. "Dien Bien Phu—Fifty Years On." *Modern and Contemporary France* 12, no. 4 (2004): 445–57.

Coulibaly, Ouezzin. *Combat pour l'Afrique: Lutte de l'R.D.A. pour une Afrique nouvelle*. Textes présentés par Claude Gérard. Abidjan: Le Nouvelles Éditions Africaines, 1988.

Deville-Danthu, Bernadette. *Le sport en noir et blanc: Du sport colonial au sport africain dans les anciens territoires français d'Afrique occidentale (1920–1965)*. Paris: L'Harmattan, 1997.

Diagne, Aissatou. "Le Sénégal et la guerre d'Indochine: Récits de vie de vétérans." Master's thesis, Université Cheikh Anta Diop, Dakar, 1992.

Dioum, Cheick Bamba. "Pèlerinage à la Mecque: Pourquoi la privatisation est la solution." http://bambadioum.seneweb.com/pelerinage-a-la-mecque-pourquoi -la-privatisation-est-la-solution_b_30.html. Accessed April 9, 2014.

Echenberg, Myron. *Colonial Conscripts: The Tirailleurs Sénégalais in French West Africa, 1857–1960*. Portsmouth NH: Heinemann, 1991.

———. "'Morts pour la France': The African Soldier in France during the Second World War." *Journal of African History* 26, no. 4 (1985): 363–80.

———. "Slaves into Soldiers: Social Origins of the Tirailleurs Sénégalais." In *Africans in Bondage: Studies in Slavery and the Slave Trade*, edited by Philip D. Curtin and Paul E. Lovejoy, 311–33. Madison: University of Wisconsin Press, 1986.

———. "Tragedy at Thiaroye: The Senegalese Soldiers' Uprising of 1944." In *African Labor History*, edited by Peter Gutkind, Robin Cohen, and Jean Copans, 109–27. Beverly Hills: Sage Publications, 1978.

Echenberg, Myron, and Jean Filipovitch. "African Military Labor and the Building of the Office du Niger Installations, 1925–1950." *Journal of African History* 27, no. 3 (1986): 533–51.

Edwards, Kathryn. "Traître au colonialisme? The Georges Boudarel Affair and the Memory of the Indochina War." *French Colonial History* 11 (2010): 193–210.

Evans, Martin. *Algeria: France's Undeclared War*. Oxford: Oxford University Press, 2012.

Evrard, Camille. "Transfer of Military Power in Mauritania: From Ecouvillon to Lamantin (1958–1978)." In *Francophone Africa at Fifty*, edited by Tony Chafer and Alexander Keese, 90–106. Manchester: Manchester University Press, 2013.

Fall, Bouboucar. *Le travail forcé en Afrique occidentale française (1900–1946)*. Paris: Karthala, 1993.

Fargettas, Julien. *Les Tirailleurs sénégalais: Les soldats noirs entre légendes et réalités, 1939–1945*. Paris: Tallandier, 2012.

Fogarty, Richard. *Race and War in France: Colonial Subjects in the French Army, 1914–1918*. Baltimore MD: Johns Hopkins University Press, 2008.

France 24. "French Army to Close Senegal Base after 50 Years." https://www.youtube .com/watch?v=_ub548mj6rg. Accessed June 9, 2010.

Galy, Michel. "Pourquoi la France est-elle intervenue au Mali?" In *La Guerre au Mali: Comprendre la crise au Sahel et au Sahara. Enjeux et zone d'ombre*, edited by Michel Gali, 76–90. Paris: La Découverte, 2013.

Ginio, Ruth. "African Colonial Soldiers between Memory and Forgetfulness: The Case of Post-colonial Senegal." *Outre-Mers: Revue d'Histoire* 94, nos. 350–51 (2006): 141–55.

———. "African Soldiers, French Women, and Colonial Fears during and after World War II." In *Africa and World War II*, edited by Judith A. Byfield, Carolyn A. Brown, Timothy Parsons, and Ahmad Alawad Sikainga, 324–38. Cambridge: Cambridge University Press, 2015.

———. "'Cherchez la femme': African Gendarmes, Quarrelsome Women and French Commanders." *International Journal of African Historical Studies* 47, no. 1 (2014): 59–75.

———. *French Colonialism Unmasked: The Vichy Years in French West Africa*. Lincoln: University of Nebraska Press, 2006.

———. "French Officers, African Officers, and the Violent Image of African Colonial Soldiers." *Historical Reflections* 36, no. 2 (2010): 59–75.

———. "La politique antijuive de Vichy en Afrique occidentale française." *Archives Juives* 36, no. 1 (2003): 109–18.

———. "Vichy Rule in French West Africa: Prelude to Decolonization?" *French Colonial History* 4 (2003): 205–26.

Goscha, Christopher. *Historical Dictionary of the Indochina War, 1945–1954*. Copenhagen: NIAS Press, 2011.

———. *Vietnam: Un état né de la guerre*. Paris: Armand Colin, 2011.

Grandhomme, Hélène. "La politique musulmane de la France au Sénégal (1936–64)." *Canadian Journal of African Studies* 38, no. 2 (2004): 237–78.

Guèye, Marc. *Un Tirailleur sénégalais dans la guerre d'Indochine, 1953–1955*. Dakar: Presses Universitaires de Dakar, 2007.

Hale, Dana S. "French Images of Race on Product Trademarks during the Third Republic." In *The Color of Liberty: Histories of Race in France*, edited by Sue Peabody and Tyler Stovall, 131–46. Durham NC: Duke University Press, 2003.

Ingold, François. *Avec les troupes noires au combat*. Paris: Berger-Levrault, 1940.

Jennings, Eric. *La France libre fut africaine*. Paris: Perrin, 2014.

Johnson, G. Wesley. "The Ascendancy of Blaise Diagne and the Beginning of African Politics in Senegal." *Africa* 36, no. 3 (1966): 235–53.

Joly, Vincent. "The French Army and Malian Independence (1956–1961)." In *Francophone Africa at Fifty*, edited by Tony Chafer and Alexander Keese, 75–89. Manchester: Manchester University Press, 2013.

Jones, Hilary. *The Métis of Senegal: Urban Life and Politics in French West Africa*. Bloomington: Indiana University Press, 2013.

———. "Rethinking Politics in the Colony: The Métis of Senegal and Urban Politics in the Late Nineteenth and Early Twentieth Centuries." *Journal of African History* 53, no. 3 (2012): 325–44.

Keese, Alexander. "First Lessons in Neo-colonialism: The Personalisation of Relations between African Politicians and French Officials in Sub-Saharan Africa, 1956–66." *Journal of Imperial and Commonwealth History* 35, no. 4 (2007): 593–613.

———. "French Officials and the Insecurities of Change in Sub-Saharan Africa: Dakar, 19 August 1960 Revisited." In *Francophone Africa at Fifty*, edited by Tony Chafer and Alexander Keese, 44–60. Manchester: Manchester University Press, 2013.

Killingray, David, and Michael Hadley. *Samori Touré: Warrior King*. Amersham: Hulton, 1973.

Koller, Christian. "The Recruitment of Colonial Troops in Africa and Asia and Their Deployment in Europe in the First World War." *Immigrants and Minorities* 26, nos. 1/2 (2008): 111–33.

Kuisel, Richard F. "Coca-Cola and the Cold War: The French Face of Americanization, 1948–1953." *French Historical Studies* 17, no. 1 (1991): 96–116.

Lambert, Michael C. "From Citizenship to Negritude: 'Making a Difference' in Elite Ideologies of Colonized Francophone West Africa." *Comparative Studies in Society and History* 35, no. 2 (1993): 239–62.

Launey, Stephan. "Les services cinématographiques militaires français pendant la Seconde guerre mondiale." *Revue Historique des Armées* 252 (2008): 27–40.

Le Naour, Jean-Yves. *La honte noire: L'Allemagne et les troupes coloniales françaises, 1914–1945*. Paris: Hachette, 2004.

Lunn, Joe. "'Les races guerrières': Racial Preconceptions in the French Military about West African Soldiers during the First World War." *Journal of Contemporary History* 34, no. 4 (1999): 517–36.

Mabon, Armelle. *Prisonniers de guerre "indigènes": Visages oubliée de la France occupée.* Paris: La Découverte, 2010.

———. "Synthèse sur le massacre de Thiaroye (Sénégal 1 décembre, 1944)." http://sfhomoutremers.free.fr/spip.php?article632. Accessed November 29, 2014.

MacDonald, Mairi. "A Vocation for Independence: Guinean Nationalism in the 1950s." In *Francophone Africa at Fifty,* edited by Tony Chafer and Alexander Keese, 30-43. Manchester: Manchester University Press, 2013.

Mangin, Charles. *La force noire.* Paris: Hachette, 1910.

Mann, Gregory. "Immigrants and Arguments in France and West Africa." *Comparative Studies in Society and History* 45, no. 2 (2003): 362-85.

———. "Locating Colonial Histories: Between France and West Africa." *American Historical Review* 110, no. 2 (2005): 409-34.

———. *Native Sons: West African Veterans and France in the Twentieth Century.* Durham NC: Duke University Press, 2006.

———. "What Was the Indigénat? The 'Empire of Law' in French West Africa." *Journal of African History* 50, no. 3 (2009): 331-53.

Mann, Gregory, and Baz Lecocq. "Between Empire, *Umma,* and the Muslim Third World: The French Union and African Pilgrims to Mecca, 1946-1958." *Comparative Studies of South Asia, Africa and the Middle East* 27, no. 2 (2007): 367-83.

Marsot, Alain-Gerard. "The Crucial Year: Indochina 1946." *Journal of Contemporary History* 19, no. 2 (1984): 337-54.

Michel, Marc. *Les Africains et la Grande Guerre: L'appel à l'Afrique.* Paris: Karthala, 2003.

Nelson, Keith L. "The 'Black Horror on the Rhine': Race as a Factor in Post-World War I Diplomacy." *Journal of Modern History* 42, no. 4 (1970): 606-27.

Niang, Mamadou. *Mémoires synchrones du fleuve de mon destin.* Dakar: Harmattan, 2012.

Office National des Anciens Combattants et Victimes de Guerre. "Le status de pupille de la nation." http://www.onac-vg.fr/fr/missions/pupille-de-la-nation/. Accessed November 25, 2014.

Orwin, Ethan M. "Of Couscous and Control: The Bureau of Muslim Soldier Affairs and the Crisis of French Colonialism." *Historian* 70, no. 2 (2008): 263-84.

Ouellet, Eric, and Pierre Pahlavi. "Institutional Analysis and Irregular Warfare: A Case Study of the French Army in Algeria, 1954-1960." *Journal of Strategic Studies* 34, no. 6 (2011): 799-824.

Pabanel, Jean-Pierre. *Les coups d'état militaires en Afrique noire.* Paris: L'Harmattan, 1984.

Pahlavi, Pierre Cyril. *Guerre révolutionnaire de l'Armée française en Algérie, 1954-1961: Entre esprit de conquête et conquête des esprits.* Paris: L'Harmattan, 2004.

———. "Political Warfare Is a Double-Edged Sword: The Rise and Fall of the French Counter-Insurgency in Algeria." *Canadian Military Journal* 8, no. 4 (2007-8): 53-62.

Philips, William. "How the Fourth Republic Died: Sources of the Revolution of May 1958." *French Historical Studies* 3, no. 1 (1963): 1–40.

Piga, Adriana. *Les voies du soufisme au sud de Sahara: Parcours historiques et anthropologiques*. Paris: Karthala, 2006.

Pinoteau, Pascal. "Propagande cinématographique et décolonisation: L'exemple français (1949–1958)." *Vingtième Siècle: Revue d'Histoire*, no. 80 (October–December 2003): 55–69.

Proschan, Frank. "'Syphilis, Opiomania, and Pederasty': Colonial Constructions of Vietnamese (and French) Social Diseases." *Journal of the History of Sexuality* 11, no. 4 (October 2002): 610–36.

Robinson, David. *The Holy War of Umar Tal: The Western Sudan in the Mid-Nineteenth Century*. Oxford: Oxford University Press, 1985.

Robinson, David. *Paths of Accommodation: Muslim Societies and French Colonial Authorities in Senegal and Mauritania, 1880–1920*. Athens: Ohio University Press, 2000.

Roos, Julia. "Women's Rights, Nationalist Anxiety, and the 'Moral' Agenda in the Early Weimar Republic: Revisiting the 'Black Horror' Campaign against France's African Occupation Troops." *Central European History* 42 (2009): 473–508.

Rouvez, Alain. *Disconsolate Empires: French, British and Belgian Military Involvement in Post-colonial Sub-Saharan Africa*. Lanham MD: University Press of America, 1994.

Scheck, Raffael. *French Colonial Soldiers in German Captivity during World War II*. Cambridge: Cambridge University Press, 2014.

———. "French Colonial Soldiers in German Prisoner-of-War Camps (1940–1945)." *French History* 24, no. 3 (2010): 420–46.

———. *Hitler's African Victims: The German Army Massacres of Black French Soldiers in 1940*. Cambridge: Cambridge University Press, 2006.

Schmidt, Elizabeth. *Cold War and Decolonization in Guinea, 1946–1958*. Athens: Ohio University Press, 2007.

Sharp, Thomas. "The Changing Boundaries of Resistance: The UPC and France in Cameroonian History and Memory." In *Francophone Africa at Fifty*, edited by Tony Chafer and Alexander Keese, 189–203. Manchester: Manchester University Press, 2013.

Shepard, Todd. *The Invention of Decolonization: The Algerian War and the Remaking of France*. Ithaca NY: Cornell University Press, 2006.

Shipway, Martin. *Decolonization and Its Impact: A Comparative Approach to the End of the Colonial Empires*. Oxford: Blackwell, 2008.

Stoler, Ann Laura. "Sexual Affronts and Racial Frontiers: European Identities and the Cultural Politics of Exclusion in Colonial Southeast Asia." In *Tensions of Empire: Colonial Cultures in a Bourgeois World*, edited by Frederick Cooper and Ann Laura Stoler, 198–237. Berkeley: University of California Press, 1997.

Thomas, Martin. *Fight or Flight: Britain, France and Their Roads from Empire*. Oxford: Oxford University Press, 2014.

Tronchon, Jacques. *L'insurrection malgache de 1947*. Paris: François Maspero, 1974.

Van Beusekon, Monica M. "Disjunctures in Theory and Practice: Making Sense of Change in Agricultural Development at the Office du Niger, 1920–1960." *Journal of African History* 41, no. 1 (2000): 79–99.

Vandervort, Bruce. *Wars of Imperial Conquest in Africa*. Bloomington: Indiana University Press, 1998.

Villatoux, Marie-Catherine. *Guerre et action psychologique en Algérie*. Paris: Service Historique de la Défense, 2007.

Whitfield, Lee. "Algeria in France: French Citizens, the War, and Right-Wing Populism in the Reckoning of the Republic in Languedoc, 1954–1962." *Proceedings of the Western Society for French History* 33 (2005): 412–32.

Woodfork, Jacquelin. "'It Is a Crime to Be a Tirailleur in the Army': The Impact of Senegalese Civilian Status in the French Colonial Army during the Second World War." *Journal of Military History* 77 (2013): 115–39.

Zimmerman, Sarah Jean. "Living beyond Boundaries: West African Servicemen in French Colonial Conflicts, 1908–1962." PhD dissertation, University of California, Berkeley, 2011.

INDEX

Page numbers in italic indicate figures; page numbers in italic followed by "t" refer to tables.

military monitoring of civilians. *See* monitoring of civilians, military

military of Franco-African Community: Guinea and, 178–80; Mali federation and, 180–83; national armies establishment and, 183–88; overview of, 177, 178

military reform. *See* reform, military

military schools, 48–55, 162–63; acceptance into, 49, 52–54; EET, 36, 48–49, 137, 216n34; enlistment requirements for, 49, 216n34; EFORTOM, 57–58, 217n57; EMPA, 36–37, 49–55, 56–57, 73, 154–55, 164–65, 216n34; exams in, 49, 52–54; Grands Ecoles' graduates, 48, 50–51; punishment in, 51

military tours, 66–69, 73, 166

Ministry of Cooperation, 177, 184

Ministry of Defense, 151

Ministry of Overseas France, 154, 157, 177

Minté, Karamako, 64

mistresses, 97, 222n58

Mitterrand, François, 10

mixed-race children, 97–98

modernization of military, 70–74

Le Monde (newspaper), 185

monitoring morale, 91, 122

monitoring of civilians by military: colonial administration and, 165–70; labor unions and, 163; National Assembly representatives and, 160–63; overview of, 159–60, 170; students and, 163–65, 227n42

Monnerville, Gaston, 225n49

monuments, 7, 156, 204–5, 212n15

moral education, 50

morale of African soldiers: in Algerian war, 111, 112, 122; in Indochina war, 87, 89, 90–96; monitoring, 91, 122; political activity and, 164

Morocco, 107, 116, 130, 131, 144

Mouvement Démocratique de la Rénovation Maglache (MDRM), 79–80

murder of French commanders in Indochina, 89–90

music lessons in military schools, 50

Muslims: Algerian war and, 112–13, 123–25; students, 118, 119–20. *See also* Islam; pilgrimage trips

Nasser, Gamal Abdul, 133

national armies, 146, 172, 180, 183–88, 201, 208

National Assembly, French. *See* French National Assembly

Native Sons (Mann), xxiii, 191

Navarre, Henri, 94

Nazis, 28, 135, 161

NCOs (noncommissioned officers), 36, 49, 54, 57, 70, 87

Ndar. *See* Saint Louis

neocolonialism, 204

newspapers, 91–92, 94. *See also specific newspapers*

Niang, Mamadou, 59, 72–73, 82, 109–10, 138, 189

Niang, Ousmane, 88

Niasse, Abdoulaye, 225n55

Niasse, Cheick Ibrahima, 135, 225n55

Niger: coup d'états in, xvii, 199, 200t; Franco-African Community and, 181, 182, 186, 187; soldiers from, 28–29, 43, 45

Nkrumah, Kwame, 118

Norodom, 95

North Africa, 4, 5, 128, 144–45. *See also* Algerian war; *specific countries of*

Nos Soldats en Afrique noire (film), 152

N'Tchoreré, Charles, 137

Nyo, Georges Yves-Marie, 146, 148–49

propaganda (cont.)
  military, 67, 69, 149–53; of Nazis, 23–24, 25, 27–28, 135; of unions and student movement, 116–20. See also pilgrimage trips
prostitutes, 97, 98
psychological operations, 67, 111, 149–53. See also action psychologique; propaganda
psychological warfare, xviii, xxvii, 87, 100, 106, 111–14. See also action psychologique
"pupils of the nation," 39

racism, 15–16, 89–90, 193
radio, 93–94, 114, 118–19, 130–31, 176
Radio Dakar, 94, 176
Radio Royal, 130–31
Radio Tangier, 118–19
RDA. See Rassemblement Démocratique Africain (RDA)
Rassemblement Démocratique Africain (RDA), 120; AERDA and, 117–18; Algerian war and, 163; background of, 9–10; military monitoring of, 159–60; military reform and, 41, 43; Papa Seck Douta and, 191–92; Upper Volta and, 199
recruitment of African soldiers: and false identities, 47; and height requirements, 42; and heterogeneity of recruit distribution, 45; for Indochina War, 86; military reform and, 36, 42–48, 55–59, 75; in World War I, 6
Red Cross, 94, 102
reform, military: African military elite and, 55–59; education and, 48–55; initiating, 37–42; Loi-Cadre and, 173; overview of, xxii, xxvi, 12, 35–37, 207; presenting the new army and, 66–73; recruitment and, 36, 42–48,

55–59, 75; results of, 73–76, 81; veteran relations and, 60–66
Republic of Mali, 182–83
Le Reveil (newspaper), 41, 43
RIM (infantry regiments of the marines), 177
Robinson, David, 126
Rufisque, 1
rumors about African soldiers, 99, 100
Rwanda, xvii

safety in cities during Indochina War, 95
Saiba, François, 64
Saigon, 95
Saint-Cyr military academy, 162–63
Saint Louis, 1, 158
Sakiet, 174
Salan, Raoul, 94
Sall, Sadiq, 136–38
Sano, Mamba, 194
Sarr, Ibrahima, 74
Saudi Arabia, 128, 131, 132–35
Sawaba, 181
Scheck, Raffael, 16
Schmidt, Elizabeth, xxiv, 179
Schoelcher, Victor, 162
scholarship on French military in AOF, xix–xx, xxiii–xxv, 211n6, 211n10
Seck, Mbaye, 159–60
Seck Douta, Papa, 54, 191–92
second portion soldiers, 43–45, 47, 75
Section Française de l'Internationale Ouvrière (SFIO), 43, 191
segregation, 64, 75
Senegal: colonization of, 1; independence of, 203–5; Mali federation and, 180–82; national army of, 185, 188, 189; soldiers from, 43, 45
Senghor, Léopold Sédar, 10, 24, 55, 157, 159–60, 173, 216n27
Serer, 47, 216n27

IN THE FRANCE OVERSEAS SERIES

French Mediterraneans: Transnational and Imperial Histories
Edited and with an introduction by Patricia M. E. Lorcin and Todd Shepard

The Cult of the Modern: Trans-Mediterranean France and the Construction of French Modernity
Gavin Murray-Miller

Cinema in an Age of Terror: North Africa, Victimization, and Colonial History
Michael F. O'Riley

Making the Voyageur World: Travelers and Traders in the North American Fur Trade
Carolyn Podruchny

A Workman Is Worthy of His Meat: Food and Colonialism in Gabon
Jeremy Rich

The Moroccan Soul: French Education, Colonial Ethnology, and Muslim Resistance, 1912–1956
Spencer D. Segalla

Silence Is Death: The Life and Work of Tahar Djaout
Julija Šukys

The French Colonial Mind, Volume 1: Mental Maps of Empire and Colonial Encounters
Edited and with an introduction by Martin Thomas

The French Colonial Mind, Volume 2: Violence, Military Encounters, and Colonialism
Edited and with an introduction by Martin Thomas

Beyond Papillon: The French Overseas Penal Colonies, 1854–1952
Stephen A. Toth

Madah-Sartre: The Kidnapping, Trial, and Conver(sat/s)ion of Jean-Paul Sartre and Simone de Beauvoir
Written and translated by Alek Baylee Toumi
With an introduction by James D. Le Sueur

To order or obtain more information on these or other University of Nebraska Press titles, visit nebraskapress.unl.edu.

CPSIA information can be obtained
at www.ICGtesting.com
Printed in the USA
LVHW030727291122
734171LV00020B/519/J

9 780803 253391